the cinema of TERRENCE MALICK

DIRECTORS' CUTS

the cinema of

TERRENCE MALICK

poetic visions of america

(second edition)

edited by
HANNAH PATTERSON

 **WALLFLOWER PRESS** LONDON & NEW YORK

A Wallflower Book
Published by
Columbia University Press
Publishers Since 1893
New York • Chichester, West Sussex
cup.columbia.edu

A complete CIP record is available from the Library of Congress

ISBN 978-1-905674-26-8 (cloth : alk. paper)
ISBN 978-1-905674-25-1 (pbk. : alk. paper)
ISBN 978-0-231-85011-7 (e-book)

Columbia University Press books are printed on permanent and durable acid-free paper.
This book is printed on paper with recycled content.

Printed in the United States of America

c 10 9 8 7 6 5 4 3 2 1
p 10 9 8 7 6 5 4 3

CONTENTS

ACKNOWLEDGEMENTS

The editor would like to thank everyone at Wallflower Press for their support and encouragement, in particular Yoram Allon, John Atkinson, Del Cullen, Howard Seal, Jacqueline Downs and Eleanor McKeown. Thanks also to Victor Perkins, whose classes on *Badlands* sparked the original idea, my family, who fostered a love of cinema, and to Ian Haydn Smith for valuable advice and boundless enthusiasm.

NOTES ON CONTRIBUTORS

Neil Campbell is Senior Research Fellow and Reader in American Studies at the University of Derby, UK. His publications include, as author, *The Cultures of the American New West* (2000), as co-author, *American Cultural Studies* (1997, 2006), as editor, *American Youth Cultures* (2004) and as co-editor, *Issues in Americanisation and Culture* (2005). He his currently completing a new volume entitled *The Rhizomatic West*.

Mark Cousins is a filmmaker, author and festival director. His last book, *The Story of Film*, was published in ten languages, including Mandarin; his last documentary was made with Abbas Kiarostami; and his last curated festival, 'Cinema China', covered eight decades of Chinese film history and played in twenty UK cities. He is presently compiling an anthology of film criticism entitled *Widescreen: Watching. Real. People. Elsewhere.*

Martin Flanagan is Senior Lecturer in Film and Media Studies at the University of Bolton, UK. He has recently published on issues around authorship, the blockbuster and cinematic adaptations of comics, and his work has appeared in the *New Review of Film and Television Studies* as well as in a number of edited collections.

Marc Furstenau is Assistant Professor of Film Studies in the School for Studies in Art and Culture at Carleton University, Ottawa, Canada.

Anne Latto was born in Australia, trained at RADA, acted professionally, and later gained a BA and MA in Film and Drama at the University of Reading, UK. She has taught Theatre Studies and has just completed an MPhil research project examining the young woman's voice-over in the films of Terrence Malick.

Leslie MacAvoy is Associate Professor of Philosophy at East Tennessee State University. She has published articles on the philosophical work of Heidegger and Levinas, and specialises in nineteenth- and twentieth-century continental philosophy.

Adrian Martin is Senior Research Fellow in Film and Television Studies, Monash University, Australia, and co-editor of the internet film journal *Rouge* (www.rouge.com.au). He is the author of books on Sergio Leone, the Mad Max movies and Raúl Ruiz, and is currently completing studies of Terrence Malick and Brian De Palma.

Ben McCann is Lecturer in French and Film Studies at the University of Adelaide. He has recently written articles on French animation, Michael Mann and set design in French poetic realist films, and is currently completing an in-depth study of *Le Jour se lève*, and is co-editor of a forthcoming anthology on the films of Michael Haneke.

Joan McGettigan is Assistant Professor of Radio-TV-Film at Texas Christian University. She has published articles on the narrative strategies of television coverage of high-profile trials; on characterisation in literature, film, radio drama and legal discourse; and on the uses of voice-over narration in Terrence Malick's films. She is currently working on a history of the economic and cultural role of movie theatres in working-class Philadelphia during the 1930s.

James Morrison is the author of *Broken Fever*, a memoir, and *The Lost Girl*, a novel, as well as several books on film, including *Roman Polanski* (2007). He is also editor of *The Cinema of Todd Haynes: All That Heaven Allows* (2007). He teaches film, literature and creative writing at Claremont McKenna College, California.

Ron Mottram is Professor of Film Studies in the School of Art at Illinois State University. He is the author of *Inner Landscapes: The Theater of Sam Shepard* (1984) and *The Danish Cinema Before Dreyer* (1988), as well as articles which have appeared in *Cinema Journal*, *Film History*, *Kosmorama* and *Texas Studies in Literature and Language*, and in a number of anthologies on film. He has also written for the CBS television series *Camera Three*, has been a guest curator for the the Department of Film at the Museum of Modern Art (New York), the Danish Film Museum (Copenhagen) and the Art Gallery of Ontario (Canada), and been a recipient of Fulbright, George C. Marshall and American Film Institute fellowships.

John Orr is Professor Emeritus at Edinburgh University and has published widely on many aspects of modern cinema. He is the author of *Cinema and Modernity* (1993), *Contemporary Cinema* (1998) and *Hitchcock and Twentieth Century Cinema* (2005). He is also co-editor of *The Cinema of Roman Polanski: Dark Sapces of the World* (2006).

Hannah Patterson is commissioning editor of Kamera Books and Creative Essentials, and co-editor of Wallflower Critical Guides on *Contemporary North American Film Directors* (2000, 2002) and *Contemporary British and Irish Film Directors* (2001). As a freelance journalist she has contributed to publications such as *Sight & Sound*, *Guardian*, *Vertigo*, *DOX* and *Time Out's 1000 Films to Change Your Life*.

Stacey Peebles is Visiting Assistant Professor in the Honors College at the University of Houston. Her research interests include modern American literature, the representation of violence and Texas arts and culture; she has published articles on violence in film and the fiction of Cormac McCarthy.

Richard Power is a composer, saxophonist and music theorist. His other research interests include the music of György Ligeti and Elliott Carter, musical applications of semiotics and the writings of Carl Jung.

Robert Silberman is Associate Professor of Art History at the University of Minnesota and the co-author of *American Photography: A Century of Images* (1999).

John Streamas is Assistant Professor of Comparative Ethnic Studies at Washington State University. He has published poems and stories as well as scholarly pieces on racism and Asian American literature, and is the author of *Japanese Americans and Cultures of Effacement* (forthcoming).

James Wierzbicki is an adjunct Associate Professor at the University of Michigan and Executive Editor of the Music of the United States (MUSA) series of critical editions.

Poetic Visions of America

Hannah Patterson

> I remember the first time the search occurred to me. I came to myself under a chindolea bush. Everything is upside down for me as I shall explain later. What are generally considered to be the best times are for me the worst times, and that worst of times was one of the best. My shoulder didn't hurt but it was pressed hard against the ground as if somebody sat on me. Six inches from my nose a dung beetle was scratching around under the leaves. As I watched, there awoke in me an immense curiosity. I was onto something. I vowed that if I ever got out of this fix, I would pursue the search.
>
> – Walker Percy, *The Moviegoer* (1998: 10–11)

The central protagonists in Terrence Malick's films are caught up in, or driven by, a search: for a different kind of life, a sense of self, a reason for being, or a spiritual presence in the world. 'The search is what anyone would undertake if he were not sunk in the everydayness of his own life', deliberates Binx Bolling, the dissatisfied hero of Walker Percy's *The Moviegoer*, a novel that Malick was at one time rumoured to be adapting for the screen. From *Badlands* (1973) through *Days of Heaven* (1978) and *The Thin Red Line* (1998) to *The New World* (2005), characters are taken out of their everydayness; their subsequent journeys form the films' narrative impetus and existential enquiry. At its most extreme, the search is manifest in the myriad voices of the soldiers in Guadalcanal. Pushed to the outer limits of themselves, they journey inwards to discover the kernel of their being, in all likelihood to kill or be killed.

Of course, the notion of a character's search is not at all unusual in cinema, or any art form, but the manner of Malick's particular vision, his conjuring of such journeys, is. Though it may be uncommon to compose a book devoted to a filmmaker who has made such a small number of features, as the chapters here testify it is precisely because of his unique vision that his work is worthy of further investigation. Some commentators have suggested that the paucity of critical writings on his films is due to the difficulty of defining them.[1] It is in an attempt to redress this balance, to articulate the concerns behind his films, that this collection seeks to bring some specificity to his work, probing each facet to illuminate our perception of the whole.

Again and again, writers use the word 'poetic' to describe Malick's work, usually in admiration, sometimes in derision, often in bafflement. Ideas about the manifestation and intention of their poetry – how and why his films are poetic – vary, and are worth identifying. The term itself is slippery, particularly within the context of film criticism. Taking many forms and educing multiple meanings, historically it has been used most often in relation to 'avant-garde' or 'art-house' cinema. John Madden, in his short book *The Poetry of Cinema*, lists a range of elements which he believes apply to poetic cinema films: '1. Open forms, 2. Ambiguity, 3. Expressionism, 4. Non-linearity, 5. Psychology, 6. Digressions, 7. Subjectivity, 8. Revision of a genre.' All of these, he argues, are 'hallmarks of the European art cinema' (1994: 1). Some are certainly useful in any analysis of Malick's work – open forms, ambiguity, revision of genre – and position him within a certain 'poetic' European tradition. His emphasis on the landscape, use of scant dialogue and unclear character motivations are just a few of the cinematic choices that could align him with a director such as Michelangelo Antonioni.

John Orr, however, in *Contemporary Cinema*, one of the few book-length studies to seriously consider Malick's work and deal specifically with the notion of cinema and poetry, conceives his output as emphatically American. He places his films alongside those of David Lynch, Robert Altman and Martin Scorsese in a chapter entitled 'American Reveries' (1998: 162–87) and points out that unlike the European cinema of poetry, the 'American cinema of poetry … is inseparable from the mythologies of the American Dream' (1998: 173). In this respect, Malick's handling of myth and his rendering of time and place – of the sublime – is intrinsic to his poetry.

Venturing into the realm of moral or spiritual value, further links have been drawn between Malick's poetic filmmaking and his preoccupations with existence beyond the material world. Geoff Andrew refers to him as 'the modern American cinema's great poet-philosopher, whose images … speak of a fascination with – and, perhaps, a faith in – the transcendent' (1999: 140). In their chapter in this collection, Marc Furstenau and Leslie MacAvoy delve even deeper into the relationship between the philosophical and the poetic. Viewing him as the embodiment of Martin Heidegger's 'poet in destitute times', they argue that through the very nature of his poetic vision Malick is ultimately an artist who reawakens and restores our sense of mystery and philosophical rumination.

Several understandings of the term 'poetic', then, and each pertinent and illuminating in any assessment of Malick's work; but it is interesting to consider where such distinctions place him practically. He would certainly seem to be unusual within Hollywood – an 'esoteric visual poet' as Martin Flanagan notes here, rather than a 'crafter of popular entertainments'. To this extent, he can best be viewed as Hollywood's arthouse director, hardly commercially successful and insistent in refusing to compromise his own vision. The specifics of that vision, the nature and extent of his 'poetic' cinemas, will be further elucidated and discussed throughout these pages.

Terrence Malick's reclusiveness, his reluctance to comment on his own work or be interviewed, has become the stuff of myth and legend within cinema, fuelled by a twenty-year 'absence' from the industry during which time he did not complete a feature. Likened to literary figures such as J. D. Salinger, Thomas Pynchon and Donna Tartt, media hype has fed this image. Just what was he doing during those twenty years? Was he indeed, as one favoured rumour would have it, a hairdresser in Paris? There are various biographical accounts of Malick's life and details are indeed scant and often contradictory.[3] A brief summary here, incorporating a précis of his films, will be followed by an overview of the chapters included and a summation of their inquiry. Readers will find a full bibliography of writings on Malick at the back of the book.

Growing up in Oklahoma and Texas, Malick attended Harvard University and studied philosophy as a Rhodes scholar at Magdalen College, Oxford. Having written for *Life* magazine and *The New Yorker*, he taught at MIT in 1968 and translated Martin Heidegger's *Vom Wesen des Grundes* (1929) as *The Essence of Reasons* (1969), published by Northwestern University Press. He enrolled at the Center for Advanced Film Studies at the American Film Institute, and his short, *Lanton Mills* (1969), which was made during his time there, remains unreleased. Working on scripts for films such as *Drive, He Said* (1971), Jack Nicholson's directorial debut – uncredited – and *Deadhead Miles* (Vernon Zimmerman, 1972) and *Pocket Money* (Stuart Rosenberg, 1972), he subsequently made his first feature, *Badlands*, which was produced by Edward R. Pressman.

Loosely based on the Charlie Starkweather and Caril Ann Fugate mid-West killings of 1958, *Badlands* stars Martin Sheen as Kit, a garbage collector, and Sissy Spacek as fifteen-year-old Holly who lives with her father (played by Warren Oates), a sign-painter, in Fort Dupre, South Dakota. She relates the events of the story in voice-over some time after their occurrence. Following a casual meeting with Kit, they begin a relationship. Her father does not approve and Kit subsequently shoots him; he and Holly take to the road. They make their temporary home in the forest but are soon discovered by bounty hunters, whom Kit kills. Having also shot his friend Cato (Ramon Bieri), and possibly two teenagers, they make their way across the badlands of Montana, and are tracked down heading for the Canadian border. Holly gives herself up and Kit is caught. He is given the electric chair and she marries the son of her lawyer who gets her off with probation.

The majority of critics at the time of the film's release were in agreement that *Badlands* was an assured debut, heralding a new and original talent. Malick went on to make *Days of Heaven* using many of the same crew in what was reportedly a more problematic shoot.[4] Following an extended editing period, the film was released in 1978. The story is set in 1916. Following a fight with a factory foreman in Chicago,

Bill (Richard Gere) flees with his lover Abby (Brooke Adams), who pretends to be his sister, and his real sister Linda (Linda Manz). They travel on the railway with other migrant workers to a farm in the Texas Panhandle to work in the wheatfields. The Farmer (Sam Shepard) is attracted to Abby and when the other workers leave after the season is over, he asks her to stay. Believing him to be dying, Bill persuades Abby to marry him so that they can inherit the farm on his demise. For a while, the three live with the Farmer; Bill and Abby continue their relationship in secret. Complications ensue as the Farmer and Abby become more intimate and Bill subsequently leaves the farm. On his return, the Farmer suspects that Bill and Abby are not in fact siblings. After a locust attack, during which the wheat is burned, he and Bill fight and the Farmer is killed. Bill, Abby and Linda flee. They are tracked down by a posse, and Bill is shot. Abby places Linda in a boarding school for girls, from which she subsequently escapes. We last see Abby boarding a train with soldiers heading for action in World War One.

Once again, the film received critical acclaim, winning an award for Best Direction at Cannes in 1979; it was also nominated for four Academy Awards and won one, Best Cinematography, for Nestor Almendros. With *Days of Heaven* complete, Malick ostensibly left Hollywood. Various rumours abounded about different projects he might undertake, including, for instance, his theatrical adaptation of *Sansho the Bailiff*, which would be directed by Andrzej Wajda.[5] Also in the early 1990s came the announcement that he would adapt James Jones' 1963 novel, *The Thin Red Line*. Stories about the background to the making of *The Thin Red Line* conflict. Peter Biskind's article 'The Runaway Genius' (1998a), which appeared in *Vanity Fair*, provides a version of its production history and discusses the roles of producers Bobby Geisler and John Roberdeau in bringing Malick back to filmmaking. Michel Chion discusses the film at length in his BFI Modern Classic *The Thin Red Line* (2004).

Set in 1942, *The Thin Red Line* follows an American rifle company, C-Company, from the moment they land on the island of Guadalcanal to fight the Japanese. During a proposed battle for Hill 210, Lt Colonel Tall (Nick Nolte) maintains that they should advance; Captain Staros (Elias Koteas), who is convinced the offensive will result in the loss of too many lives, disobeys his orders. They eventually take the hill. The soldiers are given leave and Tall relieves Staros of his command. Private Witt (Jim Caviezel), who can be seen as the film's main protagonist, dies attempting to lure the Japanese away from his fellow soldiers. The film ends with their departure from the island. *The Thin Red Line* greatly divided critical opinion and was endlessly compared to Steven Spielberg's World War Two picture *Saving Private Ryan*, which was released five months earlier. Martin Flanagan provides a comprehensive review of the film's critical reception and association in his chapter in this volume.

For a time, Malick's fourth, and most recent feature, looked set to be a biopic on Che Guevara but instead he chose to embark on a project he had originally written in the 1970s, *The New World*. The story of the first English settlers in Jamestown, Virginia, in 1607, his version of these events charts Captain John Smith's (Colin Farrell) love affair with Native American 'princess' Pocahontas (Q'Orianka Kilcher), the daughter of local chief Powhatan of the Algonquin tribe. Following her banishment from the tribe, and believing Smith to be dead, Pocahontas marries John Rolfe (Christian Bale), with whom she has a child, and travels to England. There she meets Smith once more, falls ill and dies. The film's critical reception was split and its 150-minute festival version was cut for general release.

Aside from his work as writer/director, since returning to the filmmaking industry in the 1990s, Malick has also become involved as a producer, setting up a company with Edward R. Pressman, Sunflower Productions. He has worked as an executive producer on *The Endurance: Shackleton's Legendary Antarctic Expedition* (George Butler, 2000), a documentary based on Caroline Alexander's book about the legendary 1914–16 expedition, Zhang Yimou's *Happy Times* (2001), David Gordon Green's *Undertow* (2004) and *Amazing Grace* (2006), Michael Apted's film about slavery abolitionist William Wilberforce. He also conceived the story for *Beautiful Country* (Hans Petter Moland, 2003), a narrative concerning a half-Vietnamese, half-American man who is searching for his father. At the time of writing Malick is reported to be working on *Tree of Life*, a film about the origins of the world, originally titled *Q*.

Aside from a range of essays on Malick's work that already exist in print and on-line journals, and various articles in magazines, the last few years have seen the publication of Michel Chion's aforementioned monograph on *The Thin Red Line*, and James Morrison and Thomas Schur's comprehensive study of the director's first three films, *The Films of Terrence Malick* (2003). Another, authored by Adrian Martin, is forthcoming from the British Film Institute. Citrullo International has also made a documentary, *Rosy-Fingered Dawn: A Film on Terrence Malick* (2002), which features a range of insightful interviews with actors such as Martin Sheen, Sissy Spacek, Sean Penn, Sam Shepard, Jim Caveziel, Elias Koteas and John Savage, directors Sergei Bodrov and Arthur Penn, cinematographer Haskell Wexler, editor Billy Weber, art director Jack Fisk and composer Ennio Morricone. Malick himself does not appear.

The chapters that make up this volume draw upon the expertise of a range of scholars and practitioners. Casting light on a variety of under-explored areas of Malick's filmmaking, historically, thematically and formatively, taken together they fashion a comprehensive, although by no means definitive, picture of his body of work. Like their cinematic subject, they raise questions, offering alternative points of view and ways of seeing. Where necessary for clarity of analysis, some material may be repeated across chapters.

Beginning with a single chapter that considers the progression of Malick's filmmaking across all four features, the next section focuses on his work in the 1970s, engaging with *Badlands* and *Days of Heaven* generically and mythically to encompass notions of identity and gender, and formally and stylistically to consider the uses of narrative, voice-over, sound and music, and the positioning of the landscape. The five chapters that make up the second section of the volume – 'Negotiating *The Thin Red Line*' – also touch upon these aspects, but their focus is on Malick's third feature. These chapters highlight the anticipation surrounding, and the importance of, Malick's 'return' to cinema, and reflect the divided, often bemused, critical and commercial responses to the film. They interrogate its status as a 'war' movie and the manner of its philosophical and spiritual enquiry. The third section 'Discovering *The New World*' is devoted to Malick's most recent film.

An apt opening to the collection, Ron Mottram's chapter links Malick to American intellectual writers such as Henry David Thoreau, Walt Whitman, Herman Melville and James Agee, and asserts that the director engages with the kinds of serious questions which remain largely unexplored within the mainstream North American film industry. Strategically employing a dual chronology, he first considers all four of Malick's films in the order of their making and through the formal development of his concerns as filmmaker, singling out his preoccupation with mythologies that have been central to American culture: among these, the 'appearance of evil', the loss of paradise and the 'search for redemption'. He subsequently identifies Malick's films as forming 'a kind of American history', spanning the European destruction of Native American culture, the end of the pastoral myth, the encroachment of industrialisation – specifically in one of its most extreme and destructive forms, that of war – and the society which emerged post-war, with its values uncertain and a faltering sense of identity.

My own chapter focuses on a single aspect of Malick's work, that of identity. Concerned with the formal qualities of *Badlands* and the manner in which a filmmaker can adequately present a 'sense' of characters whose motivations may be unclear, the chapter concentrates on Kit and Holly, challenging assertions such as Pauline Kael's that 'they are kept at a distance, doing things for no explained purpose ... as if the director had taped gauze over their characters, so that we wouldn't be able to take a reading of them' (1977: 304). Drawing on the work of George M. Wilson (1988), and through detailed analysis of two central scenes, the chapter seeks to prove that this lack of motivational clarity should not be viewed as a flaw but a strength of the film, coming to the conclusion that it is Kit who manages to more successfully establish a sense of identity for himself, however empty it may be, through his appropriation as a celebrity criminal, while it is Holly, the 'narrator' of the story, who is left still searching for hers.

Neil Campbell's chapter also engages with the issue of identity in *Badlands*, particularly the complexity of its representation within the generic forms it mixes – youth rebellion text, road movie and western. Having invoked these genres, he argues that Malick uses a dialogical structure to interrogate the myths of youth, road and frontier that have been commonly promulgated, inviting the audience to consider the significance of these oppositional values. Referring to the work of Frederick Turner Jackson, he demonstrates how, on one level, *Badlands* incorporates the frontier dream of the West – the call for rebellion, newness and escape from the past, and the possibility of transformation. Tracing the history of the connection between road and youth through fiction, film and music, he points to the idea of the road as a place of freedom, away from societal and adult constraint, and how subjects are invariably drawn back into the social order, unable to fully transform.

In support of his argument, and to reinforce Malick's 'suspicion' of such myths of renewal – a response Campbell reads as a societal doubt about the viability of the counter-culture – he focuses textually on the confinement and entrapment of Holly and Kit by their surroundings at the beginning of the film. The spaces they go on to attempt to inhabit are outside and in-between the normal societal spaces but by the film's outcome and their readmittance into social order – she to marry, and he to be punished by law – a central question is raised about the possibility of change and 'the impossibility of fulfilling myths that assert mobility and settlement, freedom and restraint, individualism and conformity'.

Both Joan McGettigan and John Orr consider the place of Malick's films within the western genre – a topic which has been underexplored – and his approach to myth: McGettigan through an analysis of *Days of Heaven* and its relationship to the classic western, and Orr through an exploration of Malick's 1970s films and their similarities to the contemporaneous work of Arthur Penn.

Pointing out Malick's propensity to challenge generic expectation, McGettigan argues that *Days of Heaven* establishes and heightens familiar aspects of the western and then exposes them as illusions. She refers to Robert Ray's 1985 study *A Certain Tendency of the Hollywood Cinema*, and his breakdown of the genre's archetypes, and uses examples from traditional westerns such as *My Darling Clementine* (John Ford, 1946), *Red River* (Howard Hawks, 1948) and *Shane* (George Stevens, 1953) to establish the standard model and its mythical enterprise. She subsequently deconstructs *Days of Heaven*'s plot, characters and imagining of the landscape to demonstrate these 'failures' in the 'fixtures of the western myth'. Drawing on a wide range of examples to shape her argument, McGettigan believes that it is by subverting these 'principle ideologies of the western' that Malick shows how the myths they propagate are not only untenable but actually unrealisable.

Working along similar lines, John Orr offers an alternative perspective. Like McGettigan, he maintains that Malick deconstructs the genre, but for another purpose: to reclaim it and self-consciously transform it. In this respect, he argues, Malick is akin to Arthur Penn and unlike directors such as Sergio Leone, Sam Peckinpah and Clint Eastwood who simply reinvent the western and create variations on a myth, reflecting the cynicism of their own age in the tone of their films.

Focusing on *Badlands*, *Bonnie and Clyde* (1967), *Days of Heaven* and *The Missouri Breaks* (1976), he notes first the difference of Malick and Penn's filmmaking style, looking specifically at the historical factors and manner of working which affected their output, along the way discussing the significance of their auteurism, the genesis of their films and the subsequent effect of their releases on the directors' careers. Crucially, however, he argues that both directors 'lay bare … the process of American myth-making as a practice of historic becoming'; they show the moments that history becomes myth and is caught as such within the realm of the spectacle. Not only a fascinating analysis of the films themselves, Orr's chapter thus provides a comprehensive and intriguing overview of filmmaking at the end of the 1960s and throughout the 1970s, and a riposte to Peter Biskind's 'burnout' myth, as promoted in *Easy Riders, Raging Bulls* (1998b).

Continuing with an analysis of both *Badlands* and *Days of Heaven*, Ben McCann focuses on Malick's use of landscape. Not merely beautiful images, he maintains that the director's careful framing of the landscape imparts 'a lyrical intensity, an emotional texture and a narrative depth'. Looking at the interplay between humans and nature – how the environment shapes and affects individuals – he explains how 'image-events' invite us to make comparisons between the protagonist and his/her environment, and how the landscape takes on a symbolic weight to the point where it becomes a protagonist. Concentrating on key elements of nature's indifference to human chaos, the externalisation of inner emotions, and the mythic rumination on violence and death in nature, he examines Malick's imagining of beauty, power and conflict.

Turning to an examination of Malick's aural landscape, Anne Latto spotlights his decision to use young female narrators in both *Badlands* and *Days of Heaven*. Unusually for Hollywood, where the voice is typically male and adult, she argues that this choice centralises the question of point of view, its limitation and reliability. This notion of the 'innocent abroad', more common in American literature in characters such as Holden Caulfield and Huckleberry Finn, becomes her main concern, and how the notion of 'innocence' can be interpreted. She also includes an afterword on the voice of Pocahontas in *The New World*.

Drawing on feminist theory and writings from Simone de Beauvoir (1949) to Judith Butler (1990), Latto points to the differences between Linda and Holly as gendered subjects and the implications of this divergence. Through textual analysis – the cadence, rhythm and content of the girls' speech – she demonstrates that Linda has been less constrained by the accepted societal norms of female behaviour, while Holly has more fully embraced her 'performance' as a middle-class young female of the 1950s. Attempting to fathom Malick's intentions regarding point of view and the viewer's apprehension of their respective worlds, she usefully applies Murray Smith's work (1995) on the three stages of the 'identification process' – recognition, alignment and allegiance – to the texts.

Having touched on one aspect of the aural, in complementary chapters Richard Power and James Wierzbicki explore Malick's use of sound and music, again areas that have been under-researched. Both centre their investigation on *Days of Heaven*; Power its symbolic use of music, and Wierzbicki its use of sound as music.

Power first locates the three main areas of the film's music: Camille Saint-Saëns's pre-composed classical-style piece *The Aquarium*, examples of folk music and Ennio Morricone's score, which was composed for the film. The first two elements work together, he argues, to delineate class, *The Aquarium* associated with the upper class – the Farmer – and the folk music with the working classes – Bill, Abby and Linda. They also function on another metaphorical level. Saint-Saëns's music is a character piece, 'designed to convey the image of life within an aquarium as it floats slowly along', and the idea of aquariums run throughout the film, he points out, from the wheat fields of 'ocean waves' to the coach car of President Wilson's train. Through a specific association, the folk music is connected to the idea of the devil, hell and the flames that eventually engulf the farm. At key moments, the music variously reflects the status of the protagonists, their shift in status or their desire to alter their status. Morricone's score, rather than embodying the overarching thematics of the film, complements, informs and drives the narrative. To support this reading, Power breaks the music down into its separate components, linking scenes where segments of the music may be repeated to explore the thrust and meaning of the narrative, and the relationship of the characters.

James Wierzbicki opens his chapter with an assertion made by Charles Schreger in an article about the new Dolby technology of the 1970s that 'there's no more intelligent use of sound than in *Days of Heaven*' (1985: 352), and goes on to test the value and truth of this assertion. Drawing on the work of theorists such as Michel

Chion and Raymond Bellour, he contextualises the customary uses of the score within the film narrative: how it can inform the dramatic content of a scene, paralleling the drama or countering it, and establish 'dramatic-psychological' links between scenes. Making reference to *Badlands* and *The Thin Red Line* but concentrating in-depth on *Days of Heaven*, he considers the manner in which noises and sounds are unusually foregrounded and function musically. He contests Rick Altman's assertions that musical terms should not be used in reference to film sound, and goes on to demonstrate that filmic sounds 'can serve as a score', performing 'functions similar to those normally assigned to non-diegetic music'. The film's opening for instance, in the steel mill, consists only of diegetic sound – 'clinks', 'hisses', 'clangs' and 'screeches' – yet is, Wierzbicki states, a musical experience. Extremely detailed textual analysis of these opening sequences and the scenes when the locusts attack the farm are illustrated by figures that usefully chart the duration and effect of the sound organisation in seconds, unpacking the film's complex synthesis of the aural and visual, upholding, if not wholly endorsing, Schreger's claim.

An appropriate opening to the section on *The Thin Red Line*, Martin Flanagan's chapter contextualises the state of the filmmaking business in the 1970s, the 'golden age' in which Malick initially came to prominence, and examines the industrial and critical context of his return in the mid-1990s. Pointing to his status as a director with a personal – and not necessarily commercial – vision, he initially considers the relationship of *The Thin Red Line* to *Saving Private Ryan*. Where Twentieth Century Fox had problems creating a clear-cut identity for *The Thin Red Line*, from the beginning, he argues, *Saving Private Ryan* won out with the public because of its marketing campaign; he cites, for instance, the success of *Schindler's List* (1993) and Spielberg's public involvement with 'recording' World War Two, and the differences between *Saving Private Ryan*'s palpable moral position and *The Thin Red Line*'s ambiguity.

He also details the problematic critical responses to the film, the implications of its financial underachievement and Malick's return to cinema as an 'event'. Recognising that the film does not fit easily into the genre of the war film, Flanagan considers *The Thin Red Line* textually in relation to existing generic and narrative modes, and the discourses surrounding it, both critical and promotional; to test the veracity of responses, he examines one of the film's crucial segments, the capture of Hill 210. By way of an update, Flanagan dissects the critical reception and performance of *The New World*, and Malick's now singular role within Hollywood given the tendency of his more notable 'movie brat' peers towards conformity.

John Streamas also considers *The Thin Red Line*'s relationship to history and defines it as a film 'better suited … to the culture of demythologising that characterised the 1970s', citing films such as *The Deer Hunter* (Michael Cimino, 1978) and *Apocalypse Now* (Francis Ford Coppola, 1979) that dealt with the Bad War that was Vietnam. He investigates the myth of the Good War that has grown up since that time, and specifically from the 1990s with the fiftieth anniversary of World War Two, promulgated by *Saving Private Ryan* and Tom Brokaw's book *The Greatest Generation* (2001). He contests that Malick's film does deal with certain aspects of historical particularity but seems to prefer, when faced with the competing Good War myth, to use myth as a narrative mode better able to 'expose and resist the most brutal aspects of human nature';

he concludes, however, that *The Thin Red Line* is at its most persuasive in debunking the Good War myth, in its moments of historical particularity.

Exploring the relationship of *The Thin Red Line* to James Jones' source novel and also Andrew Marton's 1964 film adaptation, Stacey Peebles argues that Malick transcends the war film genre, making the claim that he 'completely excise[s] the body from [his] war story'. While Jones' book (and to an extent Marton's film) focuses on the corporeal aspects of war – with sexuality and violence grounded in the physical – Malick, she insists, expunges these aspects to privilege, and concentrate on, the spiritual, transcendental nature of war. It is Private Witt, heroic and redemptive, who is the film's clear protagonist, and the majority of the film, the framing of the action and the backdrop of Guadalcanal, is seen from his perspective. Encompassing the ideals promulgated in Ralph Waldo Emerson's *Nature* (1836), for Malick and Witt, alongside Emerson, she proposes that 'nature and spirituality are inextricably entwined'. Comparing instances in the book with sequences in the film, she draws on the war genre work of Stanley Solomon, Stuart Kaminsky and Thomas Doherty.

Developing Ben McCann's analysis of Malick's 1970s films, Robert Silberman recognises the central importance of landscape and the natural world in *The Thin Red Line* and how its representation expresses the director's central concerns. As in *Badlands* and *Days of Heaven*, landscape in his third film provides an appropriate backdrop 'for a movement from innocence to experience haunted by a dream of Paradise', dramatising the opposition between nature as paradise and modern human society as paradise lost. For Malick, he argues, nature and war are inextricably linked and he thus refutes claims such as Tom Whalen's (1999) that the film is nothing to do with war and all about man's relationship to nature. Landscape is not merely a backdrop to events in the film, but intrinsic to Malick's vision of war, a war of territory and terrain. This is evident not only in battle scenes, which he analyses, but in the dialogue between characters and the interior monologues. The nature of nature – whether it is essentially cruel or not – is manifested in the conflict between Staros and Tall; Witt and Welsh, one a spiritualist, the other a materialist, argue about their divergent attitudes towards nature and human nature. Exploring the film's imaginings of Eden and its references to the new world (quoting from the original script), Silberman asserts the presence of both paradise and paradise lost in Malick's cinematic world, one which is dark but has the possibility for redemption. He also includes discussion of *The New World*'s positioning of landscape in relation to *The Thin Red Line*.

Like Martin Flanagan, Marc Furstenau and Leslie MacAvoy assert that critics have been more concerned with the 'trifling issues' of Malick's long-term absence and return to cinema; their primary concern is with *The Thin Red Line* as a philosophical project, one which prompts a dialogue between the film and its audience. Citing Malick's background in philosophy, specifically the work of Martin Heidegger, they define the film as an example of Heideggerian cinema, which manifests several of the philosopher's teachings in its key themes. They refer to the work of Stanley Cavell, a leading philosopher who has observed the connection between metaphysical and cinematic representation, and written on Malick's cinema as one such example. Unpacking the complexity of Heidegger's philosophy, essential concepts such as the Being of beings and the Presence of beings are elucidated. The director uses poetry as a mode of representation, they believe, to defy generic expectation and by choosing that genre 'draws attention to the film as a mode of presentation or presence', thus moving beyond the realm of 'representation'. Examining the dynamics and interchanges both between Tall/Staros and Welsh/Witt as an example of his strategy, they convey the context of war as one of alienation through technology and modernity, and conclude that he is a 'poet in destitute times' who reminds us of our mortality and humanity.

This second edition of *The Cinema of Terrence Malick* welcomes the addition of three new essays on *The New World*. Mark Cousins adopts a personal approach, mapping out his shifting, conflicting responses to the film. He describes the powerful emotions it provoked on first viewing, and his later frustration and irritation at its lack of innovation, similarity to Malick's previous work and preoccupation with America. On re-viewing the film, however, its stature rose as he recognised and engaged with its Humeanism nature, of 'impressions accumulating into ideas', as these characters construct their sense of the world/s around them.

James Morrison considers the characterisation of Smith and Pocahontas and how each are positioned within and in relation to their worlds, but with reference to the work of Heidegger and Hannah Arendt. He contests that *The New World* sees a new kind of sophistication in Malick's filmmaking, which 'explores the ways in which history, legend and ideology combine to produce possibilities for a pluralistic 'worldview' – and to subvert them'. Unlike his previous films, where nature imagery featured between narrative segments, here it becomes 'an essential component of narrative progress', raising the possibility for the first time 'that nature really could be somehow accessible to the people who inhabit it'.

Adrian Martin contends that *The New World* is structured around 'a displacement of – and investigation into – personal identity'. He demonstrates how Smith and Pocahontas are constructed ambiguously, like previous Malick characters – not fixed, or 'three-dimensional' but as ghostly, 'cinematic'. Though figures of history and/or myth, Malick portrays them in the 'becoming state before such a congealing of identity' that the passage of time allows. Martin attributes Malick's achievement, in part, to the fact that he is so knowledgeable about his films' subject-matter, which gives 'his work a palpable depth or volume that is rare in world cinema'; comparable, for example, only with Kubrick, Dreyer and Erice. Following an analysis of the film's philosophy of love, he also considers the critical backlash to *The New World* and the impossibility of quickly knowing or understanding one of the director's films, struck ultimately by the notion that 'love for a Malick film is rather like love in a Malick film'.

Notes

1   See, for instance, Hwanhee Lee (2002) who has surmised that 'the lack of much critical work on Malick's films is partly due to the fact that ... it is hard to articulate the motivations or concerns behind them'.

2   Published in 1998, Orr's book only deals with *Badlands* and *Days of Heaven*. He returned to a discussion of poetry and Malick to look at all three films after the release of *The Thin Red Line* (Orr, 1999: 24–6). Usually *Badlands* is mentioned within sections on the road movie or the outlaw couple (See Corrigan 1991: 151–

3; Sargeant 1999: 148–68; Laderman 2002: 117–27), *Days of Heaven* receives scant mention and *The Thin Red Line* is now included within discussions of war movies (see Doherty 1999: 300–15; McCrisken & Pepper 2005: 89–130; Polan 2005: 53–61) or philosophy and cinema (see Bersani & Dutoit 2004: 124–78). References to Malick's authorship as a whole tend to be brief but Ryan Gilbey has recently explored the director's work in his study of 1970s cinema, *It Don't Worry Me* (2003), and James Morrison and Thomas Schur have devoted a book-length study to the topic (2003).

3   See Biskind (1998a), Gillis (1995), Handy (1997), Young (1998) and Walker (1976). Most accounts state Malick's birth place as as Waco, Texas, some others as Ottowa, Illinois. Most are in agreement that his date of birth is 30 November, 1943, although occasionally it is cited as 1945. For further biographical detail about his upbringing see Chion (2004: 15–16).

4   See *Rosy-Fingered Dawn: A Film on Terrence Malick* (2002) and Biskind (1998b: 296–8).

5   See Biskind (1998a) for a version of events, and also Shtier (1994).

References

Andrew, Geoff (1999) *Directors A–Z: A Concise Guide to the Art of 250 Great Film-makers*. London: Prion Books.

Bersani, Leo & Ulysse Dutoit (2004) *Forms of Being: Cinema, Aesthetics, Subjectivity*. London: British Film Institute.

Biskind, Peter (1998a) 'The Runaway Genius', *Vanity Fair*, December, 460, 116–25.
_____ (1998b) *Easy Riders, Raging Bulls*. London: Bloomsbury.

Chion, Michel (2004) *The Thin Red Line*. London: British Film Institute.

Corrigan, Timothy (1991) *A Cinema Without Walls: Movies and Culture After Vietnam*. London: Routledge.

Doherty, Thomas (1999) *Projections of War: Hollywood, American Culture, and World War II*, revised edition. New York: Columbia University Press.

Gilbey, Ryan (2003) *It Don't Worry Me: Nashville, Jaws, Star Wars and Beyond*. London: Faber & Faber.

Gillis, Joe (1995) 'Waiting for Godot'. Available at: http://www.eskimo.com/~toates/malick/art5.html [Accessed: 25 October 2002]

Handy, Bruce (1998) 'Back from the Badlands', *Daily Telegraph Weekend Magazine*, 15 August, 20, 22, 24.

Kael, Pauline (1977) *Reeling*. London: Marion Boyars.

Laderman, David (2002) *Driving Visions: Exploring the Road Movie*. Texas: University of Texas Press.

Lee, Hwanhee (2002) 'Terrence Malick'. Available at: http://www.senses ofcinema.com/contents/directors/02/malick.html [Accessed: 18 December 2002]

Madden, John (1994) *The Poetry of Cinema*. Kidderminster: Crescent Moon Publishing.

McCrisken, Trevor & Andrew Pepper (2005) 'Saving the Good War: Hollywood and World War II in the post-Cold War world', in *American History and Contemporary*

Hollywood Film. Edinburgh: Edinburgh University Press, 89–130.

Morrison, James & Thomas Schur (2003) *The Films of Terrence Malick*. Westport, CT: Praeger.

Orr, John (1998) *Contemporary Cinema*. Edinburgh: Edinburgh University Press.

____ (1999) 'Poetic Enigma: The Films of Terrence Malick', *Film West*, 37, 24–6.

Percy, Walker (1998) [1961] *The Moviegoer*. New York: Vintage Books.

Pfeil, John (2004) 'Terrence Malick's war film sutra: meditating on *The Thin Red Line*', in Steven Schneider (ed.) *New Hollywood Violence*. Manchester: Manchester University Press, 165–182.

Polan, Dana (2005) 'Auteurism and War-teurism: Terrence Malick's War Movie', in Robert Eberwein (ed.) *The War Film*. New Brunswick: Rutgers University Press, 53–61.

Rosy-Fingered Dawn: A Film on Terrence Malick (2002) Directed by Luciano Barcaroli, Carlo Hinterman, Gerardo Panichi & Daniele Villa. Italy, Citrullo International.

Sargeant, Jack (1999) 'Killer Couples: From Nebraska to Route 666', in Jack Sargeant & Stephanie Watson (eds) *Lost Highways: An Illustrated History of Road Movies*. London: Creation Books, 148–68.

Shtier, Rachel (1994) 'The Elusive Playwright', *The Village Voice*, 11 January, 84, 86.

Thompson, Della (1998) *The Concise Oxford English Dictionary*. New York: Oxford University Press.

Walker, Beverly (1976) 'Malick on Badlands', *Sight and Sound*, 44, 2, 82–3.

Wilson, George M. (1988) *Narration in Light: Studies in Cinematic Point of View*. Baltimore: The John Hopkins University Press.

Young, Josh (1998) 'Hollywood's Prodigal Son', *Sunday Telegraph Review*, 5 July, 7.

Zaller, Robert (1999) 'Raising the Seventies: The Early Films of Terrence Malick', *Boulevard*, 15, 1–2, 141–55.

CHAPTER ONE

All Things Shining: The Struggle for Wholeness, Redemption and Transcendence in the Films of Terrence Malick

Ron Mottram

> Why should we be in such desperate haste to succeed and in such desperate enterprise? If a man does not keep pace with his companions, perhaps it is because he hears a different drummer.
>
> – Henry David Thoreau, *Walden* (1861)

Although this question is raised in one of the seminal works of nineteenth-century American thought and letters, it helps define the character and vision of Terrence Malick, who has avoided being swallowed up in the desperate enterprise of American commercial cinema and who has truly moved to the sound of a different drummer. That the result is the limited output of only four films over more than a quarter of a century simply reinforces the uniqueness of his vision and the seriousness of his purpose. The thoughtful consideration of philosophical, social and personal issues that is so evident in Malick's films does not mesh well with the formulaic preoccupations of an industry largely devoted to profit and the fleeting value of glamour and fame.

In an age and culture dominated by the simplified lies of commercial and political speech, and the desire for diversion, Malick asks the kind of difficult questions that, in American intellectual history, link him to such writers as Henry David Thoreau, Walt Whitman, Herman Melville and James Agee. In a period in the history of the visual arts in which the image is often sacrificed to a shallow conceptualism, he restores the beauty and power of the image as a carrier of meaning. In so doing, he has revived one of the strengths of the silent cinema, linking it to a sophisticated use of sound in voice-over narration and music.

This essay will elucidate some of the formal characteristics of Malick's films while linking his work to a number of the essential concerns and mythologies that have been central to American culture. Among these are the problem of the appearance of evil, the violation of nature in the world and in ourselves, the loss of paradise and the search for redemption, the barrenness of contemporary American life and the existence of violence as a reaction, the impingement of the urban and industrial on the pastoral, and the nature and meaning of war. It will explore the character of Malick's imagery, narrative structures, voice-over narration, non-narrative events and images, and figure to landscape relationships.

Among the strategies that will be used in making this analysis will be that of a dual chronology. The films will be considered both in the order of their making (*Badlands* (1973), *Days of Heaven* (1978), *The Thin Red Line* (1998), *The New World* (2005)) and in order of the time period of their stories (*The New World* (1607–1616), *Days of Heaven* (early 1910s), *The Thin Red Line* (World War Two), *Badlands* (1950s)). The chronology of production dates will allow an analysis of his development as a film-maker and the evolution of his style and formal strategies. The chronology of story time and setting will allow the films to be seen as a kind of American history that deals with issues such as the European imposition on and destruction of Native American culture, the passing of the pastoral myth, the questioning of belief in essential good-ness and meaning, and the potential loss of meaning in the media-saturated environ-ment of post-modern culture. As a body of work, considered from the vantage point of both chronologies, the films reveal an increasing difficulty in finding a human link to the natural world, personal and social 'redemption', peace and truth in a place and culture that was originally perceived by some of its founders to be a new Promised Land, and significance in a world in which the problem of evil has emerged in apoca-lyptic terms.

At the heart of all four films is an Edenic yearning to recapture a lost wholeness of being, an idyllic state of integration with the natural and good both within and with-out ourselves. Even *Badlands*, which on the surface seems bereft of acts or thoughts of goodness or wholeness, treats this yearning metaphorically and to a degree ironically. Holly's father paints a billboard that renders a peaceful rural scene with an idealised family. In his own house he has created a shelter from the contemporary world, simple and nostalgic in its decoration. Even Kit's murderous journey is a perverted struggle to find wholeness and a desperate attempt to define selfhood. In place of a real identity, he imitates James Dean. While Dean became an icon of alienated youth, Kit is only an image of an icon, trapped by his apparent nature and, from the perspective of the time of the film's making, by a popular and violent culture recently emerged from the Vietnam War, unsure of its present and its future, and unable to understand its past.

Everything in Kit and Holly's world is played out in a moral vacuum framed by Holly's naïve narration and analysis of events. The only things that stand in contrast to their world are the bits of the natural that survive amid the detritus of industriali-sation. Animals still live in the grass, the plains are still vast and empty, sunsets still light up the sky and birds still circle overhead, but what is their relation to the events and actions to which they bear witness? More than a simple opposition, Malick's use of nature and natural beauty rises to the level of a powerful sign for a higher good. Although most evident in *The Thin Red Line* and *The New World*, this signification is also present in *Badlands* and *Days of Heaven* and reveals an aspiration to understand the essential contradiction of darkness and light and to transcend it. In this is also revealed a high seriousness of purpose that links Malick to both Melville's exploration of the origin and meaning of evil and Thoreau's transcendental vision of nature as a link to a deeper reality.

'What's this war in the heart of nature?' asks Private Witt in the first narration of *The Thin Red Line*. 'Why does nature vie with itself? The land contend with the sea? Is there an avenging power in nature? Not one power but two?' As these words are being spoken, we see no images of war, just those of a peaceful nature and human community. The island paradise of the opening, however, is quickly replaced by the fear and horror of battle.

In each of the films, a character attempts to create and live in an idyllic world. In *Badlands*, Holly's father seeks order and a past in his house; the Farmer in *Days of Heaven* lives in a pristine Victorian mansion in the middle of vast and fruitful wheat fields; and Private Witt is AWOL in a native village in which all appears to be harmonious. Surrounding these three idyllic refuges, however, are dangerous and violent modern worlds that call into question the possibility of redemption from evil and the achievement of a sense of the wholeness and integration of all things. Even more conflicted, Captain John Smith in *The New World* is torn between his life and past as an English soldier and adventurer and his love for Pocahontas and the world of the 'Naturals', a world that is progressively lost for both him and the Naturals themselves. Nevertheless, the images of light shining through leaves and glancing off water, of wind blowing through wheat and grass, and of deep blue skies and sunsets suspended over the land function as a bridge to another world and as a sign of its existence.

At the same time, Malick does not close his eyes to the problem of evil. 'This great evil, where does it come from?' Witt asks in *The Thin Red Line*. 'How did it steal into the world? What seed, what root did it grow from? Who's doin' this? What's killin' us? Robbin' us of life and light? Mockin' us with the sight of what we might have known? Does our ruin benefit the earth? Does it help the grass to grow or the sun to shine? Is this darkness in you, too? Have you passed through this night?'

These questions and speculations are those of the viewers, too. The journeys are the viewers' journeys, which are also a pathway that leads through night. For this reason, Malick's and the characters' stories are the viewers' stories, even if the immediate events are unfamiliar and set in the past. And for this reason and because of their high seriousness and fundamental importance as questions, the issues raised resonate in a way that is the province of very few films.

Badlands begins with Holly, a lonely teenage girl sitting on her bed, who, in voice-over narration, succinctly defines her alienated relationship with her father. It immediately cuts to Kit, a young man working on a garbage truck. Between their initial meeting and their final parting, the relationship between these two isolated people is played out against a backdrop of the Dakota badlands, empty, beautiful and full of promise, while leading nowhere and dotted with remnants of civilisation and industrialisation. It is a landscape punctuated by brief idyllic moments and sudden violent acts. Above all, there is a perpetual sense of alienation and isolation of every character in the film, from each other, their environments, society and themselves. It is represented in a variety of ways: for Holly's father in his solitary work painting the billboard and in the interior of his house, drenched in the past; for Holly in her self-professed lack of friends and in the number of times she is seen framed by elements of the film's architecture, between parted curtains, in doorways, in windows and reflected in mirrors; for Kit in his moody pacing and staring, lack of ambition and concern, the number of times he is seen alone, and in his sudden and unprovoked acts of violence; and for Cato in his slow reactions and sedentary life in the small house set apart outside of town.

The emptiness of the characters' lives, their emotionless reaction to death and violence, their overall detachment from events, and the casual indifference with which they face the future are matched by their physical surroundings. The general emptiness of the streets in towns, the expansive barren landscapes through which they travel, and the vacant roads, as if existing only for their use, act as metaphors for separation and for the absence of any structure for the nurturing or sustaining of a human community and its individual members.

Early in the film, Holly is seen looking out of her bedroom window at night watching two boys on a street corner. It is not clear what they are doing or saying to each other, but it is clear that Holly's world is completely cut off from theirs, as she is cut off from her own childhood. This brief sequence is directly followed by one of Kit entering the almost deserted bus station to make a phonograph recording in a pay booth. While telling of their intended suicide, Kit is seen through the shattered glass of the booth, which is set in the middle of the space surrounded by darkness. The two sequences are the culminating images of the alienation of these two young people and set the stage for their flight.

Leaving Fort Dupree ends what can be thought of as the first idyllic section of the film, brought to finish by sudden violence. Two events precede this transition, the killing of Holly's dog by her father, in punishment for her lying to him about Kit, and the launching of the red balloon that Kit had found in the garbage. The shooting of the dog presages the murderous acts to come, and the releasing of the balloon, at least from Holly's point of view, the inevitable end of her relationship with Kit and of his ability to find redemption. As the balloon rises higher into a blue sky, Holly's commentary invests the moment with meaning: 'His heart was filled with longing as he watched it drift off. Something must have told him that we would never live these days of happiness again, that they were gone forever.'

Having lost 'these days of happiness', the romantic idyll gives way to Kit and Holly hiding out in the woods, where they build a tree house. In a sense they create a natural parallel to the artifice of the father's house, their own separate world free from the demands of society. Yet, they are not really separate. They have rescued a romantic landscape painting, an Art Nouveau lamp, and a stereoscope and slides from the house and brought them into their wooded encampment; Holly still puts curlers in her hair; and they dance to Mickey and Silva's song 'Love is Strange'. As a sign of their adventure, Holly reads to Kit from *Kon-Tiki*, but the reality is that they continue to carry, as they will throughout the film, tokens of the world they have abandoned.

Like the earlier idyllic section, this one also ends in violence – the killing of the three men who have come looking for them. From now on their journey allows them only brief moments of respite: eating dinner with Cato; resting and re-supplying at the Rich Man's house; and dancing to a Nat King Cole song in the light of the car's headlamps. As they head for Canada, it becomes clear that the goal of the narrative is not to resolve the couple's relationship or the issue of their crimes but to clarify the meaning of Kit's actions and his growing celebrity in a world in which heroes no longer have to be good, they just have to be successful. In order to become heroes two decades earlier, Bonnie and Clyde had to link their crime to a battle against oppressive banks, which were foreclosing on poor people's farms. Kit and Holly simply have to appeal to others' desire to escape boredom and the ordinary and to lash out against the difficulty of making sense of things.

Their last two days together mark the climax of the story and a major turning point for Kit. While stopped for the night, Kit is seen with his back to the camera and with his rifle across his shoulders and his arms draped over it, looking like a crucified figure or a scarecrow in the middle of an empty field. It is sunset, and he appears to be staring at the horizon. The image suggests reflection and a conscious and transitional moment. It is followed the next day by their encounter with a train, the first appearance of the world outside theirs in some time, and the burial of a bucket containing artifacts and proofs of their existence. A brief and forced moment of kissing in the car just before the train first appears in the distance and dancing in the headlights that night mark the end of the relationship. The next day, she refuses to leave with him when the helicopter carrying lawmen arrives at the oil camp, and he takes off on his own.

Although Holly's narration continues, Kit takes control of his own story. He discards Holly's clothes and suitcase, and after a chase by the sheriff, he stages his capture by shooting out his own tyres, making a stone marker of the place of capture, and surrendering. No sooner do they have him in custody than the deputy remarks on how much Kit looks likes James Dean. In a way, the deputy becomes as taken with Kit's self-constructed identity as was Holly. It is clear that Kit receives not only recognition in this sequence but also a strange kind of admiration and, from his own perspective, even sanctification. He has chosen to trade his life for a fleeting recognition of his existence, and in so doing he redeems himself in his own eyes. Had Kit lived in the late 1990s and had the film been made 20 years later, his status as a celebrity might have been confirmed in becoming a subject for reality television. As it is, the film stands as a commentary on the difficulty, if not the impossibility, of transcendence in the post-modern, post-Vietnam world.

In *Days of Heaven*, Malick returns to many of the ideas he explored in *Badlands* but on a more philosophical level and couched in imagery and events that are Biblical in nature. Like the earlier film, an act of violence initiates flight and a journey in search of a better life, which takes Bill, Abby and Linda to an idyllic natural environment that has the potential of becoming their Canaan. Like Abram and Sarai in the Old Testament, Bill and Abby pretend to be brother and sister, and the result of their subterfuge parallels that of the original story in the Book of Genesis. As God 'plagued Pharaoh and his house with great plagues' because he took Sarai into his house, thinking she was Abram's sister instead of his wife (Genesis 12), the Farmer in *Days of Heaven* is also plagued, first by locusts which begin to destroy his wheat crop and then by fire as the result of his own violent response to the trick played on him.

The events in the Texas panhandle are foreshadowed in the apocalyptic descriptions of the end of the world that Bill's young sister gives in her narration and which she says were prophesied by a friend named Ding Dong. On a larger scale this death and destruction models the immediate sufferings of the people she saw in Chicago: 'We used to roam the streets; there was people suffering in pain and hunger; some people their tongues are hanging out of their mouth.' In an attempt to flee this world of suffering, the trio run away from the streets of Chicago, from jobs in the steel mill, and from the consequences of Bill's killing of the foreman. They travel with other migrant workers by freight train, seen at first in the distance crossing a bridge, much in the way the train appears crossing the plains in *Badlands*.

In the earlier film, the train signifies the existence of that permanent world beyond the immediate, temporary world that Kit and Holly construct in their flight. In the later film, it functions more as a link between the idyllic world of the wheat fields and the world outside, as does the airplane of the flying circus, the motorcycle that Bill rides on his return to the farm, and the car used for the honeymoon and later for escape after the Farmer is killed. The train carrying President Wilson on his whistle-stop tour also brings in the outer world and especially suggests the world war, which seems so far away. As idyllic as their lives appear to be, there is both trouble in paradise, seen in Bill's and the Farmer's mutual jealousies over Abby, and trouble in the world at large. The personal conflict and the international conflict are versions of the same problem, though different in scale. The national insignia on the planes of the flying circus and, especially, Abby's leaving on the troop train at the end of the film signify the impossibility of escaping this interrelationship.

This interplay of elements and ideas is encoded in the structure of the film itself. The opening, including the credit sequence with its photographs, introduces the urban world of poverty and industrial work, the world of 'people suffering in pain and hunger'. Nature is absent, the only water runs past a slagheap, fire is contained in a furnace, and the sky is darkened by factory smoke. In contrast, the wheat fields of the second section of the film present a world in which people seem to live in harmony with nature, the water is pure and cleansing, and the skies are defined in striking colours. Yet within this great natural beauty, human motives and passions pose the same danger of bringing suffering. The farm is also a world of exploitive work and war-induced profits in which power resides in wealth and the machine encroaches on the garden.

With the end of the harvest, the farm and its remaining inhabitants settle into an idyllic life in which play and leisure dominate, passions and deception slip into the background, and the cycle of the seasons brings nature to the forefront. Bill's departure and apparent acceptance of the growing love of Abby for the Farmer removes for a time the remaining threat to this pastoral scene. However, like the return of planting and harvest, which culminates in the plague of locusts, Bill's return reintroduces the seed of jealousy and conflict, which results in the conflagration of fire and the deaths of both Bill and the Farmer. In light of the Biblical connections of this narrative, the arrival of the locusts and the destruction they bring to the wheat suggests the possible existence of judgement and punishment for human actions or, at least, a joint appearance of evil in both the human and natural spheres.

Structurally, the fire which destroys the crop and the fire which destroys the house in *Badlands* serve a similar purpose, as do the killing of the Farmer and the killing of the father. The fires destroy worlds which can no longer exist and, in a sense, never existed in an ideal state, and the killings force the main characters to flee and result in death at the hands of the law. They also cause the main female characters to create new lives for themselves. The final sequence in the town reintroduces the world at large and elevates the primal conflicts in the characters' lives to the wider scale of war. Although Linda's world remains personal as she walks along the railroad tracks with her friend into an uncertain future, Abby boards a troop train and joins the country as it moves into even greater uncertainty of participation in the 'war to end all wars'.

More than the first two films, *The Thin Red Line* transcends the immediate setting and action of the narrative to ask questions that penetrate to the heart of the Western mythos, such as the source and nature of evil, the existence of the spiritual, and the role and meaning of love. The existence of war as a great evil, especially on a world scale, raises the stakes of the discussion far beyond Kit's murder spree and the interlaced jealousies and conflicts of Bill and the Farmer. The characters struggle with war itself more than they do with the Japanese enemy. Unlike most films about World War Two, *The Thin Red Line* is not concerned with the right or wrong of a cause but with the horror and meaning of the conflict for all involved. The war functions more like the great white whale in Melville's *Moby Dick*, as a force that needs to be explained, than as a setting for the defence of political and cultural values or a theatre for personal courage.

The film begins with a metaphor. The island paradise, which serves as a hideaway and refuge for Witt, points to another world, one that Witt maintains a belief in despite the immediate horror of the war and Sergeant Welsh's ongoing counter argument that there is no world other than the one they are experiencing. In a sense, Witt has seen this other world, partly in his mother's calm facing of death and partly in his own good-natured faith, stated in his narration and signified throughout the film in the use of light seen through the vegetation, reflected off the tall grass, and shimmering in the water. Witt's 'spark', as Welsh refers to it, is never extinguished, even in his own death at the end of the film.

This philosophical conflict, best represented in the world-views of Private Witt and Sergeant Welsh, is paralleled by the conflict between the personal and the professional that operates on a number of levels. It is most forcibly seen in Colonel Tall, who has been skipped over for promotion because he had no prior war experience. In his frustrated desire to fulfil his professional life, he has squandered the possibilities of family life. Over the sequence of his conversation with the general on the deck of the troop ship, his voice is heard lamenting his loss: 'All they sacrificed for me. Poured out like water on the ground. All I might have given for love's sake. Too late.' For Captain Staros, this conflict has to do with his attempts to protect the lives of his men and the demands of combat, which require their deaths to achieve a military objective. It culminates in his refusing to obey Tall's order for a frontal attack. For Private Bell, the conflict is in his longing for his wife and the life they had before the war and his fearful participation in the battle.

The most powerful aspect of the conflict between the personal and the professional, and the one that most clearly feeds into the larger philosophical and moral issues of the film, is that which pits human beings against each other as enemies. Although the idea of the other as enemy is essential to war, it violates an even more essential idea. In Witt's words, we are 'all faces of the same man. One big self'. This humanistic concept is the personal put in universal terms and cannot co-exist with the professional in war. The contradiction is most poignantly implied in an image of a dead Japanese soldier's face peering out of the earth shortly after the bunkers are taken by the American troops. The voice-over narration, speaking for the dead soldier, asks, 'Are you righteous? Kind? Does your confidence lie in this? Are you loved by all? Know that I was, too. Do you imagine that your sufferings will be less because you loved goodness? Truth?' These pointed questions, which apply to all the soldiers, American and Japanese, are reinforced in the sequence of the attack on the Japanese encampment. The killing, the suffering and the fear are presented in terms so remarkably personal that the very idea of an enemy as other disappears. What remains is simply a human tragedy.

Whatever the ultimate answers to the questions the film raises, there is a sense of inevitability that drives the action of the narrative and the futures of the characters as much as it does the great contradictions that exist in human nature and the world. One scene in particular seems to signify this inevitability. As the small group of soldiers who are sent to find the bunker move through the grass and up the hill, they are followed by the camera, which shows them from behind and moves above them and the grass. At first it seems as if the camera is just tracking them, but it becomes evident that it is not tied to their movement. It passes over some of the soldiers as the others begin to move off to the right. The camera continues its movement, as if under its own motivation, towards the top of the hill where the bunker is located. This camera movement, as brief as it is, speaks to this inevitability because it is so completely free of the characters' actions. It suggests that war itself, or the contradiction in nature that war may represent, drives these men forward to their battle for the bunker and to their confrontation with the Japanese and the conflicted elements within themselves.

The climax of the narrative comes with the taking of the Japanese encampment. It is the most immediate and revealing of all the battle sequences. It presents a powerful image of war as the destruction of the personal and of the humanity within us. This is seen most clearly in the reactions of the fearful and wounded Japanese soldiers and in the American soldier who goes around with pliers pulling and collecting the gold teeth of the Japanese dead. As if to wash away this horror and perhaps the guilt, the Americans are seen at the edge of a stream washing and filling canteens. Witt pours water over one soldier's head, almost in baptism. Following this, the Americans use flamethrowers to burn the encampment, an image that calls up the burning of the house in *Badlands*, the burning of the wheat in *Days of Heaven*, and the burning of the Naturals' crops and village in *The New World*. All four sequences suggest the attempt to wipe something away: Kit's crime and Holly's past life; the Farmer's pain and jealousy in having been betrayed; the hideous images and acts of killing in battle; and the

Naturals' more integrated life and their right to the land which the English colonisers neither recognise nor are able to harmoniously share.

In summary to what we have seen, a voice-over narration concludes, 'War don't ennoble men. It turns them into dogs. Poisons the soul.' Despite this dark truth, another truth is immediately placed in contradiction to it. Over shots of his wife and himself, Bell muses, 'Love. Where does it come from? This flame in us. No war can put it out, conquer it.'

As the narrative moves towards its conclusion, these two sentiments are tested in Witt. At twilight he walks through a native village, but unlike the opening sequence, he encounters fear and conflict among the villagers. His narration brings questionings and doubts to his mind, like Jesus in the Garden of Gethsemane on the night before his crucifixion. He talks about people as a family that had to break up, 'each standing in the other's light'. He asks, 'How did we lose the good that was given us? Let it slip away? Scattered. Careless. What's keeping us from reaching out? Touching the glory?' Arriving back at the camp, he encounters Welsh for the last time, and once again Welsh questions Witt's belief in the light, in something beyond the immediate evidence of a pervading darkness.

Although Witt is killed in the last battle sequence, his death is immediately contradicted metaphorically by the image of him, from the beginning of the film, swimming underwater with the villagers. This, combined with his final voice-over narration, suggests some triumph over both the questions he repeatedly asks and the materially-bound perspective of Welsh. Welsh's final question, as he crouches over Witt's makeshift grave, 'Where's your spark now?' is answered in that final narration: 'Look out through my eyes. Look out at the things you made. All things shining.' Is Malick asking us to look though Witt's eyes, to discover all things shining, despite what our senses and experience of the world tell us? The answer to this question and to the greater question of whether the grand redemption that Witt is seeking is actually possible, especially in light of the great evils of the twentieth century, lie beyond the scope of Malick's film. Nevertheless, the film's willingness to raise such issues is part of its greatness and make it one of the truly thoughtful and intelligent films of our time.

The New World has much in common with Malick's first three films, while, at the same time, it goes further than they in its use of nature as a narrative element and, in some ways, demands more of its audience by shifting the focus, significantly, from character and action to nature itself as a carrier of meaning. The very title of the film suggests what its subject matter is. It proposes not just a place of character action and development, though it includes that as well, but a world view that is more than new territory and a colonial extension of an old world, or even a chance for a new beginning. Rather, the film is primarily about a new land, or, more precisely, a new concept of the land and human beings' relationship to it. The colonial concept of a new geographical and political entity, which this new world ultimately becomes, misses an important requirement for it to become truly a new world for the English settlers. From the point of view of the film, it requires a transformation of thought, which none of the English characters, including John Smith, finally prove capable of accomplishing because of the cultural, religious, social and political baggage they bring to Virginia with them.

The means the film uses to explore this issue focuses on the character of Pocahontas and, in a correlative way, on that of John Smith. The love story of Pocahontas and Smith constitutes the principal narrative thread of the film, and in a metaphoric way, its principal signifier. This romantic relationship contradicts the historical reality on which it is based, despite the fact that Malick, in general, has attempted to recreate the Jamestown experience physically in great historical detail. The set, shooting location, costumes, make-up, movement of the Naturals, natural elements on the soundtrack and use of historical sources are central to the film's realism. His free treatment of characters, historical events and time frame, although certainly resting on a foundation of historical truth, reinvents the story of Jamestown to suit Malick's own interests as a filmmaker and artist.

At the heart of this reinvention is the story of Pocahontas and John Smith, which he treats in terms of the traditional and non-historical mythology of her saving his life and of the romance between them that followed. James Horn points out in his book, *A Land As God Made It: Jamestown and the Birth of America*, that since Pocahontas was only eleven years old when this incident took place and had never seen Smith before, that 'given her age and background it was not romantic love; but she may have seen him as a father figure or special friend (he once called her his 'dearest jewel and daughter'), and he may have viewed her as an exceptionally bright young girl who had the ear of Wahunsonacock [her father and chief of the Powhatans]' (2005: 68–9).

The mythic/romantic approach does not in the least damage the film. On the contrary, it is one of its great strengths because it functions as an expression of something deeper, the issue of humans' relations to nature and the land. Pocahontas emerges as the central character of the film and the purest expression of a harmonious integration of the human and the natural environment that is presented as characteristic of the Naturals, at least as seen from Smith's point of view. The opening images state this integration visually. Pocahontas and her brother are seen swimming underwater, and the sky and clouds are reflected in water. Juxtaposed to the images is her voice-over narration in which she calls on the Spirit: 'Help us sing the story of our land. You are our mother, we your field of corn. We rise from out of the soul of you.' Smith is presented as not only drawn to Pocahontas romantically but also to the Naturals as a people, their autochthonous view of themselves, and the integrated, harmonious nature of their society. What makes *The New World* so extraordinary from an aesthetic point of view is how the cinematography integrates character and environment in complex, unified signs of the human, natural, philosophical and religious meanings that are brought together under the central concept of the land. The film itself can be seen as the song of the land that Pocahontas prays for.

A consideration of the four films in chronologically-ordered narrative and historical time allows the construction of a particular history of America that charts the establishment of the earliest permanent colony and the conflicts and contradictions that entailed (which remain yet to be resolved), the end of the pastoral myth in the early 19th century (a Europeanised version of the Naturals' relationship to the land that greeted the first settlers), the triumph of industrialisation in its most virulent form (mechanised, global war) and the emergence of a post-war culture that is without a defined sense of identity and values. The films also mark a progressive violation of the natural world and of the natural within the human being, as well as a growing difficulty of maintaining a moral code and a belief in meaning.

The New World places in opposition the two mythologies that collided as the first English adventurers and settlers arrived with their complex goals of establishing a new Promised Land, that on one hand would offer them unlimited opportunities for human development and the creation of a more egalitarian society and on the other to increase their wealth through the exploitation of the land and their religion through the conversion of the native inhabitants. This new world, of course, was only a new world for the colonists and from a European perspective. For the Native Americans it meant the loss of their land and world. Thrust against the mythos of a nature-based society, represented in the film as peaceful, integrated and harmonious, though, in reality, often warlike before the arrival of the Europeans, was the power-based, politicised and expansionist society of the English, represented as largely unconcerned with the native peoples, except as a potential enemy.

For the English the land was a physical fact to be developed not just as a place to live but as a generator of wealth and political power, especially against Spain which had already established itself on the North American continent. Although not clearly expressed in the film, land for the Powhatans was also a political entity. Horn points out that 'the rise of the Powhatan chiefdom was the central political development of the late sixteenth and early seventeenth centuries, shaping the lives of Indian peoples throughout the coastal plain (tidewater) of Virginia, as well as of these strangers who arrived from across the ocean' (2005: 11–12). He also stresses that to maintain this dominant position, 'Powhatan society was organized for war, a response to the threat posed by powerful enemies to the north and west ... and Wahunsonacock's (Pocahontas's father) territorial ambitions' (ibid.). The film ignores this aspect of the Naturals' history by focusing on the religious and philosophical integration of a life lived as a part of nature with only positive social outcomes. The Powhatans' capacity for war is presented as defensive.

Keeping with the focus of the film was the Powhatans' religious practice. According to Horn, 'Religion and spirituality were of fundamental importance to Indian peoples and were expressed in a rich variety of beliefs about powerful deities, local spirits, myths, and prophecies. The Powhatans revered a 'great, good God', Ahone, who lived in the heavens above and whose perfection was boundless. Ahone had created the cosmos, the Earth, and lesser gods; had taught the Indians how to plant corn; he was the 'author of their good'. He made 'the Sun to shine'; through his 'virtues and Influences the under earth is tempered, and brings forth her fruictes according to her seasons". In addition, there was a second powerful god, Okeus, who was a not god of peace, but one who was the "malitious enemy of mankind' ... the origin of all harm and misfortune'. He also 'stirred up wars" (2005: 20–21).

Pocahontas's periodic prayers addressed to 'Mother' are at the heart of the film's religious considerations and are clearly linked to Ahone through their accompanying images and to the description of the Naturals' fundamental goodness that one of Smith's voice-over narrations provides. Malick's historical recreation of the settling of Jamestown, though accurate in its physical rendering and many of its essential events, shifts the overall meaning of the events and those who participated in them away from history to a broader mythic and philosophical significance, much as he did with the Battle of Guadalcanal in *The Thin Red Line*.

The very title *Days of Heaven*, suggests both a harmonious state of existence and the impossibility of its lasting beyond a short time. Although most of the narrative takes place in a pastoral setting, the film begins in that industrialised world which, by the mid-1910s setting of the story, had already replaced the earlier dominance of the agricultural. The Sam Shepard character runs a large, mechanised farming operation, which is a far cry from Thomas Jefferson's ideal of the yeoman farmer. As idyllic as the farm seems to be for its off-season inhabitants, it is an island in a land of factories and world war, and as a wheat producer, especially in wartime, it is actually part of the industrial system. Yet the land is beautiful and the farming activity, with all its accompanying human conflicts and emotions, exists in relation to the natural world that goes on despite the incursions made upon it. Ultimately, however, this semi-pastoral world cannot be sustained. It is attacked by a true force of nature, the locusts, and is destroyed by a fire caused by human actions. The locusts are not a problem in nature because the planted and cultivated wheat is not truly natural, and its loss would be a financial, not a natural, disaster. The man-made fire consumes everything, the locusts, the animals that live amid the growing wheat, and the hope for a peaceful life. The myth of the pastoral ideal, like the actual events of history, cannot be reclaimed, and the only place for Abby and Linda is somewhere in the modern world. Abby vows to redeem herself by somehow making up for what she has done. Linda, less conscious of the need to do this, allows the railroad tracks to take her wherever they might lead. There is a sense at the end of the film that there are still possibilities for them, that a moral order still exists that can be used to reconstruct their lives.

The two decades after the end of the period presented in *Days of Heaven* saw America's participation in World War One, the frenzied modernity of the 1920s and the sobering reality of the Great Depression, and culminated in the catastrophe of World War Two, a human conflict of such great proportions that it shook the foundations of American belief systems. The material and destructive capacity of the industrialised nations overwhelmed their moral structures to such a degree that there was no escaping the profound philosophical, religious and moral questioning that inevitably took place. To a degree unseen before, the war destroyed cities, people, nature and our mythologies about civilisation, human conduct and meaning, and challenged the belief in a moral order.

Most films dealing with World War Two have concerned themselves with the struggle against Fascism and the preservation of democratic systems and values. *The Thin Red Line*, however, puts aside the political issues and adopts a distanced stance in relation to the historical events that allows the war to be viewed as both the outcome of a deeper problem and as a testing ground of faith in essential goodness, the significance of the individual, and higher meaning. The war brings the individuals fighting it to the edge of the absurd and requires that they either abandon explanation or find a way to look beyond the immediate. As the historical event that is the field for this struggle, the war divides the first half of America's twentieth-century experience, with its inherited belief in fixed meaning and moral order, however strained, from the second half, which gives birth to a world cut loose from the moorings of cultural, social, behavioural and moral norms.

The struggle to preserve meaning and the belief in the possibility of redemption runs throughout *The Thin Red Line*. This war in the heart of nature and in the hearts and minds of the individual soldiers cannot be won by defeating the enemy and taking control of the island. It can only be won, if at all, by defeating the despair brought on by the apparent absurdity of the war itself. Although the film raises questions and examines points of view, it does not attempt to provide definitive answers. That it was made over fifty years after the end of the war indicates that the fundamental questions it asks are still vitally relevant in Malick's mind. Despite the pessimism expressed by many of the characters, the film does not adopt cynicism or the self-absorbed amorality of the post-modern world. Nor does it, like Spielberg's *Saving Private Ryan* (1998), resort to a nostalgic celebration of an earlier mythos of heroism and self-sacrifice. *The Thin Red Line* stands unashamedly as a present call for serious ontological thinking, and, as such, it not only references a period of historical change and moral crisis, but claims a higher ground of thought for our own time.

Set in the 1950s, *Badlands* looks back to that period of malaise in American culture which was defined by the aftershock of world war, the fears engendered by the Cold War, and the questioning of both cultural and individual identity. Among the manifestations of this were the rise of a rebellious youth culture, most strongly represented in the screen persona of James Dean and in the emergence of rock'n'roll, two elements that play a significant part in *Badlands*. The real issues raised by the war were submerged by the rapid growth of a consumer economy, the American response to communism, and the alienation of young people from mainstream American values and behaviour. Kit and Holly are signifiers of this alienation taken to the extreme. On one level, Kit's murder spree, as coldly casual as it is, is a minor issue in comparison to the slaughter of War World Two; Kit is only an amateur at killing when compared to the nations of the world, and a symptom of the moral ambiguity of his time. At his trial, something chilling is provided for Kit. He becomes a celebrity, liked by his captors and sent off to the electric chair with a wish of good luck.

The period in which *Badlands* is set marks the transition to post-modern America. The conflagration of war, like the burning of Holly's father's house, had cleared away the past and its certainties, leaving a future of great uncertainty that would include the social and political turmoil of the 1960s and the Vietnam War. Made shortly after the end of that war, *Badlands* serves as a link between the two post-war decades of the 1950s and the 1970s and suggests that, despite the desire for fundamental change that motivated the intervening decade, the country was once again facing a time in which important issues would simply be submerged in a new homogenisation of culture and in which the desire and hope for a new world forgotten.

Reference

Horn, James (2005) *A Land As God Made It: Jamestown and the Birth of America*. New York: Basic Books.

CHAPTER TWO

Two Characters in Search of a Direction: Motivation and the Construction of Identity in Badlands

Hannah Patterson

It all goes to show how you can know a person and not really know him at the same time.
    – Holly, *Badlands* (1973)

Since its release, *Badlands* has received limited critical attention, particularly in comparison to other generically similar films such as the earlier *Bonnie and Clyde* (Arthur Penn, 1967), and more recent variants *Wild at Heart* (David Lynch, 1990), *True Romance* (Tony Scott, 1993) and *Natural Born Killers* (Oliver Stone, 1994). Critics who have offered comment agree that the central characters display unusually motiveless, seemingly surface or 'blank' personalities. They disagree, however, as to the validity and effectiveness of this mode of characterisation and any value that can subsequently be awarded the film.

In an unfavourable review of the film, Pauline Kael explicitly refers to the characters' lack of motivational clarity as a flaw, asserting that

Kit and Holly are kept at a distance, doing things for no explained purpose; it's as if the director had taped gauze over their characters, so that we wouldn't be able to take a reading of them. (1977: 304)

In light of this statement, it is my intention to examine how Terrence Malick consistently and successfully establishes a sense of Kit and Holly's characters without drawing comprehensive, psychological portraits of them. Through com-binations of *mise-en-scène* – their actions and their spoken (and unspoken) words – we are offered various ways of reading their characters; what we are not offered are emphatically clear or definitive readings. For, as will emerge from a more sustained study of the film, these characters are fundamentally lacking a strong or clear sense of *their own* identity. Their apparent apathy and their ambiguous emotions are symptomatic of this lack and it is by virtue of their opacity that we achieve a greater sense of their own equivocal state of being. Although they may appear motiveless, it is possible to view their actions in the film as motivated by their need to find, and more fully construct, identities for themselves. As William Johnson points out, '*they* form part of the phenomena that challenge *us*. As we try to make sense of their actions we see them trying to do the same with the phenomena of their world' (1974: 44). As an adjunct to this, I would argue against Kael that their opacity, rather than disinterest us as viewers, actually serves to make us more curious about, and compelled by, their behaviour.

Before looking more closely at two scenes it is useful to explicitly define this con-ception of opacity by referring to the work already undertaken in this area of study by George M. Wilson. In *Narration in Light: Studies in Cinematic Points of View* he asserts that when attempting to analyse certain types of films – of which *Badlands* would be an example – 'we are frequently unable, no matter how much has been observed, to make out the true causes of an event or the motivations that really prompted an agent to his act' (1986: 45). He attempts to clarify the different forms of opacity that can be present in a film. The one which most closely concerns us here is that which he believes occurs when 'a filmmaker wishes to repudiate widespread practices of closure which yield, as it seems to him, only the false semblance of an honest explanation' (*ibid.*). Malick's filmmaking style in *Badlands* certainly signals his choice to work outside these more conventional parameters. In such a case, Wilson asserts that 'narrative and narra-tion must together achieve a structure that appropriately weights the favoured explana-tory factors and traces out their relevance to the dramatic questions they purport to answer' (*ibid.*). Part of the difficulty with *Badlands* is, however, as already stated, its refusal to clearly or readably answer the dramatic questions it poses. Why, for instance, does Kit feel the compulsion to kill? For this question we are never given a clear answer or conclusive explanation; his motivation is made deliberately opaque because he him-self does not seem to know why he kills. Wilson goes some way to allowing for this style of unreadability:

> But if it is part of the point that these factors are not immediately open to perception, then the system of weighting and the network of tracing may themselves be less than obvious to first inspection. The factors are present but presented only opaquely. (*ibid.*)

We may hazard a guess then, through the factors present in the film which we will return to, that Kit performs the extreme act of killing as a way of attempting to draw attention to himself and more fully assert a sense of his own identity.

To illustrate a more specific moment of such character opacity in *Badlands*, and a way in which it may be penetrated, it is helpful to draw upon a specific instance of character *revelation* in another film – *Wild at Heart*. David Lynch – ironically a director who is well known for his unconventional and often surrealist mode of filmmaking – creates in the central protagonist, Sailor, a character who, like Kit, displays an unease with conforming to the societal norm. When challenged about his snakeskin jacket he remarks, 'For me it's a symbol of my individuality and my belief in personal freedom', thus simultaneously asserting a motivation for his way of life and his own clear sense of identity. A strikingly similar allusion to attire occurs in *Badlands* when Kit makes a reference to Holly about his cowboy boots and his new job at the feed lot: 'Yeah, well, at least nobody can get at me about wearing these boots anymore.' Unlike Sailor, Kit gives no clear indication as to why he wears the boots – what they may or may not symbolically mean to him. Malick leaves this point deliberately ambiguous, on the one hand creating an enigmatic quality in Kit and, on the other, significantly hinting that perhaps, after all, Kit *does not know* why he wears the boots. He thus manages to achieve a sense of Kit's difference whilst also highlighting the fact that he does not know himself.

This accent on the enigma and mystery of character is signalled from the very beginning of the film by Malick's denial of an explanation of their past, either factually or emotionally. The details of Holly's past life are brief – she says a little in her opening voice-over about her mother's death and her move from Texas to South Dakota – and of Kit's they are almost nonexistent. The characters do not become defined by their past either for us or each other. We may assume that their past has had a psychological effect on their character and personality, but they do not seem to feel defined by it – if they do, they certainly do not speak of it. This lack or omission becomes apparent when they encounter each other for the first time.

The scene of their initial meeting is of interest for obvious reasons as the moment when the audience, having been introduced to both characters separately, actually see them coming together. The repercussions of this meeting are vast in the narrative scheme of the film: Holly's father objects to Kit's character; when threatened, Kit kills him; the couple flee, on the run from the law; Kit commits more murders; they are eventually captured; and he is subsequently executed. More importantly though (for us) it also sets the tone and style of the film: a dynamic is created between the surface of the characters – the apparent unreadability of the way in which they act – and their real emotional motivations. Their inscrutability forces us to dig a little deeper in order to achieve a fuller grasp of their essence and because of their opacity we question their mode of communication, the reasons why they are attracted to one another, and the implications of this for their actions in the rest of the film.

On the surface this scene could – and on a practical level does – function as a traditionally romantic one: the boy seeing the girl and desiring her; his subsequent wooing of her; their mutual flirtation; and a coming together on screen. Kit exhibits a physical discomfort and awkwardness, which could be interpreted as embarrassment – he shuffles around inside the frame and some parts of his body disappear beyond it. He stumbles over his invitation to her, 'You, er, I dunno … wanna take a walk with me?' She is more passive, saying very little, and smiling in a coy, girlish fashion. The scene is made up mostly of medium shots, medium close-ups and close-ups and it is as the characters become more acquainted that the camera conventionally closes in on them.

It is highly probable that we would be inclined to see it in merely romantic terms had Malick not already introduced a more ominous note, prior to the scene, in the form of Holly's voice-over. She has significantly stated, 'Little did I realise that what began in the alleys and backways of this little town would end in the badlands of Montana', hinting at a far more sinister outcome to (and potential reading of) their meeting. Her words colour the scene, hanging portentously over it. Having already been introduced to Kit in 'the alleys and backways' of the town, he is therefore implicated in the literal and metaphorical shift that will take place to the 'badlands of Montana' and it is his actions which will directly result in the 'end' of their relationship and the 'end' of Kit.

Initially, the town is presented as a safe place for Holly to play on the street: small, sleepy and uneventful. The atmosphere is warm and hazy. The colours are muted. We see very few people. The only sounds we hear around her are the quiet hum of insects. The accompanying music is lighthearted and simple. An emphasis is placed on Holly's adolescence: we have already seen her playing with her dog and here she practices with her baton. She is dressed simply in shorts and T-shirt, her hair naturally down, wearing no make-up; the stress is on the harmlessness of the place and of her.

The peace and tranquillity of this environment has already been shattered though, through the garbage collection, which has taken place in the unclean, disordered streets behind these. It is a noisy and dirty occupation in which Kit has been fully implicated; he has been directly responsible then for this intrusion. We see him grubby, aimlessly wandering, out of place next to these large houses with their perfectly mowed gardens. When he then enters Holly's world, walking quite deliberately into her space, he carries these associations with him, tainting her clean, childlike image, destroying the innocuousness of the setting.

The title 'Badlands' has appeared on the screen as Kit walks towards her, evoking Holly's prophetic voice-over, directly insinuating him in the subsequent shift of location and also the shift which will take place within Holly through her association with him. Later in the film we will witness the consequences of this as her identity (and her own sense of it) begins to alter. She becomes very interested in attempting different ways of looking: in the forest she tries on make-up and later she puts curlers in her hair. She also begins to smoke – an action she performs in her father's house – displaying a blatant disregard for authority/convention.

The fact that she is impressionable is emphasised here through the use of speech in their conversation: her lack of it and Kit's comparative abundance of it. Her replies are monosyllabic and she only answers when it is necessary, offering the minimal amount of information. Her reticent character is stressed through her reluctance to proffer her name to Kit: he is forced to ask her before she will disclose it. As a result, Kit appears the more dominating; he is the more proactive of the two, leading and defining their relationship. He is an opportunist, as he himself states, 'I'll try anything once'. His actions in the rest of the film stand as testament to the truth of this statement. Although he never at any juncture forces her to follow him, it is by trying anything once – and in fact more than once – that he will lead them both into trouble.

Paradoxically, we can also see the seeds of Holly's strength and later revolt here. She does question him, asking 'what for?' when he suggests they take a walk. She is not afraid to tell him later that her father would not approve of their association because he is a garbage man. At various moments throughout the film she tries to stop him from moulding her identity too much when she resists the various nicknames – such as 'red' and 'tex' – that he attempts to pin on her. Manifest in these instances is the pivotal moment when she defies Kit towards the end of the film and chooses to give herself up to the authorities rather than carry on with him. She may initially be led by him but ultimately she finds a way to assert herself and her will, separating from him and trying to take a firmer grasp of her own identity.

We are warned in this scene of the dangers of reading too much into characters by taking what they say at face value. It is a mistake that Kit alludes to and makes himself when he says to Holly, 'Oh, I got some stuff to say. Guess I'm kinda lucky that way. Most people don't have anything on their minds do they?' Kit clearly equates people having something interesting to say with them saying it out loud. Out of his assumption we could question exactly how much *he* actually has on his mind. This is a central and revealing paradox of his character which Stanley Cavell alludes to when he questions, 'In what spirit does the killer in *Badlands* say that he "has a lot to say"? – In what spirit does Malick baffle this claim by showing the boy unable even to fill a sixty-second recording in a vandalised Record-Your-Own-Voice booth?' (1979: 245). Is Kit's compulsion to speak then an over-compensatory measure on his part for the fact that he actually has little of great interest or import to say? If we see communication as a way of trying to make people understand then his attempts at it are not terribly successful: he does not really *communicate* very much when he speaks. As Brian Henderson points out, however, 'Much of the conversation in the film is phatic communication – empty of content, concerned with maintaining contact and keeping the channel of communication open' (1983: 40). It is in his attempts to speak then – his urgent need to display his words to others – that he actually reveals his faltering sense of identity.

This makes more sense when we consider that he clearly has a desire for other people to be aware of him. He expresses this need here when he launches into speech, eager to make Holly's acquaintance, assuming that she will want to know him. We see it also in the way he interacts with everyone he comes into contact with, saying 'hi' to people on the street;[1] in the recordings he makes; and most particularly at the end of the film when he chats to the soldiers, handing out his belongings, revelling in their attention. Ultimately we will see him coming into his own; as he spends so much of the film searching through and trying on other people's identities – the rich man's clothes, for instance – the public will finally seek parts of *his*: they will seek out his words and his opinions. Holly, by contrast, actually has quite a lot on her mind – we know this through the various instances of her voice-over which occur throughout the film – but she, unlike Kit, does not say a great deal of it out loud. In a moment of extreme irony, when Kit says 'do they?' there is a cut to a close-up of Holly, during which she says nothing. Her silence raises the question of why Kit – who seems to perceive talking as such a positive attribute – is attracted to Holly, who says very little? Why in fact is he attracted to Holly at all?

In *Bonnie and Clyde*, a film that constructs a very similar situation of attraction – that of a man seeing a woman and wanting her, and his subsequent leading of her outside the law and on the run – the hero states his intentions unequivocally and cogently. Clyde explains precisely to Bonnie (and the audience) his motives for choosing her and his vision of their future together: 'You're different. You got something better than being a waitress. You and me travelling together, we'd cut a path clean across this state … and everybody'd know about it.' In *Bonnie and Clyde*, however, the characters are quite clear about the fact that they want to change their identities; they are dissatisfied with who they are and wish to reinvent themselves.

In *Badlands*, Malick denies us this type of lucid information, suggesting that the characters may be drawn to each other, not through a conscious desire to change or reinvent, but because neither of them has any clear sense of self in the first place. Kit never at any point states his reasons for wanting to be with Holly. The only information that we are ever directly given about the subject is through one of Holly's subsequent voice-overs:

> He'd never met a fifteen-year-old girl who behaved more like a grown up and wasn't giggly. He didn't care what anybody else thought. I looked good to him and whatever I did was okay. And if I didn't have a lot to say well that was okay too.

It is possible to infer through this statement, and Kit and Holly's interaction, that he is drawn to her *because* she does not say very much. If she does not have 'a lot to say' then she does not provide him with too great a challenge. In a later scene when they have had intercourse for the first time, Holly is blatantly dissatisfied but does not cause a fuss. Here, albeit rather unenthusiastically, she agrees to go for a walk with him. She becomes a blank canvas on which he can begin to draw his own identity. With her, he is able to more easily attempt ways of constructing his sense of self. He is, in a very obvious and conventional way, allowed a form of identity simply by being one half of a couple.

In addition, Holly actually seems to validate him. When, in a moment of identity crisis, he betrays how uncomfortable he is with his surname and its ambiguity, stressing how he had no choice in the matter – how it was 'hung' on him – she assures him, 'It's okay'. She accepts his strange behaviour and outlook. As Brian Henderson points out, 'Holly doesn't respond much, but she tolerates his impersonation; for him this is encouragement enough' (1983: 39). This arrangement also serves to satisfy some of her needs. She is presented as a loner, with no friends and a rather disinterested, cold father. In Kit, she has someone who wants her, who wants to be in her company; she too is validated and allowed a stronger sense of identity by her association with him.

Their subsequent coming together is strongly implied in the first shot of them walking along the road. Prior to this shot they have, throughout their conversation, been visually separated from one another. He is an outsider, out of place here, awkwardly located at the edge of her property next to the road. She is situated with her home behind her and the security that it represents. Only after they have had a chance to negotiate and size each other up does Holly accept his invitation and make the decision to follow him, off her father's land. She must shift her identity, deny her past and all that it represents here to be with him. It is only then that he can take her – after he has killed her father, broken the bonds and shattered this security – quite literally *on the road* with him.

In a scene which occurs about a quarter of the way into the film, we see Kit and Holly, after they have been alone together and on the run for a while, come into contact with another couple, a boy and girl of roughly the same age. This scene offers no clear narrative function; we already know that Kit is a killer, they pose him no real threat, and two more deaths will not substantially affect his fate. Rather, it seems to function as a means whereby we can further probe the current state of Kit and Holly's identities, using the other couple as a reference point.

There are several visual and verbal parallels which are suggestively drawn between the two couples (Figs. 1–11) and implied within these similarities are the ways in which Kit and Holly could be perceived as potentially aligned with, or typical of, their generation and society. Other elements of the scene, however, work in opposition to this reading, undercutting it, to stress their difference and estrangement, thus ultimately reaffirming their identities as constructed, at this stage of the film, outside society and their place as firmly outside the law. Any efforts they may have been making to seek a more conventional identity – through their building of a 'home', for example, in the forest – are in this scene proven to be fruitless; their unlawful and unsociable actions have only isolated them even further.

Their superficial and surface similarities are implicit in the first shot of the couple's arrival in the car, which evokes Kit and Holly's arrival at Cato's. When we initially see the couple (Fig. 1) we are struck by their physical resemblances. The boy, like Kit, wears jeans and a white T-shirt. Kit's difference is of course marked by his cowboy boots, the significance of which has already been highlighted. Although the girl wears a skirt and Holly trousers, her white ruffled shirt is almost identical to one which Holly later wears in the scene by the train tracks. Their language is duplicated through their use of the customary 'hi' and the repetition of 'yeah', the casualness of their greeting and their monosyllabic tendencies.

The dynamics of the couple's relationship also bear striking similarities. Jack is the more proactive, coming forward to talk to Kit while the girl, like Holly, remains passively in the background. Both girls, in a matching action (Figs. 7 & 9), have to negotiate their way around obstacles, neither of them talking in fact until the men have moved away. Significantly though the girl actually gets out of the car making herself more visible (Fig. 6) while Holly remains shielded behind the wire mesh of the door, allowing Kit to do the talking (Fig. 5). Although this is a typical feature of their relationship – she waiting for him to establish what will happen before subsequently falling in line – it also stresses her impenetrability and her own uncertainty.

Their politeness – a fact which is highlighted throughout the film in their attempts to communicate pleasantly with other people – signals their desire not only to be liked and accepted but also to conform to the rules of convention. Revealed here is a paradox of their character and indeterminate identity, one which Henderson points out: 'Although Kit and Holly break violently with society they still cling to fragments of its structure, as if they might one day discover the meaning it seems to carry for other

1

Jack: Hi.

2

Kit: Hi.
Jack: Where's Cato?

3

Kit: Well, he's gone.
Jack: Gone?
Kit: Yeah.
Jack: Where?
Kit: He said not to tell.

4

Jack: Oh, yeah?

5

Kit: He said for you to give us a lift into town. You're the ones with the Studebaker aren't you?

6

Jack: Well, I just need to pick up something in the house.
Kit: I can't allow that.
Jack: What?
Kit: If you go in there I'm gonna have to kill you.
Jack: What's going on?
Kit: Can't afford to take chances.

7

Kit: Come out of there young lady.

8

Kit: Let's just go out into this field here. Come on. I'm gonna have to keep my eye on you though. You don't mind?

9

Holly: Hi.

10

Girl: What's gonna happen to Jack and me?
Holly: Have to ask Kit. He says frog I jump.
Girl: Okay.
Holly: What's your friend's name?
Girl: Jack.
Holly: Oh. You love him?
Girl: I dunno.

11

Holly: I gotta stick by Kit. He feels trapped.
Girl: I can imagine.
Holly: I've felt that way, haven't you?

people' (1974: 44). Even when he is pointing a gun at the boy, Kit absurdly states, 'I'm gonna have to keep my eyes on you though. You don't mind?' His efforts to be 'normal' are undercut: despite this verbal familiarity he betrays a physical unease. He moves cautiously, lurking half in and half out of the frame (Fig. 2), circling warily, like an animal, around Jack (Fig. 8). The most obvious reason for his anxiety is the fact that Cato is dying inside the house, but more significant is its accentuation of the discomfort he feels around more accepted notions of intimacy. Although he may have an urge to behave like them, his way of being betrays the fact of his difference. By moving in and out of their space, his isolation and separateness from them is amplified.

Kit and Holly's isolation is further signalled by the air of mystery which shrouds them. Holly is loathe to show herself. Kit's words are wilfully enigmatic and unrevealing, even more so than usual: when Jack asks him where Cato has gone he replies, 'He said not to tell'. They lurk near the house, within its shadows while the other couple appear more open, brightly lit by the sun and clear blue sky, more comfortable within their environment.

As the two girls move away from the camera across the field, we are struck again by the relatedness of the four characters brought together amid this vast rural expanse, their diminutive statures stressed by the size of the dwarfing wind machine – the sound of the wind is actually the only sound we can make out whining in the background of the otherwise rather suspenseful silence. Kit and Jack are located in the background as two barely-distinguishable figures so that it becomes almost impossible to know which is sitting and which is standing. This unreliable image provides us with another warning against believing what we think we see. Later in the scene it will be revealed that Kit is in fact sitting and Jack is standing: an unexpected physical dynamic given that Kit has a gun and is the more threatening and powerful in this situation.

Holly and the girl, with their backs to the camera and their words barely audible to us, seem on the surface to have a mutual understanding of each other, brought close together (Fig. 10) by their shared outlooks and attitudes. Holly's overly bright (and somewhat suspiciously false) smile – again a sign of politeness – indicates her intention to welcome, suggesting that perhaps she feels able to fit in now and communicate with other girls her own age. When they discuss, as if engaged in small talk, what may potentially happen to the couple, despite the delicate and alarming nature of their subject matter, the girl speaks in a vague and indecisive manner, typical of Holly's usual mode of verbal address. She displays Holly's customary apathy and emits the same flat tones, to the point where on first viewing it is difficult to know which of the two is actually speaking. When Holly asks her if she loves Jack she is noncommittal, saying, 'I dunno', just as Holly would if questioned about Kit.

Is the film suggesting that this rather dulled and indifferent mode of speaking is not peculiar to Kit and Holly, but representative of others their age? Should we assume by the carefully executed paralleling in this scene that if circumstances were different – if Kit for instance had never killed Holly's father – this could have been Holly and Kit getting out of the car, greeting people in a pleasant manner? Or is it that they are supposed to be representative of their generation: that this couple could very easily be like Kit and Holly if their circumstances were different – that they too have this capacity within them? Although Malick creates these conundrums he does not provide us with any solid solutions to them. What he does provide is strong evidence to support the reading that Kit and Holly are fundamentally alienated from this couple, that they are not and cannot be wholly like them.

In one of the most subtly significant and revealing moments of the film, as Holly declares that she has to 'stick by Kit', the other girl moves away from her, creating a visual and emotional void between them (Fig. 11). At Holly's declaration of her intent, the girl betrays her unease by separating herself from Holly. When Holly justifies Kit, saying 'I've felt that way, haven't you?' the girl does not answer, the implication being that she has never felt that way and that she is, therefore, not like Holly. So, it is by sticking with Kit that Holly isolates herself from 'normal' society and is prevented from pursuing any form of average existence and human contact. If, even before meeting Kit, she felt herself to be an isolated individual, by her association with him and through her search for an identity, she has at this stage only further complicated and exacerbated her situation.

In order to achieve a more substantial and conclusive reading of Kit and Holly's characters – and the extent to which they may or may not have shifted – it is useful to look at how they are represented at the end of the film. If their journey, as thus far argued, has been prompted by their need to seek out a clearer identity then to what extent has that journey been a successful one? Have they been able to find and more fully construct identities for themselves? Although the ending is, in keeping with the rest of the film, ambiguous and equivocal, there are several factors present – both visual and verbal – which suggest that Kit has managed, more successfully than Holly, to develop a clearer sense of identity, one which does not fit into this society but is an identity nonetheless. We can assume that Holly, by choosing to break away from Kit, is making an effort to re-enter conventional society alone, denying him and what she has become by her association with him. Kit, who is consequently bereft of companion/partner and audience, then makes a very deliberate choice to be captured. Having tried, unsuccessfully, to negotiate satisfactory identities for themselves outside the law/society they make the shift to seek them within it. Although Kit comes into clearer focus (both for us and himself) after his capture, Holly remains just as enigmatic and elusive.

He is given a defined role, constructed by those around him as dangerously criminal and psychologically fascinating, and becomes the centre of attention and curiosity. Tom, one of his captors, is captivated by him and eager to understand his motivation, asking, 'Do you like people … then why did you do it?', drawing visual parallels between Kit and James Dean, a fact which clearly gives Kit enormous pleasure. Even more gratifying, it seems, is the feeling Kit derives from standing in chains – centre-screen, on the wing of a plane – confident while being looked at by the sheriffs and soldiers, fielding questions about himself and dispersing his personal possessions. Holly, by contrast, appears less knowable, standing apart from the group and in background, fidgety and uncomfortable, wearing only handcuffs and causing very little interest amongst the soldiers – no one questions her. She is kept at the periphery, sidelined and overshadowed by Kit's celebrity status as indeed she has been throughout the film by the extremity of his actions. She seems to have returned to the kind of obscurity from which Kit claimed her. The only way she is able to define and construct her identity is through her voice-over, retrospectively and romantically in relation to him/his.

If we consider that their opacity as characters signalled their fundamental lack of a strong sense of identity and their actions prompted by their need to find one then Kit has indeed succeeded where Holly has failed. It is by virtue of the fact that Kit has become less opaque – more conspicuously at ease with his role as criminal – that we know he has achieved a stronger sense of identity and because Holly remains as unclear – enigmatic and impenetrable – that we infer she has not.

Note

1   Brian Henderson asserts that 'the film's dialogue, among other things, contains a

rather complete study of the American greeting "Hi!"' and that it can and does 'constitute a sort of etiquette of expression' (1983: 40). When the characters say 'hi' it allows them moments of normality in extraordinary circumstances; it becomes a point of reference for them, a shared commonality.

References

Cavell, Stanley (1979) *The World Viewed*, revised edition. Harvard: Harvard University Press.

Henderson, Brian (1983) 'Exploring *Badlands*', *Wide Angle* 5, 4, 38–51.

Johnson, William (1974) '*Badlands*', *Film Quarterly* 27, 3, 43–6.

Kael, Pauline (1977) *Reeling*. London: Calder and Boyars Ltd.

Kinder, Marsha (1974) 'The Return of the Outlaw Couple', *Film Quarterly*, 27, 4, 2–10.

Wilson, George M. (1988) *Narration in Light: Studies in Cinematic Point of View*. Baltimore: The Johns Hopkins University Press.

CHAPTER THREE

The Highway Kind: Badlands, Youth, Space and the Road

Neil Campbell

> My days they are the highway kind
> They only come to leave
> But the leavin' I don't mind
> It's the comin' that I crave ...
> — Townes Van Zandt, 'The Highway Kind'[1]

Terrence Malick's *Badlands* (1973) is a hybrid mix of youth rebellion text, road movie and western, drawing upon and interrogating these traditional forms to construct an ambiguous and provocative film that resists comforting resolutions or moral closure. Deliberately borrowing from these very American genres, the film's dialogical structure invites its audience to experience and examine the, often contradictory, value systems and assumptions that constitute the mythic territories of frontier, youth and the road. Hence mobility and stasis, inside and outside, youth and age, work and adventure, individual and social, and several other such oppositions are engaged with and explored throughout the course of the film. In its attention to such archetypes, the film consciously examines wider ideologies of identity, gender and power that are fundamental to the way in which these genres have operated in the construction of an American national imaginary. For example, at one level, *Badlands* is about re-experiencing the formative frontier dream of the West through the eyes of disconnected, alienated youth in 1959, acting out Frederick Jackson Turner's mythic definition that each frontier furnished 'a new field of opportunity, a gate of escape from the bondage of the past; and freshness, and confidence, and scorn of older society, impatience of its restraints and its ideas, and indifference to its lessons' (in Milner 1989: 21).

Inscribed in these myths of the West is youth's restless desire to usurp the past and rejuvenate the future as an essential characteristic of American identity formation, suggested by David Lowenthal's comment that 'inherited wisdom should be assimilated and transformed, not simply revered and repeated' (1985: 72). However, at the heart of *Badlands* is a cycle of repetition forcing us to question the validity of received notions of youthful rebellion, regeneration and inevitable progress inherent in these mythic American themes of transformation, making us revise these beliefs and ask different, complex, existential questions that destabilise the genre assumptions and values implicit in these very American forms. Ultimately, the suspicion of such myths indicates Malick's film is a response to wider cultural doubts over the viability of the counter-culture, the involvement in Vietnam and the long-term prospects for the 'New Frontier' announced by Kennedy in 1960, as well as a comment on the film industry's own reproduction of particular ideologies within its most popular forms.[2] In the final analysis, youth rebellion and the questioning of 'inherited wisdom' in this dark and troubling film comes to nothing as its circularity erases change and transforms dreams of escape into captivity, conformity and celebrity.

However, the road and youth have long been connected in American culture, from Mark Twain to Jack Kerouac to J. D. Salinger, through *Easy Rider* (Dennis Hopper, 1969), *True Romance* (Tony Scott, 1993) and *Natural Born Killers* (Oliver Stone, 1994) to Woody Guthrie and Bruce Springsteen, setting 'the liberation of the road against the oppression of hegemonic norms' (Cohan and Hark 1997: 1) whilst re-working the picaresque and *bildungsroman* traditions.[3] In such texts of development and education, protagonists traditionally encounter the world through adventure, contact and compromise, being shaped and possibly transformed, before being drawn back into the social order. Indeed Fredric Jameson has termed *bildungsroman*, 'machines for producing subjectivity … designed to construct "centred subjects"'(1996: 182), reflecting and reinforcing the process through which the young are disciplined into the officially sanctioned discourse of their elders. However, the assumption in conventional youth texts is that they represent opposition to, or at least temporarily test out, the power and authority of this discourse. In *Badlands* Malick utilises these genres to examine dialogically the powers of normalisation against the disruptive intervention of Kit and Holly's journey, so as to unravel the implicit mythic assumptions and values contained within this collision. Holly's framing narrative seems to justify Jameson's claim, for by the end of the film Kit awaits his death at the hands of the authorities statically and Holly tells her romanticised story from the safety of a suburban life married to the son of the lawyer who defended her in court. This circularity suggests that the social code with its 'machines for producing subjectivity' has reasserted itself over the disruptive violence and insubordinate will of Kit and Holly and done its work by reclaiming her and disciplining him back into the system.

Edgar Z. Friedenberg wrote that 'human life is a continuous thread which each of us spins to his own pattern, rich and complex in meaning. There are no natural knots in it. Yet knots form, nearly always in adolescence' (1963: 3). Youth texts are conventionally concerned with these existential tensions between the desire for self-generated 'pattern', to 'be oneself', and the 'knots' that seek to fix and bind youth into others' definitions and norms of social acceptability. The idea of being fixed and tied inherent in the notion of 'knots', implies a version of identity formation based in rootedness, stability and predictable development, locating youth within a social code of official, adult spaces. These encoded spaces define the boundaries of normalised identity: the domestic house, the suburb, the school, and the workplace, where subjectivity forms according to specific 'regimes of jurisdiction' (Grossberg 1992: 106). Within *Badlands*, spatiality emphasises these tensions, beginning with images of confinement, such as cages, pens and enclosures that symbolise Kit and Holly's limited lives, from the circling shots around her bed in the opening scene, to his work at the feed lot penning cattle, to the traps and cages that echo through the film, including one taken from the father's house and another at Cato's where he also keeps a spider in a bottle.

Holly's bedroom, in the opening scene, illustrates her containment, with its patterned wallpaper, lace, quilt and brass bed-frame forming a model of Victorian America, from where she delivers her first voice-over:

My mother died of pneumonia ... My father had kept their wedding cake in the freezer for ten whole years. After the funeral he gave it to the yardman. He tried to be cheerful but he could never be consoled by the little stranger he found in his house.

Here is a lonely 'little stranger' used to her own company, to talking inside her head rather than outwardly with others, emphasised by the contained space of her barred bed, within her room, within the family house, associated with coldness (pneumonia, death and the freezer[4]) and adrift from her remaining parent struggling with his own loss and confusion. She appears powerless within this domestic cage, ruled by her father and by the memory of her mother's love for him. Holly evolves negligibly throughout the film, seeming, like so much in *Badlands*, trapped in cycles of repetition, attempting to be 'for Kit what her mother was for her father', to 're-live her parents' brief romantic idyll' (McGettigan 2001: 25). Yet because Kit controls the journey just like her father does her life, it is only through her narration she gains power, transforming events into a romantic fantasy of love and honour. Holly remains alienated, existing within her mind and creating her own story to fulfill her particular dreams, 'spelling out with my tongue on the roof of my mouth whole sentences where no one could read them'. Whilst on the road, she reads a magazine article to Kit where celebrities' lives are determined by the differences between 'rumour' and 'fact', imitating her practice of constructing a mythic 'rumour' from fragments of naïve youth rebel romance rather than reality: 'He was handsomer than anybody I'd ever met. He looked just like James Dean'; 'He wanted to die with me ... I dreamt of being lost forever in his arms.' Holly longs for space beyond the confines of home and her friendless existence and Kit provides a conduit for her desires. In an interview, Malick has said that the main influences on *Badlands* were 'books like *The Hardy Boys, Swiss Family Robinson, Tom Sawyer, Huck Finn* – all involving an innocent in a drama over his or her head' (in Walker 1975). These youth texts desire spaces of difference where young lives define themselves away from the constraints and boundaries of the adult world. As Twain wrote, 'the elastic heart of youth cannot be kept compressed into one shape long at a time' (1986: 60), for it yearns to explore identities outside the normalised cages of everyday life. Thus in *Tom Sawyer*, youth desires alternative Edenic spaces like 'Cardiff Hill', '*beyond* the village and *above* it ... *green* with vegetation ... *just far enough away* to seem a Delectable Land, *dreamy, reposeful*, and *inviting*', representing 'the seductive outside' that 'civilization' discourages them from entering (1986: 15, 37 – my emphases). This is the restless, 'outcast' space of Huck Finn who 'came and went at his own free will ... did not have to go to school or to church, or call any being master, or obey anybody' (1986: 46). In these early literary conceptualisations of American youth space, inertia is associated with the adult, familial, official world while 'beyond' or 'between' always represents a risky but exciting potentiality for self-definition and the tantalising promise of 'freedom'. As Lawrence Grossberg has written,

> youth could construct its own places in *the spaces of transition between* ...
> institutions ... spaces located between the domestic, public and social spaces
> of the adult world. What the dominant society assumes to be no place at all ...
> (1992: 179 – my emphasis)

Contested spaces dramatise and represent these tensions over adolescent conditioning and socialisation and are a particular feature of *Badlands* where the realms of home, work and family are contrasted to other spaces 'outside'; the river, the woods, the road and finally the 'badlands' themselves.

For Holly, the 'seductive outside' is about the romance her narrative invents to explain Kit's eccentric (and possibly insane) actions, imitating the 'dreamy quality' of children's texts,[5] like her claim that 'my destiny now lay with Kit' for 'it was better to spend a week with the one who loved me for what I was, than years of loneliness'. Having changed their names to 'James' [Dean] and 'Priscilla' [Presley], she says they would 'hide out like spies in the North' and live in the 'wilderness, down by a river, in a grove of cottonwoods', further demonstrating her capacity for sentimental clichés and images drawn firstly from idealised literary sources, secondly, from myths of freedom epitomised by a view of nature as Edenic with her as Eve to Kit's Adam – 'there wasn't a plant in the forest that didn't come in handy', 'let's not pick them, they're so nice' she says – and thirdly, by her particular fascination with exotic, faraway spaces. Throughout the film, Holly finds an imagined spatial locus through exotic travel literature, like Thor Heyerdahl's *Kon-Tiki* (that she reads to Kit in the woods) and *The Adventures of Marco Polo*, which she refers to in her narration when comparing the trains on the Plains to the caravans across the desert. For her, Kit offers adventure, like Huck does for Tom Sawyer, but, as with the latter, she demands everything to have 'style' conforming to the patterns learned in her reading. Tom says, 'I've seen it in books; and so of course that's what we've got to do ... Do you want to go doing different from what's in the books, and get all muddled up?' (Twain 1985: 57). Tom's 'rebellion' is conditioned by his ultimate need for the order he appears to reject and the same is true for Holly who longs for the exotic but becomes increasingly worried by Kit's uncontrolled violence as their 'adventure' turns into a 'muddle'. At one point, whilst living in the woods, Holly looks at her father's stereopticon with its exotic 'vistas'

Holly voices her misgivings to Kit on the road in *Badlands*

of 'otherness', of Egypt, languorous women and foreign places, and comments 'I was just a little girl with so many years to live' and 'where would I be at this very moment if Kit had never met me?' Her adventure with Kit is a disappointment compared to these vistas, for she adds 'sometimes I wished I could fall asleep and dream I was being taken off to some magical land, but this had never happened'. Ironically, Holly re-states Kit's own 'seductive outside' of a 'magical land beyond the law' only to remind us that it has not been achieved and that her imagined space of contented romance can only exist as images in the stereopticon, pictures in the fan magazines, or words in the travelogues she reads. Her desire for 'style' and exotic 'rumour' are transformed into more 'cages' of 'fact', as Kit and her migrate westward on the dusty desert roads of the Great Plains.[6] Kit's increasingly violent actions and the couple's gradual, cyclical return to geographical and symbolic South Dakota signifies in Holly's case, a return to the life she was born into; domesticity, marriage and gendered dependence, and within the film as a whole, further questions the potential for change and regeneration.

Holly's romantic longings form part of the youthful intersection within the film completed by Kit – who also yearns for spaces beyond the workaday world in which he too feels trapped. Kit's name suggests his efforts to construct himself throughout the film from the debris all around him, but unlike James Dean's Jim Stark in *Rebel Without a Cause* (Nicholas Ray, 1955), clearly an influence on *Badlands*, there is no father to reintegrate Kit back into the social order. However, Kit's search is, to some degree, about *becoming* a father to Holly and about finding a level of acceptability within the community in which he lives. His violence can be seen as a displacement of this urge to belong and to find a place within the immense spaces of America, or as part of a desire to purge the world and bury its 'waste' below the ground.[7] Contrary to the assumed traditions of youth and road movies as subversive texts, Kit's actions can be read as his quest for conformity and responsibility rather than as a counter-cultural rebel, for what he desires, above all, is a return to some ideal lost time of manners, respect and honesty. In fact many youth texts have concerned themselves with rediscovering forms of stability, authenticity and values perceived as lost in the 'phoney' adult world, as in *The Catcher in the Rye, Rebel Without a Cause* and *The Outsiders*.[8]

Thus *Badlands* plays consistently with the iconography of youth rebellion and the road movie using their stock characteristics to provoke the audience into a wider consideration of the ideological values contained and articulated in these genres. Kit *performs* James Dean, adding him to the identities he is trying out, appearing to be in love with the *idea* of freedom, of 'lighting out for the Territory' in search of alternative spatiality beyond the boundaries of the static, adult world he associates with the institutions of home, work, school and to this end he too constructs a 'narrative' of action wherein his identity assumes multiple and contradictory aspects rather than any single 'self'; as cowboy, James Dean, guerilla warrior, Robin Hood or Nat King Cole. Ironically, he even resembles Holly's father who once gave away his frozen wedding cake to the 'yardman' as he will 'give' his emotionless daughter to Kit (the garbage-man), and whose own migratory pattern of flight from pain (from Texas to South Dakota) will be replicated as Kit takes Holly on the road. Curiously, it is as if Kit kills the father only to become a repeated version of him in his own zealous protection of Holly, his increasingly 'fatherly' attitudes and comments, and even his adoption of a white Panama hat.

As he attempts to construct a 'kit-identity' along the road, these startling contra-dictions surface to destabilise any attainable, single self, until as 'surrogate father' and dreamer of a 'magical land beyond the law', Kit assumes the voice of reason and lawfulness, in imitation of the 'adult' acceptability his violent actions undermine. Hence, he is disturbed by a paper bag dropped on the sidewalk, commenting that 'if everyone did that the whole town'd be in a mess', or preaching to a Dictaphone that children should 'listen to … parents and teachers … don't treat them like enemies … you can learn something … keep an open mind … get along with the majority of opinion once its accepted'. In all these humorous moments, Kit is not rebellious or anti-social, but 'an Eisenhower conservative' and a very conventional American Dreamer, if *in extremis*, troubled by the loss of moral direction in community and family whose individual action and 'frontier spirit' is his way of purging the world. Like the frontiersman his gunplay suggests, Kit's amoral actions resonate with classic, mythic American traits – 'dominant individualism', freedom, anti-authoritarian, 'a practical, inventive turn of mind', 'restless, nervous energy' and 'a masterful grasp of material things'.[9] F. J. Turner argued that such traits emerged on the frontier, becoming the essence of American entrepreneurial spirit and democracy, and in true rags-to-riches style, can be seen in Kit's 'cowboy' aspiring to be a respectable, well-known citizen. In his confused mind, his actions are true to Turner's evolving American character, for as Malick has said, ultimately 'he wants to be like them, like the rich man he locks in the closet, the only man he doesn't kill, the only man he *sympathises* with…' (in Walker 1975).

Kit's life is 'routine like anything' and so he wants to belong and achieve celebrity, empowered by marking the world with his own story and performance instead of being defined by clearing away the remains of others' lives. He says early on, 'I've got some stuff to say … most people don't have anything on their minds' and 'no-one asked what I thought, they just stuck it on me', he claims about his name, Kit Carruthers, 'it sounds a little too much like *your others*'. Following the tradition of so many youth texts, Kit resents restrictive controls and being 'too much like your others', for he has 'stuff to say' but fears no one was 'going to listen'. So Holly becomes both his audience and mythographer, providing her romantic narration to their journey out West: 'through desert and mesas, across endless miles of range', while Kit marks his 'history' with symbolic gestures: a balloon full of tokens released into the air, a 'Voice-o-graph' message left in the burning house, a Dictaphone 'diary', a time-capsule buried for posterity and a of pile rocks to memorialise his capture. With these acts, Kit records his life by inscribing his otherwise anonymous identity into space for others to know, since, someone 'might dig them up a thousand years from now, and wouldn't they wonder?' Emerging from the garbage he collects, with its associated sense of deathly suburban waste and consumerist inauthenticity, Kit longs for a vital authentic being whose presence and 'wonder' is marked in space by his own acts and language. He wishes to be more than those objects that surround him and that he collects throughout the film, from garbage, to rocks, to 'tokens', and to achieve this he must articulate his subjectivity as set out above but also, more disturbingly, through his taking of others' lives. In a perverse way Kit enacts his version of the myth of regeneration through violence, strengthening his own identity by denying it to others who, he believes, deserve to die.[10]

Kit longs for something out there beyond the 'frenetic inertia' of the everyday,[11] manifested, according to Holly's narration, in the imagined, migratory 'West' of Montana, in the temporary, displaced spaces of flight, and in the iconic road as the American dreamscape of fluid identity unchecked and unfixed by the 'authorities' – 'a magical land beyond the law'. Kit is a mixture of the existentialist living for the present in the sure knowledge of death, a 'being-towards-its-own-end' (Steiner 1978: 101), and the all-American, gun-toting cowboy moving on to the next horizon.[12] Increasingly, Kit's 'beyond' translates into motion and the road itself as the route away from 'rooted', static home-places with their panoptic regulatory systems and established histories, towards alternative 'youth' spaces to enact one's own 'history' through a direct and immediate 'writing' of the self into the world, constructing and inscribing one's own narrative rather than being slotted into a pre-existing family and social text. The road becomes the pathway to those neo-Edenic 'other spaces' imagined in youth texts as opportunities for escape and fulfilment because it was *not* where home was and, like the river with which it is often compared, it offers a fluid, untamed and open energy with the power to 'wash the roots away', as Kit says, like their flight itself.

Kit's first gesture against containment is to destroy Holly's father, an authoritarian sign-writer whose job projects approved social codes, such as the billboard for an idealised family with house, domestic animals and the word 'Friendly' clearly in the frame that he is painting when Kit visits him. Kit's erasure of the 'sign' of the father appears a radical act and an assault on the containment he represents, but as so often

'Beyond the law': Kit stalks through his makeshift home in the woods in *Badlands*

in the film, one is made uncertain of such assumptions by the way the sequence is filmed and how the characters respond. Malick frames Kit and the father in doorways, windows and mirrors to suggest confinement and tension, but also to remind us of their similarities, emphasised by the father's Panama hat repeated throughout the film, in the Rich Man's house where Kit steals a similar one and wears it until his capture when the police throw it from the car. In killing the father Kit asserts his youthful authority, visually, by looking down on his victim from the top of the stairs, and verbally by claiming 'I can't allow that' when the father says 'I'm turning you in to the authorities'. Empowered through his usurpation of the father, by possessing his house and stealing his daughter, Kit is troubled that 'they're not going to listen to me' and so narrates his own 'story' of suicide and 'fun' via the Voice-o-graph that he will leave for 'the DA to find' when he has burned down the house. Meanwhile, Holly alone in the house, looks at two children playing in the dark street below, symbolic of her lost childhood and of things to come as her and Kit 'play' more dangerous games in the sunlit seductive outside of the 'badlands'. As the house burns to a religious, choral soundtrack, Malick emphasises the sacrificial rites of purgation; flames engulf dolls, a doll's house, a piano, Holly's bed and her father, all signs of her disciplined childhood containment within the space of domesticity and adult law.

In rescuing a lamp, a radio, a toaster and a Bierstadt-like Edenic painting from the burning house, the runaways show they cannot sever all links with the domestic world, soon establishing their version of that space in the wilderness. Here the camera lingers over their tree house with its remnants of suburbia reconfigured as their own 'home' in an idyllic, natural world connecting them with images of beetles, trees and water, as though they have created a new Eden away from the suburban regime of father, school and work. Yet Malick undercuts this idyll through Holly's naïveté and Kit's barely suppressed violence, for she tells of their 'secret passwords' and tunnels and being able to 'sneak out at night' while he practices guerilla warfare and trains for combat.

As the outlaw couple run from the law, movement becomes more significant than direction and when they stop, it is as though the world catches up with them and Kit's only response is violence; first killing Cato, then the couple who arrive at his house. In talking to the girl in the couple, a reverse image of Kit and Holly, the latter says, 'I've got to stick by Kit. He feels trapped … I've felt that way. Haven't you?' In seeking to escape one trap through transgression and romance, she has merely moved closer to another with Kit. For as she says, 'You can know a person and not know him *at the same time*', describing her own feelings for him, but illustrating simultaneously the dialogical effect of the film as it continuously unsettles the audience's sense of 'knowledge' and genre expectations by setting myth against reality and 'rumour' against 'fact'.

At the Rich Man's house, Kit and Holly prowl around restlessly touching objects, trying chairs as if alienated from any settled life and Holly comments, 'The world was like a faraway planet to which I could never return … full of things people could look at and enjoy'. Of course, despite her romance, Holly is about to return to this 'faraway place', becoming increasingly wary of Kit's behaviour as 'trigger happy' and 'hell bent'. This impending return is marked as they leave the Rich Man's house in his stolen Cadillac as a parodic married couple with Kit 'disguised' in a Panama hat and Holly in a white tablecloth veil. Yet they have found no perfect familial space, only the rugged immensity of the Great Plains with their endless horizons emphasised by extraordinary shots of empty roads, telegraph lines and pipelines dwarfing their journey. Everything seems to have direction except Kit and Holly as they find a temporary peace, building a fire on the Plains in a sequence that inter-cuts between them and animals, sky and the mountains in a moment of tranquility that repeats the wilderness idyll earlier in the film. This 'community', however, is like that of Jim and Huck on the raft in *Huckleberry Finn* existing as transitional, temporary, *between* the normalised world all around with the river representing a moment out of time in which they experience freedoms only dreamt of on the land, resembling exactly what Malick intended: 'I wanted the picture to set up like a fairy tale, outside time, like *Treasure Island*' (in

Walker 1975). As Holly comments, 'We lived in utter loneliness *neither here nor there*', for these spaces of escape epitomise an 'in-betweenness', detached from the constraining world and from any final destination. Of course, they cannot remain 'between', on Treasure Island, even if they wanted to, precisely because it is 'out of time' and to be human is to live *in* time. Holly is unhappy because she wants to stop the flight and return home, whereas Kit cannot, for as he says '*maybe* we ought to be stuck here', as they watch a train race past in the desert. To be on the road is to be 'in between', 'neither here nor there', the motion *between* spaces – between static parental origins of suburban settlement, and the unknowable but certain death – a kind of epitomised youth moment detached from social codes, existing in suspended animation before the inevitable closure to come. Kit's 'maybe' recognises they cannot remain out of time and as they dance in the dark, lit by the car headlights, out on the Plains to Nat King Cole's 'A Blossom Fell' the sense of ending dominates the sequence as the song comments on their own predicament: 'The dream has ended for true love died the night a blossom fell and touched two lips that lied.' Holly cannot sustain her romance; her voice-over comments that Kit 'dreaded the idea of being shot down alone without a girl to scream out his name'. It is no longer her name that counts, but *any* girl will do now for Kit's final performance.

With Holly left behind, Kit, 'who knew the end was coming', throws her clothes, now 'junk', into a garbage can at the One Stop gas station sitting under two prominent signs that could have been the work of her father, underscoring the circularity of events and marking his personal finale. Without Holly as an audience, Kit checks his own 'look' in the mirror, before shooting the tyre on his car to halt his motion and give himself up to the law, becoming in imminent death the celebrity he longed for in life. Appropriately, one of the policemen repeats Holly's assertion that Kit looks like James Dean, connecting his new audience with the old, as he is ushered into the limelight, giving away his possessions like a star and answering questions in a mock interview. Here Kit represents an excessive American individualism formed on the road in pursuit of independence and control, a self-construction refuting 'your others' like a vision of cowboy-youth, a 'closed book' (Walker 1975) of images garnered from dime novels and Hollywood that endows him a legendary status and gives his life some momentary meaning.

Ironically, throughout this final scene, Kit is bound and manacled, barely able to move as he spins his tales of freedom and chats to the police like a model citizen. Of course, as elsewhere in the film, Malick's dialogical approach questions these underlying visions produced by cultural myths and simulations and perpetuated in Holly's daydreams and Kit's emulations. Living a life constructed through such signs and images reveals the contradictions inherent in the values they espouse and the impossibility of fulfilling myths that assert mobility *and* settlement, freedom *and* restraint, individualism *and* conformity. Ultimately, in these joyless, brutally cold lives, youth rebellion on the road goes nowhere and offers nothing, for any hopeful spaces are temporary and transitory at best and seem only to lead back to where the social codes of normalisation and discipline wait to reclaim the highway kind. The grand myths of frontier freedom and the promise of Edenic youthful new beginnings inscribed in the individual self are dialogised in *Badlands* by more ambiguous, mundane and bleak endings. Like Holly, Kit's journey is circular, merely repeating unconvincingly the credo spoken to her father earlier, 'It takes all kinds I guess', whilst clinging to the debris of 'teen-rebel' myths, telling her 'Boy, we rang the bell didn't we?' In the film's final conversation, a police officer says 'You're quite an individual Kit', to which he replies, 'Do you think they'll take that into consideration?' In Kit's darkly humorous articulation of American myths: of wilful, arrogant youth, the value of individuality, diversity and the fantasy of the road, his last flight is, ironically, to isolation, incarceration and execution. Rising above the world in this final movement, Malick re-positions the audience where we have been for much of the film, poised between the promising spatiality of dreams and the harsh reality of social control and staticity over the horizon. As the film's rebellious 'subjects' are 'centred' again, contained by home and the law, and all their potential energy and imagination turned to waste, what remains is a chilling circularity reflecting a pessimism about society's motivating values and underlying beliefs, not least because of the generic responsibility films themselves must bear for the maintenance, perpetuation and unquestioned reinforcement of these very same damaging, but persistent, American cultural myths and ideologies.

Notes

1   Townes Van Zandt, 'The Highway Kind', from *High, Low and In Between* (1972).
2   John F. Kennedy quoted in P. Nelson Limerick (1994: 80–2). Pauline Kael's 1974 unfavourable review of *Badlands* sees it as a counter-cultural film (see Kael 1977: 303–6).
3   Springsteen has referred to *Badlands* directly in two songs, 'Badlands' (1978) and 'Nebraska' (1982), or to the real-life story that Malick draws upon for the film, that of Charlie Starkweather and Caril Ann Fugate, who in 1958 went on a killing spree across Nebraska and Wyoming. Both *Natural Born Killers* and *True Romance* are re-workings of *Badlands*. These typical myth-texts of the road, the West and youth are precisely what *Badlands* pre-figures and analyses.
4   Holly's association with coldness is repeated in the film in two other key moments, firstly when she is punished by her father to more music lessons and we see her staring out of a window with the word 'Frigidaire' emblazoned across the building below her, and secondly, when she stands in front of the fridge as Kit announces her father's death.
5   There are many times in the film where Kit is referred to as mad and many visual clues to this possibility. For example, he paranoically forges his own signature and dreams of 'a noise like someone holding a sea shell to his ear', according to Holly, who also tells the 'Rich Man', 'Sometimes he acts like there's something wrong with his bean ... I dunno. He's kinda odd'. Later after they watch a train across the Plains, Holly says 'You're crazy'. He is often seen gesturing to himself, as if an inner conversation is taking place, most noticeably in the long shot behind the trailer where he locks up Cato. The 'dreamy quality' is Malick's phrase, in Walker (1975).
6   At one point, Holly tells of the 'rumours' surrounding their outlaw status in a sepia-toned sequence, ending with her words, 'It was like the Russians had invaded'.

7   Kit confines his victims in dark places, often below ground, throughout the film.
8   See Campbell & Kean (1997; chapter 8, 'Representing Youth') and Campbell (2000).
9   These terms are taken from F. Jackson Turner's 'The Significance of the Frontier in American History', in Milner (1989: 21).
10 See Slotkin (2000).
11 This is a term coined by George Steiner from his reading of Heidegger. Other translators term it 'uninhabited hustle'.
12 Death is everywhere in the film, for besides the eight killings there are dead mothers, fish, dogs, chickens, cows, and it is mentioned several times in Holly's narration.

References

Campbell, Neil & Alasdair Kean (1997) *American Cultural Studies*. London: Routledge.
Campbell, Neil (ed.) (2000) *The Radiant Hour: Versions of Youth in American Culture*. Exeter: University of Exeter Press.
Cohan, Steve & Ina Rae Hark (1997) *The Road Movie Book*. London: Routledge.
Friedenberg, Edgar Z. (1963) *Coming of Age in America*. New York: Vintage.
Grossberg, Lawrence (1992) *We gotta get out of this place: Popular Conservatism and Postmodern Culture*. London: Routledge.
Henderson, Brian (1983) 'Exploring Badlands', *Wide Angle*, 5, 4, 38–51.
Jameson, Fredric (1996) 'On Literary and Cultural Import-Substitution in the Third World: The Case of the Testimonio', in G. M. Gugelberger (ed.) *The Real Thing: Testimonial Discourse and Latin America*. Durham: Duke University Press, 172–91.
Kael, Pauline (1977) *Reeling*. London: Marion Boyars.
Limerick, P. Nelson (1994) 'The Adventures of the Frontier in the Twentieth Century', in J. R. Grossman (ed.) *The Frontier in American Culture*. Berkeley: University of California Press, 67–102.
Lowenthal, David (1985) *The Past is a Foreign Country*. Cambridge: Cambridge University Press.
McGettigan, Joan (2001) 'Interpreting a Man's World: Female Voices in *Badlands* and *Days of Heaven*', *Journal of Film and Video*, 52, 4, Winter, 22–32.
Slotkin, Richard (2000) *Regeneration Through Violence: The Mythology of the American Frontier, 1600–1860*. Middletown: Wesleyan University Press.
Steiner, George (1978) *Heidegger*. Glasgow: Fontana/Collins.
Turner, Frederick Jackson (1989) 'The Significance of the Frontier in American History', in C. Milner (ed.) *Major Problems in American Western History*. DC Heath: Lexington, 2–34.
Twain, Mark (1985) [1884] *The Adventures of Huckleberry Finn*. Harmondsworth: Penguin.
_____ (1986) [1876] *The Adventures of Tom Sawyer*. Harmondsworth: Penguin.
Walker, Beverly (1975) 'Malick on *Badlands*'. Available at: http//www.eskimo.com/~toates/malick/art6.html [Accessed 21 May 2002]

CHAPTER FOUR

Days of Heaven and the Myth of the West

Joan McGettigan

Terrence Malick's films share a fundamental insistence on challenging generic expectations in ways that can be puzzling and disturbing to viewers. Regarding *Badlands* (1973), for instance, Michael Filippidis argues that Malick employs the road movie framework and yet 'defamiliarises and critiques its familiar coordinates' (2000), and Marsha Kinder analyses the ways in which the film uses and expands the parameters of the outlaw couple genre (1974: 2–10). Malick himself has noted that the humour in the film 'lies in Holly's misestimation of her audience', in that her voice-over rarely addresses the violent acts her boyfriend Kit commits; instead, it is rooted in road-movie typicality, describing 'what they ate and what it tasted like, as though we might be planning a similar trip' across the badlands (in Walker 1975: 83). Similarly, *The Thin Red Line* (1998) baffled critics prepared by years of war movies and the proximity of *Saving Private Ryan* (Steven Spielberg, 1998); they complained about 'Malick's lack of sustained interest in narrative' (Turan 1998) – that is, his refusal to conform to one narrative structure, one genre. Here at first seems to be the story of a rebel, a man gone AWOL, who will eventually prove himself in battle. Then the film is transformed into a combat movie, with each man in C-Company representing a particular cultural background and perspective on the war, except that many of the characters are indistinguishable from one another. Then there is the great battle, which seems to resolve nothing and serves as an anti-climax.

    In *Days of Heaven* (1978) Malick raises the stakes by taking on the inherently American genre, the western. In a series of reversals, the film introduces and even

elevates characteristics of the western, and then reveals them as illusions. The painful process of working the land, made meaningful through its contribution to the
communal good in traditional westerns such as *Shane* (George Stevens, 1953) and
Red River (Howard Hawks, 1948) is here performed by disenfranchised hired hands.
The familiar 'official' hero is revealed to be a hollow man, the 'outlaw' hero punished
rather than redeemed. The comradeship which sustains the Westerners in films such as
My Darling Clementine (John Ford, 1946) fails to develop in *Days of Heaven*, and the
satisfaction of revenge we so often feel in the western's third act is rendered meaningless. The familiar, vast landscape, the source of so many western characters' hopes and
dreams, is shown to be just that – a dream, a kind of heavenly apparition shared by the
characters and the viewers, amorphous and unsustainable. Malick does not so much
disprove the myth of the West as demonstrate our need for it and reinforce our desire
for it; viewers leave the film understanding why our culture developed the western. At
the end of *Days of Heaven*, we may long to start it again, hoping that all will go well
this time, hoping to recapture those glimpses of the western Malick so skilfully provides and then admits to be unrealisable.

The film begins with a journey westward, the main characters – Bill, his lover Abby
and his sister Linda – seeking an escape from old problems in a new environment.
Bill appears to be the typical 'outlaw hero' described by Robert Ray: 'Embodied in
the adventurer ... wanderer, and loner, the outlaw hero ... represented a flight from
maturity ... an anxiety about civilized life' (1985: 59–60). He faces the future with no
particular plans; 'Just gotta get fixed up' is how he vaguely describes what he foresees
for himself, Abby and Linda. When they arrive on the farm, however, there is a sense
of hope: we see a series of shots which emphasise the beauty and tranquility of the
landscape; Bill walks through tall grass, surveying the expanse with a smile; a bird soars
across a magic-hour horizon. This is a harmonious, comforting landscape, presided
over by the last of the main characters, the Farmer. In contrast to Bill as the 'outlaw'
hero, the Farmer completes Ray's formula: he is an 'official' hero, a man of few words,
a grown-up with responsibilities and plans (1985: 60).

If our first impulse is to interpret the Farmer as an 'official' hero, though, we are
soon encouraged to reconsider. Carole Zucker points out that the Farmer is 'introduced in distinctly mythic terms', but that Malick 'is at great pains to disavow this
innocent archetype' (2001: 5). The Farmer is, in fact, more like a feudal lord. 'The
richest man in the Panhandle', as he is described, he watches through a telescope as
migrant workers bring in the harvest for him. 'Malick declares the Farmer's relationship to his workers in a visual juxtaposition', Zucker writes; 'The Farmer, seated on
an upholstered chair, sips from an ornamental glass as dirty and fatigued workers file
by' (ibid.). Moreover, the film's depiction of labour not only de-mystifies the Farmer,
it has more serious implications. Westerns have traditionally been about land and
who earns the right to work on it; that work has been consistently represented as goal-
oriented, personally satisfying and ideologically driven by the desire to establish and
nurture community. Even in the most isolated circumstances, the Westerner – Joe
Starrett in *Shane*, Tom Dunson in *Red River* – sees the land as an opportunity to
achieve personal goals and to contribute to the greater good. Ray's official hero recognises these goals and works towards them; his outlaw hero frequently struggles with

his own selfish impulses but does attempt to compromise in order to participate in this ideology of civilisation – in some cases successfully integrated into the community, and in others nobly sacrificed.

This critical juncture of individual, community and land is rendered in complex terms in *Days of Heaven*. Zucker is right in describing the Farmer as a problematic figure, seemingly Godlike at first but revealed as flawed and weak. Though Linda's voice-over urges us to consider him in sympathetic terms – 'This Farmer … wasn't no harm in 'im. You give him a flower, he'd keep it forever' – we cannot ignore his apparent indifference to the stark contrast between his own privileged life and the brutal existence of the migrant workers. He does not seem naïve; rather, he appears complacent. The Farmer sees no possibility of – or reason for – change; the ways of the world are established, and he cannot conceive of anyone, himself included, challenging them. This is what primarily disqualifies him from the 'official' hero category: he appears to have no ideals. Casting Sam Shepard as the Farmer contributes to this subversion of the western type: with his thin build and reticent manner, he does not look or behave like a man who has harnessed horses and ploughed a field, or run behind a thresher as we see Abby and Bill doing. This Westerner did not earn the land, he bought it. He has never 'farmed' it himself, but overseen the work of others, through his foreman, rarely speaking to many of his employees. He has brought the East with him, in the form of his house and its civilised contents, such as paintings, books and glassware, but he has not *civilised* the West, perpetuating instead a medieval system in which he is lord of the manor and a worker may be fired at any time for expressing a complaint.

Furthermore, the Farmer's connection to the earth seems self-interested. He does appear to appreciate nature, as some scholars have pointed out; Richard Corliss, for instance, describes his association with the land and with dogs: 'They hunt with him, and we can share his pleasure, watching … [their] graceful, purposeful movements' (1978: 69). Yet he continues by attributing a romanticised vision of the Farmer's relation to nature, arguing that this is a man 'who loves the land … He's a merchant of the earth, but also its sensual lover' (1978: 69). While this description may fit a traditional western farmer, images of the Farmer with his dogs, or of him 'sniffing a stalk of wheat, moving it between his fingers' (ibid.) cannot obfuscate his exploitation of the land. It has made him rich, but that seems a hollow achievement and a misinterpretation of what Western expansion is about in our mythology, where it is a part of the development of the country, and the individual's actions are always related to the well-being of others and the community.

It is worth comparing the Farmer's attitude with the more traditional Westerner's concept of the earth: in *Red River*, for instance, Tom Dunson selects land for a purpose and with hope for the future. He envisions 'a good place to live in … the greatest ranch in Texas' on which he will raise 'enough beef to feed the whole country. Good beef, for hungry people.' Of course, he takes that land illegally and defends it by killing any challengers. Yet as long as he continues to think of his work and the land in relation to the good of others as well as himself, the movie supports him. His ambitions seem reasonable in contrast to those of the man he supplants, Diego, who lives 'over four hundred miles' from the spot Tom has chosen. Tom's faithful pal Groot says of Diego, 'Here's all this land achin' to be used and never has been. I tell ya, it ain't decent.'

Back-breaking labour for no subsistence in *Days of Heaven*

Furthermore, Tom embraces self-sacrifice in order to achieve his goals, admitting at the start that 'it takes work, it takes sweat.' Years after establishing his ranch, in the grim post-Civil War days, he plans a cattle drive to Missouri, and tells his men, 'Most of you … have come back [from the war] to nothing.' It is for them as well as himself that he takes on the challenge of the unknown, and he assures them, 'Nobody has to come along. We'll still have a job for you when we get back.' On the cattle drive, Tom endures the same privations as the other men. It is only when he loses sight of what is best for the men, and focuses obsessively on the success of the drive, that the film and his adopted son forsake him; his redemption at the film's conclusion is earned by his re-education that community comes before individual, personal desires.

This emphasis on the land and the manner in which it is worked to a noble end is also present in what many consider *the* classic western, *Shane*. When the farmers bury one of their own, brutally shot down by a gunslinger hired by their rivals, the ranchers, they consider giving up and leaving. Shane reminds them, 'You know what he [Starrett] wants you to stay for. Something that means more to you than anything else. Your families.' Starrett adds, 'This is farmin' country, a place where people can come and bring up their families … grow 'em good and grow 'em up strong the way they was meant to be grown.' Personal goals go beyond individual survival or even the attainment of a better life for one's family; they extend to the larger community, unseen but undeniably there – the nation. The settlement of the West, with the hard work it requires, is necessary and purposeful. In film after film, a harvest is brought in, sheep are sheered, cattle are driven to market: labourers are rewarded with money or stability, but also with the knowledge that they are contributing to progress, to the Americanisation of the West. The Farmer in *Days of Heaven* seems completely detached not only from the fellow humans who work his land but also from the world as a whole. He does not feed the rest of the nation, or even the rest of Texas; he merely becomes the richest man in the Panhandle.

Those who work the farm in *Days of Heaven* are only temporary help so they have no emotional investment in their work. The harvest is not an accomplishment and it provides no closure. When the Farmer asks Abby where she will go after this crop is in, she says resignedly, 'All over. Wyoming. Do you think I'll like it?' The Farmer laughs nervously, but clearly does not see the irony of using the word *like* in relation to back-breaking labour performed for subsistence wages with no hope of advancement or progress. In the cycle of work depicted in *Days of Heaven*, there is no personal satisfaction as there is in the classic western. Many westerns even feature a cathartic task, such as the removal of the tree stump in *Shane*. As thanks for the Starretts' hospitality, Shane takes an axe to a stubborn stump which Joe has been battling indefinitely. He and Starrett attack the tree as if it is a personal challenge, and when Marion makes the practical suggestion that they hitch up the horses and haul it out, the men refuse. This glorification of labour and its personal rewards is rejected by *Days of Heaven*, as it is impersonal, endless and devoid of meaning.

Both the brutal depiction of labour and the hopeless state of those who engage in it are underscored in Malick's film by the overwhelming beauty of the landscape. This is possibly the most breathtaking depiction of the Western United States ever seen on screen; Texas has never looked more lovely (and rightly so, for the movie was filmed in Canada). Critics made much at the time of the film's release about its pictorial beauty, and many considered *Days of Heaven* pretty but empty. Stanley Kauffmann's review in *The New Republic* complained that 'as the film fails to grow and as the stunning pictures continue to flow, the Beauty becomes like a lavish blanket on a coffin … (One sign of too-pretty photography is that nothing ever happens at midday, only early or late in the day when the light slants)' (1978: 16). In the early portions of the film, however, the heightened reality of this landscape makes the western myth seem not only possible, but plausible. Here at last is a landscape worth having left the safety and stability of the East for. When Tom Dunson stops in *Red River* and says 'this is it', we must take his word for it since the acreage he admires looks pretty much the same as all the land has since he left the wagon train. Yet the West of *Days of Heaven* is truly a West worth experiencing. This *is* the mythical West, shrouded in magical light, still and mysterious at daybreak, so new that we may be seeing stretches of land no other human being has yet laid eyes on. The exhilaration of these images makes it so much the worse when the illusion is destroyed by the image of sweat-soaked labourers walking past the Farmer seated in that upholstered chair, placed incongruously in the middle of the field. In the early moments of the film, as Bill, Abby and Linda flee Chicago, there is a thrill to the shots of the train wending its way West, and a buoyancy to the music and to Linda's voice-over remarks that 'all three of us been goin' places … goin' on adventures.' All of that is revealed as a dream, an illusion, both for the characters and for the viewers. This farm, this West, is not heaven after all, though it may have seemed so for a few fleeting moments.

In its plot development, *Days of Heaven* also uses conventions of the western to raise our hopes, and then reveals those conventions to be false or flawed. The fate of Bill, the film's outlaw hero, seems particularly cruel. The project of many westerns featuring an outlaw hero is to redeem him, to observe his growth and maturity. In *Stagecoach* (John Ford, 1939), for instance, Ringo must be seen to understand that his own personal whims are not paramount, that one must come to see the world through the eyes of others. When he finally does, at the end of the film, he becomes worthy of not only liberty, but of Dallas, the woman who loves him. When he grows up, he earns reward. Other outlaw heroes may be redeemed through a noble death. In *My Darling Clementine*, Doc Holliday rules the town of Tombstone through intimidation, scorns the love of saloon-girl Chihuahua but uses her anyway and rejects all overtures of friendship. He has become bitter because of the tuberculosis which is sure to cut short his life. But he is not too far gone to appreciate Shakespeare, recognise the value of Wyatt Earp as an ally, and feel love for ex-fiancee Clementine when she appears in town. He goes so far as to join the Earps in their showdown with the Clantons at the OK Corral. He acquits himself nobly and is then killed. Ready to turn over a new leaf, Doc had learned from his mistakes. As Clementine and Wyatt (the official hero) are destined for one another, the film cannot allow that to happen and so provides him with the alternative of a selfless death.

In *Days of Heaven*, Bill is rewarded with neither Ringo's happy ending nor Doc Holliday's noble death. He should qualify for one or the other, because he does learn from his mistakes, and may in fact be seen as the only character who grows up in the course of the movie. The Farmer *finds things out* – that Bill and Abby had been lovers, for instance – but is not educated or enlightened; Abby, we are told in Linda's voice-over, blames herself for all that happens and vows to live a better life, but in the final scenes of the movie we see her blithely leaving the past behind, placing Linda at a boarding school and climbing on a troop train. Linda remains a child, and perhaps always will. The voice-over is a significant element in the constancy of Linda as a child, since her voice-over, at least part of which seems to be spoken *after* the events of the film, is in the same voice she has as a character. We do not hear from Linda the adult looking back on these events, but from Linda the adolescent, with her still-limited understanding of the world around her.

Bill starts the film as the least self-aware character; he believes the world is against him and that everything happens by chance. As Linda tells us in voice-over, 'He was tired of livin' like the rest of them, nosin' around like a pig in a gutter … He figured there must be somethin' wrong with them, the way they always got no luck…' He is eager for change, but sees no opportunity. Work in the mill has been succeeded by work in the fields – tedious, mindless, endless. For Carole Zucker, who sees the Farmer as a diminished figure due to his acceptance of his privileged role as landowner, Bill's suffering humanises him. He is rendered sympathetic by the 'pathos of his class victimisation' (2001: 5). However cruel he seems when he encourages Abby to marry and await the man's death, and however petulant he seems when he eyes them jealously, he is not as bad as he might want to be. The Farmer is at their mercy and Bill could kill him any time. Faced with just such an opportunity – to kill him in a hunting 'accident' – Bill tilts his shotgun at the last second and shoots into the ground. Manipulative as he may be, he does not have what it takes to murder the man in cold blood. Soon thereafter, he leaves the farm, unable to watch Abby and the Farmer together, unable or unwilling to kill his rival.

Lovers Abby and Bill huddle against the harsh conditions in the wheatfields in *Days of Heaven*

Not only is Bill sympathetic; he develops as a character. As the seasons turn, and migrants arrive once again for the harvest, Bill reappears. Linda is excited to see him, the Farmer and Abby understandably wary. But he has not come back for a confrontation. He seems rather to be exploring his own past, assessing the relationship of the married couple, and recognising his own failures. In a significant scene, Abby meets him in the barn by chance. She says, 'I'm sorry', indicating that their relationship is over. Bill then utters his most thoughtful words of the whole film, saying regretfully, 'You didn't do nothin' to me. I didn't know what I had with you. I think about it – the things I said to you, how I pushed you into this. Got nobody to blame but myself.' Seeing the mistakes he has made, and accepting responsibility for his own actions, he understands what he has lost, and resigns himself to leave Abby in peace, saying, 'I gotta get goin', before it gets too late.'

The movie does not permit him a graceful departure, however. At this point, locusts arrive to devour the wheat crop; in the chaotic effort to 'smoke 'em out', a fire is started, which lays the farm to waste. The Farmer confronts Bill in a charred, smoky landscape, almost regretfully pulling out a pistol and then walking decisively towards Bill – too close, so that Bill lunges forward with his only weapon, a screwdriver. One might argue that Bill's actions have brought him to this pivotal moment – that he has, as he has said to Abby, no one to blame but himself. But ironically, it is only after Bill has given Abby up to him that the Farmer acts on his jealousy. The death of *either* man at this point serves no purpose, as Bill had already committed himself to leaving the farm and Abby. But the Farmer's rash desire to punish Bill results in one man dying on the burnt ground, and the other fleeing – as he had from Chicago – with Abby and Linda. This time, the Foreman and a posse pursue him, and Bill is eventually shot in the back. Despite his growth as a character, and his ultimate willingness to give up Abby, Bill dies as a fugitive.

In these events and in Bill's fate we see failures of other fixtures of the western myth – the power of male bonding and the closure achieved through the revenge narrative. In classic westerns, even loners such as Ringo, Shane, Dunson and Doc Holliday form supportive, nuanced relationships with other men. The comradeship of men is one of the inherent values of the western. In *My Darling Clementine*, Wyatt relies on his brothers and on Holliday. They enjoy each other's company and yet know when to leave one another alone. They view one another with the utmost seriousness. Wyatt respects Doc enough to try to save him from drinking himself to death; Doc may bristle at Wyatt's interference in his personal life, but can be depended on when Wyatt needs him. In the same way, Shane and Joe Starrett are worlds apart, yet understand each other perfectly, even to the point of Joe recognising that if anything were to happen to him, Marion would be well looked after – by Shane. Tom Dunson has not only a buddy in Groot, but an adopted son in Matt – quite a family for the ultimate Westerner, gruff, independent, intolerant of others.

In *Days of Heaven*, one relationship between men fails to develop, and another is abruptly terminated. The former is that between Bill and the Farmer. Once they have shifted from field help to household help, and then to 'family' by marriage, Abby, Bill and Linda enter the Farmer's world. They play improvised forms of baseball and golf together; they eat together in the gazebo and entertain each other with juggling tricks and the like. But Bill and the Farmer are seldom depicted alone together. In one rare moment of intimacy, Bill articulates – albeit in a limited manner – the disillusion he has experienced. He and the Farmer sit side by side as he confides, 'So I went to work in the mill, couldn't wait to get in there … Then one day you wake up, you find you're

Bill runs through the river, a fugitive from the law, before being shot in the back and killed

not the smartest guy in the world – never gonna come up with a big score. And when I was growing up I thought I really would.' At this point, we know that Bill believes the Farmer is dying. He hopes that this is the big score he has waited for, because Abby – and he and Linda – will inherit the farm. Still, he seems to be fishing for some reply, and the Farmer, whose past is a blank slate, says nothing. Again, we are left with the impression that Bill's disappointments are alien to him; the scene ends with a shot of Bill looking off into the distance dejectedly. They are sitting next to each other, but are not in the same world.

Other scenes of them hunting and cleaning birds are fraught with tension and mistrust; the activities which bring most Western men together serve no such purpose here. Furthermore, their love for the same woman is a typical device in conventional westerns, and frequently strengthens the male relationship. Tom Dunson and his adopted son Matt briefly vie for the same woman. More significantly, though Doc at first resents Wyatt's interest in Clementine, it seems a confirmation of the two men's similarities and status as heroes – they both admire her and both believe she is too good for them. Of course, in *Shane* the love for Marion is an integral part of Shane's relationship with Joe; each recognises the other's tenderness towards her and desire to please her. Shane prevents Joe from facing Wilson because he knows that Joe would not win; he sacrifices himself for Joe as a friend and also for Joe's family, who need and love him. In contrast, in *Days of Heaven*, the love the two men feel for Abby makes it impossible for them to become friends.

While the relationship between Bill and the Farmer is thwarted, that between the Foreman and the Farmer is abruptly renounced. Throughout the early stages of the film, the two seem to respect and care for each other. The grizzled, wary old man protects the Farmer from contact with the migrants; he attempts to prevent the Farmer from getting to know Abby, and suspiciously questions Linda about where they lived last and what they did there. There is even an indication that he docks Bill and Abby for sloppy work in the hope that they will react angrily and leave the farm altogether. Later, when the Farmer marries Abby, the Foreman expresses his doubts, saying that he does not believe Bill and Abby are 'honest people'. In response, the Farmer admits to the older man, 'We've been together a long time, and I've always felt close to you', but sends him to 'the North end' of the property – which may as well be in the next state. By exiling him, the Farmer is in effect forsaking their relationship, which is dependent exclusively on their shared experiences. In her analysis of the western, Jenni Calder describes this comradeship as the genre's only antidote to loneliness. The men who work together in the western landscape 'are extensions of each other'; they have a 'silent and instinctive appreciation of each other's feelings' (1975: 3). They seek out no one else's company, and the Westerner who rejects marriage 'protects something vital about himself' (1975: 172). In *Days of Heaven*, the Farmer seems willing to replace the Foreman with Abby, literally sending the older man away. As he departs, the Foreman makes one more effort to protect his former companion, telling Bill, 'I know what you're up to. That boy's like a son to me.' Perhaps because he cannot bear to watch the Farmer make this crucial mistake, the Foreman accepts a separation, which reduces him to the role of a witness to events. When the Farmer confronts Bill, the Foreman is not even there; he arrives too late, and weeps over the lifeless body of his 'son'.

The Foreman, however, is not so quick to accept the failure of comradeship, and he makes what can be interpreted as a final attempt to redeem his friendship with the younger man through the pursuit of revenge. In response to the Farmer's death, he organises that most western of devices, a posse. As Bill flees with Abby and Linda, the Foreman hunts them down, flanked by policemen, showing strangers a photograph of Abby and the Farmer and asking in a dead voice, 'You seen her? Where?' This impulse to seek vengeance has been, of course, one of the most fundamental characteristics of the western, from *Stagecoach* to *The Searchers* (John Ford, 1956) to Clint Eastwood's films. In *My Darling Clementine*, Wyatt's personal pursuit of revenge is 'civilised' by the town's desire to get rid of the dangerous Clantons. Shane has lived his life according to the revenge narrative, and knows all the formulas, down to the exchange of insults and the final challenge, 'Prove it'. It is to break the cycle of retribution killings in the valley that Shane takes Joe Starrett's place, disposes of the threat to the community, and then moves on. In these classic westerns, retaliation killing is used not merely for personal gratification; those who seek it hope that it will result in a greater good. Wyatt visits the grave of his youngest brother, murdered by the Clantons, and says, 'Didn't get much of a chance, did you, James? ... Can't tell, maybe when we leave this country, young kids like you will be able to grow up and live safe'. In the classic western, the personal goal becomes inseparable from the common good.

The Foreman sets out on the same path as Wyatt Earp, but for purely personal reasons, and therefore his revenge proves hollow. There is no reason to think that Bill is a further danger to anyone – especially no reason for *us* to think so. We saw him pass up an opportunity to shoot the Farmer while hunting quail, and we saw the confrontation between the two men – a clear case of self-defence. Ridding the world of Bill is not comparable to ridding the world of the Clantons, or the Rykers and Wilson of *Shane*. As Bill runs through the forest towards the river, pursued by a dozen policemen on horseback, badges prominently pinned on their blue uniforms, guns drawn, the odds seem ridiculously uneven, and there is no indication that taking him alive is an option. Even the Foreman seems to recognise the futility of this revenge killing. After Bill has been shot crossing the river, the lawmen fish him out. We cut to shots of Abby, of Linda and of the Foreman, all of whom look devastated. There is a lost expression on his face, as if he realises that this death is devoid of meaning. At the end of the scene, we see three mounted policemen calmly talking amongst themselves, but we do not get another glimpse of the Foreman. Revenge has been exacted, but there is no redemption in it; it only inflicts more pain, deepening the bitterness.

By the very fact that this act of revenge fails to provide closure, *Days of Heaven* subverts a principle ideology of the western, that violence is sometimes necessary and sometimes good. This is the final aspect of its rejection of the western formula; the closing images – of Abby boarding the troop train – point away from the West of myth and towards the future, World War One. Constantly using western conventions and then revealing their falsity, the film becomes gradually more poignant. Hopeful that this narrative may ultimately be about the glory of the West, about progress and community, and the emotional rewards of labour, in each instance, the viewer is shown the fragility and elusiveness of these ideals. The central characters deal with situations that do not face more traditional Westerners – the failed male friendship, redemption denied, revenge rendered meaningless. It is mournful, and nostalgic, though not for any true West. Rather, it confirms our need for the myth of the West. Having seen the western's practices exposed as illusions, we understand better their value, and cling to them all the more. *Days of Heaven* is not an anti-western but a homage, to the West that never was, a love letter to the West which we have created.

References

Calder, Jenni (1975) *There Must Be a Lone Ranger: The American West in Film and Reality*. New York: Taplinger.

Corliss, Richard (1978) 'Every Picture Tells a Story', *New York Times*, 2 October, 68–70.

Fillipidis, Michael (2000) 'On Malick's Subjects', *Senses of Cinema*. Available at: http://www.sensesofcinema.com/contents/00/8/malick.html [Accessed: 11 May 2001]

Kauffmann, Stanley (1978) 'Harder Times', *The New Republic*, September 16, 16–18.

Kinder, Marsha (1974) 'The Return of the Outlaw Couple', *Film Quarterly* , 27, 4, 2–10.

Ray, Robert (1985) *A Certain Tendency of the Hollywood Cinema, 1930–1980*. Princeton University Press: Princeton.

Turan, Kenneth (1998) '*Red Line*: A Distant Epic', *Los Angeles Times*, December 23. Available at http://www.calendarlive.com/home/calendarlive/hold/redline_review.html [Accessed: 22 January 1999]

Walker, Beverly (1975) 'Malick on *Badlands*', *Sight and Sound*, 44, 2, 82–3.

Zucker, Carole (2001) '"God Don't Even Hear You", or Paradise Lost: Terrence Malick's *Days of Heaven*', *Literature/Film Quarterly*, 29, 1, 2–9.

CHAPTER FIVE

Terrence Malick and Arthur Penn: The Western Re-Myth

John Orr

The movie western is a hybrid vision of the American West inseparable from the idea of Manifest Destiny, the founding of a nation based upon the movement west by settlers, ranchers, soldiers, politicians and outlaws. The myth of the West incorporates two factors, the settling of a wilderness against the threat of Indian tribes and the settlement of a civil society against the threat of Outlaws. In this double movement, the myth of the Indian is set against the myth of the Cowboy. The former is the external barbarian, at times cruel and cunning, at times noble and brave, the latter the active-heroic settler transformed by circumstance into the lone enforcer or the doomed outlaw. This division describes nobody but fascinates everybody. Mythical figures always populate our imagination, at certain times more so than others. What is intriguing about the western's relationship to the West lies in its compressed process of becoming. Silent cinema followed on from the full settlement of the West, to reinvent the figures of the frontier a generation later, a generation spanning the nineteenth and twentieth centuries. In the stream of becoming, historic figures of the West were transformed into something else, mythic heroes and villains of the western. In childhood, the hero of Clyde Barrow, Texan farm boy become 1930s bank robber, was Jesse James. Meanwhile back at the Dream Factory there was a contrary movement. With the advent of the studio system and the politics of triumphalism after World War Two, the western crystallised into its classic form, the victory of settler over renegade, sheriff over outlaw, lone avenger over psychopath, cavalry over Native-Americans, good over evil.

The films of Terrence Malick and Arthur Penn are an oblique response to the mythic aura of the classical western, all the way from *The Plainsman* (Cecil B. de Mille, 1936) and *Stagecoach* (John Ford, 1939) to *High Noon* (Fred Zinnemann, 1952) and *Shane* (George Stevens, 1953). But they are more than self-conscious transformations of genre.[1] Like Robert Altman's *McCabe and Mrs Miller* (1971), they are radical attempts to reclaim the West from the western, not merely to reinvent the genre, as Sergio Leone, Sam Peckinpah and Clint Eastwood did so inventively during the same period. The latter, a popular revisionist trio, not only challenged the optimism and high morality of the classic western; the cynicism and brutality of their films now seem a one-sided reflection on their own age, referencing a growing amorality and contempt for human life, and also a United States that saw the gun triumphant as an essential item in its civil society. In that sense they remain mythic, and conservative. We are perversely assured that the world we have lost had no higher value than our own, that it mirrors ours and was just as free with its wicked, violent ways. Penn and Malick's films, however, aim to deconstruct myth rather than to substitute one form of myth for another. Their films are neither brutal nor cynical, but sceptical and tragic. Moreover, their reclamation of the West occurs only through a basic recognition. In American culture, the West constantly reinvented itself. Thus did William Cody commodify himself as Buffalo Bill in his travelling rodeo-circus where he also reinvented his old adversary, Sitting Bull, as an exotic Noble Savage. Thus did the ageing Wyatt Earp hang around Hollywood, spinning tall tales of the gunfight at the OK Corral that would find creative issue in John Ford's *My Darling Clementine* (1946). Just as life turns itself into closed spectacle, the history of the West becomes a history of self-invention. In tough circumstances, when times are hard, individuals reinvent themselves, or are reinvented, as 'characters' of an open frontier or of borderless spaces. The nature of the game is notoriety, where there is a double movement. As life is turned into spectacle, future generations, including Hollywood, turn history into myth.

The landmark films of Penn and Malick take forward this theme of re-invention well into the twentieth century, dissecting the western legacy in the epoch of modernity. The reinvention of self cues us to the hubris of their quintessential figure of the West, the proletarian outlaw. Penn's first western, *The Left-Handed Gun* (1958), set the standard, showing how taciturn, illiterate William Bonney (Paul Newman) became notorious Billy the Kid. Thereafter, *Bonnie and Clyde* (1967) glosses Texan outlaws of the Great Depression while *Badlands* (1973) charts the rise and fall of fugitive lovers who reverse the priority of robbing and killing in a decade (the 1950s) of conformity. In Penn's Texan movie, killing is the calamitous spin-off from robbing banks. In Malick's film it is the main event. Later, in *Days of Heaven* (1978), his proletarian outlaw, played by Richard Gere, is a furnace worker from Chicago forced southwest to Texas farmlands with his lover and her young sister to escape a murder charge, a fugitive on the run forced to conceal his own identity. In Penn's film of the same period, *The Missouri Breaks* (1976), Jack Nicholson is a horse rustler 'passing' as a small-time farmer in Montana to escape arrest. His persona is equally concealed but we see both men chafing at the bit, willing themselves fatefully to things better and things new. The fugitive beyond the law acts out reluctantly the role of the ordinary settler: the nature of the West as a land and a wilderness to be worked by human hand is highlighted by default. Four films: four variations on the fugitive kind, four fugues on protean identity.

All four also seek to break with the double movement of the West as 'western', showing how reality is turned into spectacle yet *denying* that history is invariably mythic. For history is the hubris of a self-transforming reality, and in this cinematic instant, its spectacles are lucid images of the darker side of American life. Here the shift forward into the twentieth century is two things, a shift away from the frontier and a shift into modernity, above all into a mechanised age where the car has specifically replaced the horse as the outlaw's mode of getaway and generally displaced the iron horse as motor of mobility over vast Western spaces. Unlike the steam train taking seasonal workers to harvest in *Days of Heaven*, the car (or the motorbike with sidecar that Bill later drives) is not impersonal. It is motion as *mine*. *My* horse has become *my* car, and like a stolen horse the stolen cars of Bonnie and Clyde are still possessive agents of motion and sweet engines of crime.

So, what exactly does 'the West' mean here? Is it merely geographic setting? East Texas for Bonnie and Clyde: South Dakota for Kit and Holly in *Badlands*? It is clearly more, a journey in space but also in time. In Penn's film, Bonnie Parker and Clyde Barrow are re-figured as specific icons in this history. Penn saw them as models of the mobile western outlaw in the age of the automobile, driving across state lines to rob banks, de-territorial at a time when tens of thousands fled west from the Dustbowl in T-model Fords. Bankrupt farmers migrate; in their wake the Barrow gang circulates. Yet Clyde Barrow is not Robin Hood and Penn's movie gang hardly a rerun of The Magnificent Seven. They are, if anything, the Notorious Five. In *Badlands*, Kit and Holly are not romantic outlaws but a *folie à deux*, matching sociopaths beyond good and evil. Here the stakes are raised further. There is no redeeming pull of the social and no local theatre of robbery. Murder is an *acte gratuite*: whoever crosses your path, whoever you happen to meet. Penn's film signifies motive; for Malick, it is an existential void. Bonnie and Clyde elevate outlaw theatre into murderous spectacle; Kit and Holly are icon-figures of a poet's montage, numbing us through lack of affect. Penn's film is prose-narrative, edgy, fluid, high energy; Malick's is rhythmic and dreamy in its poetic delicacy.

The legend of *Badlands*, aided by that of Malick as a reclusive auteur, has aided the film's reinvention as cool, post-modern irony – who says that life is linear when film students solemnly tell you the movie is 'cool' because it shows the 'influence' of *True Romance* (Tony Scott, 1993) and *Pulp Fiction* (Quentin Tarantino, 1994)? Yet its detachment and alienation-techniques are far from self-conscious. Its glacial effect is too chilling, its dryness too laconic and the present cul-de-sac of film irony is another world. If Malick's film is too chill to be cool, it also balances irony, very finely, on the edge of romance. Worlds apart in acting style, *Badlands* and *Bonnie and Clyde* are knit together by the romance narrative, where the reckless adventure is matched by a parallel passion. And if the adventure is perverse, then so equally is the passion. Penn's Clyde is impotent on screen, not bisexual as he was in life,[2] and the cult of the gun clear compensation for the limp phallus until the very end when the gun's excess is prelude to final and joyous potency. While Faye Dunaway plays Bonnie as an active,

'The cult of the gun': compensation for the limp phallus in *Bonnie and Clyde*

sensual woman, Sissy Spacek as Malick's Holly, the fifteen-year-old deflowered, finds nothing in the act of sex at all. For both her and Kit, this is asexual romance where, almost by default, the lure of the adventure is all.

The admiration Penn and Malick have expressed for each other's work is based here on a fundament of common themes. Malick, who grew up in East Texas like Robert Benton, the co-writer of *Bonnie and Clyde*, could not fail to have been impressed by Penn's location shootings in places familiar to him, indeed in the very towns south of Dallas with very same banks where the original raids took place. Penn, in turn, advised

Lured by adventure, Holly and Kit's romance is of an asexual nature

with on-the-hoof shooting in *Badlands*, where locations in southeast Colorado stand in for South Dakota.[3] Both knew they were engaged in reversals of mythology and Malick was certainly fired by Penn's triumphant example. Yet we also see how critical are the differences which come into play. In the wake of Nicholas Ray and Elia Kazan, and with a similar start in theatre, Penn had forged a style of film acting based on intimate psychodrama. What also intrigued him was the self-dramatising power of American culture at close quarters, its flair for autonomous spectacle. His camera is thus intense, intimate, powerful, highly epic and personal at the same time, a style he forged to such great effect early on in *The Left-Handed Gun*. Malick moves away from this use of *mise-en-scène* in quite significant ways. Sissy Spacek's *faux-naïf* voice-over is one means: the narrative chronicle is another. It is not a question of device – Holly says what she means and what she feels in words that are hers and not cute interpolations – yet by way of balance the Malick chronicle lends critical distance. Time is another country, time past and time lost that cinema reinvents as art. While Penn tries to recreate the past with vivid immediacy, Malick keeps us at arm's length. Here and there, now and then, them and us are binary opposites of a film aesthetic forged sparingly over twenty-five years in just four features.

There are also contrasting shades of auteurism. Warren Beatty as hands-on producer brought Penn in to direct the screenplay of Benton and New Yorker David Newman. In general, Penn has taken over on a preformed concept or draft screenplay, then turned it into his own film. Malick's first two films, however, come from his original screenplays and even though *The Thin Red Line* (1998) was a labour of love born out of admiration for the James Jones novel, the mark of Malick's special vision is stamped all over his screen adaptation. Penn's ability to adapt and absorb preformed material secured a continuous career for him. Malick's desire only to direct his own material – though he was sometimes happy to write for others – put him on a tougher track. Even in 1970s America the single writer-director with original material was a rare thing and the only consistent creator in this vein was the maverick John Cassavetes. Like Cassavetes, Malick was closer to the auteurist model of the French New Wave than to his fellow-Americans steeped in genre.[4]

At opposite ends of the auteur spectrum, Penn and Malick share one crucial thing. They lay bare, as argued, the process of American myth-making as a practice of historic becoming, precisely because they show the movement of history *into* myth in the arena of spectacle, spectacle that can be murderous, destructive and tragic. Thus there is no romantic nostalgia for the myth of an 'old West' foundering on modernity that drives films as different in tone as *The Man Who Shot Liberty Valance* (John Ford, 1962) or *The Wild Bunch* (Sam Peckinpah, 1969). The West absorbs modernity and transforms it through the conflict that ensues, shown most clearly though the impact of changing technologies on nature in *Days of Heaven*. The change can be brutal; the change can be tragic. Human nature is flawed, romantic by inclination, murderous under threat; and in a violent world the two become inseparable.

Here, *Badlands* and *Bonnie and Clyde* play uncannily on the difference between then and now, where the unfamiliar past echoes the familiar present. Of course the gap in Penn's film is greater. Thirty years and one World War between then (early 1930s) and now (late 1960s) allow the film's clothes to recycle as fashion items out of the past for a young audience. In *Badlands*, a mere fifteen post-war years narrow the gap. James Dean, whose T-shirt, Levis and mannerisms Kit decides to copy, was still an icon to a 1970s audience. Kit's beat-up escape car could still be a relic retuned and used by members of that same audience fifteen years later. Indeed, *Badlands* as a cult movie has contributed to 1950s retro-chic that later marked the Levis 501 film-advert cycle in the 1990s and further enshrined Dean as an icon of eternal return. Martin Sheen as Malick's spectral effigy of Dean and film persona of Dean's real life imitator, the Nebraska spree killer Charlie Starkweather, presents a double lineage: the Western 'badlands' and Hollywood both resurrected in a single figure. While Penn's films echo the 1950s acting lineage, the Stanislavskian Method of the Actor's Studio and the power of psychodrama in which Dean had duly played his part, *Badlands* moves in the opposite direction, for Sheen is Dean's antithesis. His psychopathic rebel has no inner torment; instead a vacancy that is chilling. Lack of conscience, no sense of good and evil, no feel for fellow-suffering, all are embodied in the scene where Kit watches Cato slowly bleed to death.

The comparison goes deeper. *Bonnie and Clyde* transforms the earlier inarticulate rebel of *The Left-Handed Gun*, a role earmarked for Dean before his sudden death, into the cute-talking brat-outlaw that served as a key model for the American New Wave of the 1970s and the US independents of the 1990s. The western outlaw robbing banks is resurrected as a modern 1930s figure: car-wise, motel-hopping, fashion conscious, machine-gun toting. Penn's trick is to place the iconic figure of Warren Beatty in the outlaw lineage as a daredevil become folk-hero, not simply to pastiche the gangster movie. Barrow had, after all, modelled himself on Jessie James and then updated the myth. His gang's victims were unforeseen by-products of robbery for little gain or a calculated killing of law officers – 'the laws' to use the sneering term that keys in the title of that 1930s outlaw fiction, Edward Anderson's *Thieves Like Us*. For if 'the laws' were thieves like us, then for many death by shoot-out was no more then they deserved.

We can see how far in the space of seven years that Malick had moved away from Penn's film. In *Badlands*, Kit and Holly are figures pointing to a more disturbing trend in the dark side of modernity. They represent a more casual evil that leaves us mute and stupefied, whose aural and visual signifiers float on the backwash of poetic chronicle, embellished by montage, by a pure mix of image, voice-over, music and ambient sound. We can think of the mixed montage sequence that starts with the choral torching of the dead father's house, then cuts into the voice-overed, xylophoned getaway car outside Holly's high school and ends in the cartoon spectacle of an outlaw's wilderness where Kit postures like a jungle rebel fresh out of Nam. There is here a narrative synesthesia, where our experience of multiple images and sounds shade over into one another, blur and merge and float. Uncannily, we are outside our own experience of watching, going with the flow of the chronicle but also on the outside looking in, spectators from afar. It is a startling aesthetic that Malick would go on to refine and deepen in *Days of Heaven* and twenty years later in *The Thin Red Line*; an aesthetic that gives pleasure without eliminating judgement, which demands judgement without destroying pleasure.

It is also the opposite of melodrama. In *Badlands* and its dry dialogues there are no venal sheriffs, no sneering and corrupt citizens, no incidental buffoons. Instead there are victims frozen by their moment of doom, uncomprehending as death closes in. The horror of recognition is an instant that has already passed. Malick could not hope to capture Starkweather's killing spree in Nebraska, eight corpses in ten days, so his remodelled Kit is spare and austere in the measuring of catastrophe. He is creating his own legend, knowingly, yet it is legend in a vacuum. Malick makes sure the killer admired at the end as 'quite an individual' by his captors is also in awe of them, of the full power of the state and its troopers in payback mode. He is further diminished by the power of Holly's voice that worships adventure as a romantic fate beyond the mortal reach of the small-town psychopath. Here apotheosis, at best, is a cartoon that places clarity above complexity. The Image of adventure cannot hope to live up to the Word of romance and we are constantly reminded of it. It is of course not for want of trying on the part of the lovers. In the hiatus between word and image that Malick creates, there is sustained pathos. Where Bonnie and Clyde's notoriety is full and riotous, that of Kit and Holly remains fraught and frail, a deadpan destiny.

The underlay of *Badlands*, however, should not be overlooked – its faint but telling residues of Greek and Biblical myth. The killing of the Father and the torching of the ordered family home evoke the daughter's ritual abandonment of Oedipal desire, the transfer from father to lover that can be accomplished here only through the pathology of killing. In Kit's capture of the Rich Man in his Queen Anne-style home, a sign of gracious Western living, there is due repetition of this revolt against the patriarch. Sheen, from the wrong side of the tracks, strikes back twice. Here we can look at film ancestors, offspring Montgomery Clift squaring up to cattle baron John Wayne in *Red River* (Howard Hawks, 1948), James Dean agonistic in contempt for his domesticated dad in *Rebel Without a Cause* (Nicholas Ray, 1955) and again *The Left-Handed Gun* where Billy is finally gunned down by his real-life father figure, Pat Garret. In transforming this revolt against the Father, Sheen reduces the screen sensitivities of Clift, Newman and Dean to peremptory blankness. Kit's casual murder of Holly's father halfway through comes as a shock to the system, reflexive in matching Holly's abrupt departure, in the 1950s, from a normal life to Hollywood's abrupt departure, in the 1970s, from its genetic optimism.

The film form that shapes catastrophe is vital. Holly's voice-over is a chronicle of casual witnessing that echoes in Western idiom the versing of atrocities that come to pass in the Old Testament of the King James Bible. In the sacred text there is epic distance of the invisible witness (God or man?) from 'the event', and of the telling of the event passed down through time. In Malick there is the chilling distance of the visible witness who is party to the act. This quality of there-ness, the act witnessed and act spoken, that makes montage so central to Malick's art, is unnerving in its power to be numbing and lyrical at the same time. Thus the Malick narrative produces in the spectator an immense double take. We celebrate the awesome power of film in general while failing in particular to react to behaviour *in extremis*. With this double shift, Malick moves outside the carapace of melodrama in which so much American film is enclosed. But he does so through a style that some critics have seen as dangerously specific and too brittle, limitations which in their view are a key to the absence of Malick from the cinema for twenty long years.

After their encounters with recent history in *Bonnie and Clyde* and *Badlands*, both directors go back in time. Penn returns to the earlier history of the West he had tackled in *The Left-Handed Gun* but this time more expansively in *Little Big Man* (1970) and *The Missouri Breaks*. With *Days of Heaven*, Malick goes back to a later but critical juncture in American history, the time just before its entry into World War One, and here he hovers on the threshold between the old and the new. Penn's return to the nineteenth century results in a filmic theatre that is tragic-comic. In *Little Big Man*, his General Custer is a bombastic, Wagnerian figure, precursor of the fascist leaders of the next century, righteously convinced of his doomed mission yet flaunting it like a histrionic showman on inhospitable land. For some genre critics, Penn's 1970s films are dated 'progressive' westerns, either importing un-macho elements into a macho genre or smart but obvious allegories of Vietnam.[5] Yet this crude rejection ignores a key aesthetic. His western characters are new iconic figures on the edge of genre, and do something unique. They match the Wellesian aesthetic forged in *Citizen Kane* (Orson Welles, 1941) with the Stanislavskian forms Penn had encountered in 1950s theatre.

His best films fuse the disparate directions of those two great RKO rivals, Welles and Ray. Ray's films had a close-quarter intensity and use of intimate camera offset by dynamic action sequences, then sutured by montage. Welles's camera led the assault on character as such, rendering his screen figures both larger and smaller than life – famously the huge portrait-image of Kane behind the lone figure of Kane as podium-orator. His screen figures are loud, self-creating theatricals ever ready for a fall and here Kane and Susan Alexander are the iconic precursors of Penn's Bonnie and Clyde. Kane-like 'character', ever-protean, is etched even more clearly on the many faces of Dustin Hoffman's Jack Crabb, teller of tall tales and soul chameleon who starts off as a white orphan, grows up as an Indian brave, returns to the Anglo settler culture as a cheap conman and finally survives the massacre of Little Big Horn as the only paleface left to tell the tale.

This enables us to gloss the contrast between *The Missouri Breaks* and *Days of Heaven*, but first the convergence of circumstance. Both were filmed at around the same time, 1976, though Malick's film came out two years later. Both were tough to edit, in Malick's case delaying release. Both directors had to deal with lead actors, Marlon Brando and Richard Gere, obsessed with star persona. Each film marked a crisis in their respective careers. Malick gave up directing and then disappeared while Penn's western appears now as the last of his great movies. That double blow points to a general predicament of the late 1970s: to the crisis of continuous innovation afflicting cineastes as diverse as Robert Altman, Francis Ford Coppola, William Friedkin, Roman Polanski, Bob Rafelson and Martin Scorsese. This has nothing to do with the crude burnout myth propagated by Peter Biskind (1998), who has speciously sought to blame everything on sex, drugs and psychosis and blame everyone involved into the bargain. It has a lot to do with the ceaseless self-invention of art in what is ever a mass industrial form and especially so in the United States. While Penn, after a great career, had seemed to reach the point of exhaustion, Malick's art seemed stillborn, its loss an American tragedy in a minor key.

Apart from common dilemmas faced by their directors, the two films present a paradox. They share like themes but are further apart than *Bonnie and Clyde* and *Badlands*. Certainly, both were well researched and both focus on the fugitive-hero 'passing' in order to escape the law. Both too are about interloping. Abby, Bill's lover posing as his sister, marries the farmer she knows to be dying in order that she and Bill can inherit his land. In Penn's film, Logan casually seduces the daughter of Braxton, his neighbour-rancher whose horses he steals, with intimations of a like power play. Yet differences are crucial. Penn's film is a frontier movie of rustlers and ranchers while Malick portrays a later, more ordered society, where he foregrounds the juxtaposition of city and prairie, migrant and farmer, technology and nature. The train that annually dumps the harvest workers in the fields by the Farmer's house – designed by Jack Fisk in the style of Edward Hopper's *House by the Railroad* (1925) – is the metonymic link between these different worlds. In the opening sequence where it rushes across an immense viaduct, it echoes early photography and painting, evoking a tense co-existence in the West between the natural and the technological sublime. In a way, the film is an animation of that pictorial theme and Malick's characters duly bring it to life, recreating the early world of the century for the late-century viewer by turning the still image into moving narrative – an austere narrative, however, that seems at times like a montage of pure images.

Penn's vision is more specific. In *The Missouri Breaks*, Montana is a vibrant scenography of filmic theatre scripted by Thomas McGuane, who researched rancher and rustler wars in the early years of the state. Penn had difficulties with the film at every stage; with McGuane over the script where some re-writing was done by Robert Towne, with the intense summer heat of location shooting, with Brando over characterisation and cue cards and with editor Dede Allen in post-production. Yet the end result is a defining film for its decade, more compact than *Heaven's Gate* (1980), Michael Cimino's sprawling epic on similar themes that was soon to bankrupt United Artists. Even now the film divides viewers very abruptly in their response. Some decry Brando's performance as a flamboyant Regulator hired by rancher Braxton to hunt down rustlers. Others see it as a tour de force, echoing and extending the protean showmanship of Penn's earlier 'characters' Custer and Crabb, Bonnie and Clyde. In heavy buckskins concealing a huge girth, ever in love with his horse, his accent swaying between stage Irish and Southern Gentleman, Brando lives up to his preposterous name as Robert E. Lee Clayton. An outrageous impostor of frontier history, his identity lies entirely in performance and that performance is both camp and chilling, for he kills Logan's rustlers only while in costume, even when one costume is a Sunday-best frock and bonnet.

Penn's narrative is linear and parallel, the separate lives of Clayton and Logan intersecting at critical moments. Both are existential figures appearing to improvise their fate, at times dilatory yet ruthless when opportunity strikes. Penn ends the phantom contest with a sequence of extreme close-ups of the two leads, and the proximity of the two figures is deadly. Clayton wakes in the wild to stare up at Logan's leering face as the rustler tells him: 'You've just had your throat cut.' The ellipsis here, the cut from the peace of nightfall by the campfire to the horror of the morning is as shocking as the slow-motion ballet of Bonnie and Clyde's bullet-riddled corpses. There the camera recorded every shot and every bullet hole in the gangster's bodies. Here the action of Logan's knife is off-screen, elapsed but deadly. Yet the daring fixity of extreme close-up fills in the horror, suspending us in the obscene intimacy of killer and victim. Nothing could be further from this than Malick's medium-long shots of the accidental killing of his farmer-rival by Bill after fire has destroyed the harvest. In Penn we have a powerful variation on the western showdown; in Malick we have the absurdity of the un-meditated event. Penn constructs the knowing look in the eyes of killer and victim alike; Malick shows us baffled incomprehension.

Just as Penn's talent lies in conveying the tactile nearness of his characters, their daily intimacies in talk and body language, so Malick's instincts take him in a different direction. His *mise-en-scène* is an aesthetic distancing created by the medium-long shot or the telephoto lens. His wide shots convey the power of Western landscapes to swallow those whose presence inhabits them. Thus he works differently from the camera set-ups of the classic western. The wide static shots of Ford typically used deep focus, separating out a foreground and a background to create in the dynamic action of ranchers, settlers or Indians a still microcosm of the western *comedie humaine* where all movement is contained by the frame. Later, Leone's camera in *Once Upon a Time in the West* (1968) is more mobile, and more sophisticated in its use of off-screen space, showing the influence of Luchino Visconti and Michelangelo Antonioni. Yet it is also a continuation, a stage on from Ford in its re-creation of collectivities, of mountain landscape and of panoramic depth. Malick's *mise-en-scène* tends to be flatter, more horizontal. The prairie takes precedent over the mountain range and depth, where it occurs, is often a signifier of distance between solitary beings. In *Badlands*, where Cato flees back to his shack to escape the gun-toting Kit, his receding figure on the plain conveys the mute terror of an innocent victim with nowhere to hide and nowhere to run. His running figure appears to be going nowhere on a flat empty landscape and we sense at that point that Kit will see him and kill him. The openness of the image thus signifies doom.

In *Days of Heaven*, where Malick does confront the collective, the seasonal workers who come by train to bring in the harvest, he frames them in terms of panoramic tableaux, their figures pressed against the wheatfields they harvest by telephoto shot, their faces in shadow as the camera of Nestor Almendros worked the magic hour of twilight, all twenty minutes of it.[6] Where Malick used extreme mobility it was through the hand-held immediacy of the Panaglide. Newly invented in 1976, precursor of the Steadicam, it follows and moves in amongst the moving actors so that its fluent movement is constantly reducing distance, as in the fire sequences, the camera pressed close to the hurtling bodies that it tracks. Malick's insistence on natural light is also an insistence on the power of nature. The humans who populate his landscapes have no sovereignty over nature but are presented as just the last in a long line of living species. Malick the naturalist shows us through inserts their predecessors who are now their contemporaries, flesh, fish, fowl, insect. In *Days of Heaven*, he matches narrative rhythm to the rhythm of the seasons and the rhythm of work upon the land, the seeding and the harvest, the stackers and threshing machines.

The film resembles a micro-continuum of nature. The Mennonite wheatfields of Alberta (Canada, 1976) stand in for the wheatfields of the Texas Panhandle (USA, 1912) they resemble in terms of cultivation. Here Malick treads the fine line between elevating the harvesters above their fraught spaces of being and diminishing their stature beyond the point of no return. A clue to this delicate balance lies in the photo-montage of the prelude that poses a question for all Americans as inheritors of a once promised land. How do they bring the faces of their recent ancestors back to life? How do they restore them to meaning? The film attempts precisely that but the still frame of the photograph, the shape of the figure, the embodied look frozen in time combine to cause a mystery the moving image can never resolve. The film certainly brings them to life, but it does so only by elevating the image over the spoken word. In the classic western, the power of the word enhances good and the quest for justice. Here the power to articulate, beyond the snatched phrase and the half-sentence, is rare.

This paucity of words and profusion of images in Malick's narrative is fundamental. It seems to use film as a medium to invert the hallowed tradition of all sacred texts, where the Word reigns supreme. Here the Image and not the Word, is God. What can be spoken onscreen as immediate to the other, and present to the viewer's ear (though fictionally in time past) is refined by Malick to a point barely above zero. Snatched phrases, half-completed sentences, half heard words. At best we are eavesdropping, ears strained, on the little that is spoken. Almost by default there is acoustic prohibition and Linda's voice-over comes across as an act of ventriloquism on Malick's part, a young girl's deep voice purifying the observances of her creator. This becomes the film's dominant, a dialogic dominant: the sounds of conversation overridden by other sounds, the sounds of Ennio Morricone's music and Linda's voice-over, the sounds of technology and nature. Sounds of human encounter vanish on the wind, erased from history. Her voice-over, a raw cover-version for reflection in tranquillity, is also wisdom masquerading as confused nostalgia, a ventriloquist's text filling in the spaces beyond the spoken fragments outrun by Malick's images. It is American reverie of the highest order.[7] In it the mystery of the spoken Word is displaced by the poetry of commentary and the enigma of the Image. In the King James Bible, voice, verse and cadence had displayed the power of the Word to conquer through chronicle. In *Days of Heaven*, voice-over, music and montage display the power of the Image to conquer through luminescence. As viewers of this muted spectacle we are there and not there. We float between being and non-being, precariously perched yet always entranced. Malick's characters share this splitting of being in a different way. Our trio of unfortunates (Bill, Linda, Abby) are people in a Promised Land but also people on the run, newly minted by becoming what they are not, running from the Law by working themselves to the bone then living out a dream of heaven on borrowed time.

In the Bible, we know the godly by their Name and their Legend. In Malick, we know the doomed through their Bodies and their Faces, for this is how we track the signs: the face of Death on the dying Farmer, the plague of locusts and the curse of fire that follows. The ripe earth is scorched; jealous rage ends in killing and retribution. Thou shalt not commit adultery and thou shalt not kill are well known; thou shalt not mimic incest (Bill and Abby as lovers posing as siblings) less so. All three and the Farmer (their saviour and their victim) seem punished here by the deep cruelty of nature and this also has its Biblical echoes. Yet we sense in Malick something deeper: that nature's cruelty is not anthropomorphic at all for it has no ulterior God. It is nakedly there and its coincidences are as cruel as its consequences. It is a puzzle and a terror that resides in the being of an implacable world, a being that brings nonetheless the passing respite of wonder, that still permits the 'miracle' of days of heaven.

In concluding, we can now see that Penn's interest in the West ranged much wider than Malick's, from the frail settler territories before the battle of Little Bighorn to the modern outlaws of a settled but troublesome civil society in *Bonnie and Clyde* and *The Chase* (1966). In films as diverse as *Mickey One* (1965), *Alice's Restaurant* (1969) and *Night Moves* (1975), moreover, he has shown his deep interest in the contemporary world of the United States. In Malick, the historical focus is narrower. He has always explored the recent past of the twentieth century, the remembrance of modernity in earlier times, a theme echoed and repeated throughout *The Thin Red Line*. His is the spare poetic reverie forged out of the fault-lines between wilderness and civilisation and within it the changing encounters of nature and the machine. The human figures of his cinema are somehow caught in between, unsure of their own destinies, their raw romantic urge to conquer nature undermined by their conflicts with each other, flawed by their failings and by past mistakes. Here Malick's detachment is not that of Stanley Kubrick or of Andrei Tarkovsky, for he is neither clinical in his filmic sensibility nor God-like in his placement of the camera. His vision signifies a rare fusion of critical distance and empathy and it is a vision that necessitates bold and daring strategies. Though never strictly out of favour in Hollywood, this has never been the kind of vision that Hollywood easily supports. And that may be one good reason among the many we do not know as to why Malick's career to date has been so elusive and so incomplete.

Notes

1   This is how John Cawelti typically reads the 1970s transformation of genre in 'Chinatown and the generic transformation in American Film', in Mast and Cohen (eds) (1985: 503–26).
2   Lester D. Friedman points out Penn's discomfort with the bisexual aspect of the original screenplay in his monograph *Bonnie and Clyde* (2000: 19–20). Like most of Penn's critics, Friedman insists on seeing the film as a 'gangster' movie.
3   Detail on the locations for *Bonnie and Clyde*, *Little Big Man*, *Badlands* and *Days of Heaven* can all be found in Reeves (2001).
4   For general discussion of this question, see David Cook, 'Auteur Cinema and the "Film Generation" in 1970s Hollywood', in Lewis (ed.) (1998: 271–8). For the special position of Cassavetes, see Carney (1994: 271–81).
5   Recent books on the western genre have little to say about Penn and predictably, nothing about Malick at all. See, for example Kitses and Rickman (1988); worse still is Kolker's dismissal of Penn's western films at the expense of *Bonnie and Clyde* and *Night Moves*. See Kolker (1988: 17–77). An exception is Saunders (2001) which includes a case-study of *Little Big Man* (95–101).
6   Nestor Almendros (1985) '*Days of Heaven* – Terrence Malick, 1976', in *A Man with a Camera* (London: Faber & Faber), 234–47.
7   For the significance of reverie in 1970s American film, see Orr (1998: 162–77).

References

Almendros, Nestor (1985) *A Man with a Camera*. London: Faber & Faber.
Biskind, Peter (1998) *Easy Riders, Raging Bulls*. London: Bloomsbury.
Carney, Ray (1994) *The Films of John Cassavetes*. Cambridge: Cambridge University Press.
Friedman, Lester D. (2000) *Bonnie and Clyde*. London: British Film Institute.
Kitses, Jim and Gregg Rickman (eds) (1988) *The Western Reader*. New York: Lime-

light.

Kolker, Robert (1988) *A Cinema of Loneliness*, second edition. Oxford: Oxford University Press.

Lewis, Jon (ed.) (1998) *New American Cinema*. Duke, NC: Duke University Press.

Mast, Gerald and Marshall Cohen (eds) (1985) *Film Theory and Criticism*, third edition. Oxford: Oxford University Press, 503–26.

Orr, John (1998) *Contemporary Cinema*. Edinburgh: Edinburgh University Press.

Reeves, Tony (ed.) (2001) *The Worldwide Guide to Movie Locations*. London: Titan Books.

Saunders, John (2001) *The Western Genre: From Lordsburg to Big Whiskey*. London: Wallflower Press.

CHAPTER SIX

'Enjoying the Scenery': Landscape and the Fetishisation of Nature in Badlands and Days of Heaven

Ben McCann

'Kit told me to enjoy the scenery. And I did.'
 – Holly, *Badlands* (1973)

'I got to like this farm. Do anything I want. Roll in the fields. Talk to the wheat patches. When I was sleeping, they'd talk to me … They'd go in my dreams.'
 – Linda, *Days of Heaven* (1978)

Few directors have invested the American landscape with such beauty or meaning as Terrence Malick. Throughout his films, the environment plays a crucial role in the narrative, governing character emotions and motivations, providing a lyrical canvas for the action and, perhaps most importantly, offering a deeper understanding of the personal stories Malick wants to tell. He uses landscape to define what are essentially philosophical and ethical issues, and moves from tiny peripheral detail to epic perspective within a single shot. Initially harsh and unforgiving environments are thus imbued with a voluptuous significance, which conveys a unique symbiosis of word and image. His grasp of natural landscape recalls Jean Renoir and John Ford, two other filmmakers whose images also involved the fastidious framing of the landscape to effect a subtle interplay between human beings and their surroundings.

This chapter will focus on the representation of landscape in Malick's two films of the 1970s, *Badlands* and *Days of Heaven*, and explore the way in which he inscribes his painterly images with a lyrical intensity, an emotional texture, and a narrative depth. Although such thematic concerns resurface in *The Thin Red Line* (1998) and *The New World* (2005) – where the beauty and violence of nature are transposed into the context of modern warfare[1] and a prelapsarian America – it is in *Badlands* and *Days of Heaven* that the scorched intimacy of the natural landscape and the ecstatic flow of imagery provides an extraordinary visual framework within which Malick's oblique approach to genre and iconography functions. 'Enjoying the scenery' may be fundamental to his cinematic repertoire, but it is clear that nature and landscape are also key co-ordinates in mapping the geographical and emotional journeys of his characters. In this respect, *Badlands* and *Days of Heaven* corroborate Steven Spielberg's observation that the 1970s 'was a time when the environment was crucial to the storytelling' (Biskind 1998: 263).

The cinematic environment is fundamental to the creation of the self, a notion reinforced by P. Adams Sitney in his study of landscape in the cinema: 'as the syntax of filmic narrative congealed, genres emerged which were predicated upon dramatising the situation of individuals in distinctive landscapes' (1993: 189). The western, say, or film noir, are manifestations of Sitney's 'emerging genres'. A clearly recognisable visual atmosphere is constructed and the narrative is driven as much by setting as character, so that nature, or more abstractly, the construction and use of natural space, assumes a vital aesthetic and narratological function.[2] As Frank McConnell suggests, any form of storytelling is always the story 'of the individual in some sort of relationship to his social, political or cultural environment' (1979: 6). Thus Malick's settings, and the manner in which these settings are portrayed, produce a kind of common meaning and reaction in the audience, precisely because the use of a certain recognisable place as a finite geographical and narratorial context anchors the spectator into a clearly defined setting.

Throughout *Badlands* and *Days of Heaven*, landscape assumes a symbolic weight. Christina Kennedy has noted that 'we are, in an important sense, the places that we inhabit' (1994: 163). In her analysis of *Lawrence of Arabia* (David Lean, 1962) she refers to the mutuality of self and space and the way in which a person-environment interdependence is created by a succession of 'image-events'. These 'image-events' are defined as a series of shots that distort or enhance the rhythm of a film so that a basic rapport can be created between the spectator and the filmmaker. Her examples include the film's desert vistas which act as an objective co-relative, inviting the viewer to make mental connections between the protagonist and his environment. Kennedy argues that through this technique, the filmmaker can begin to suture the viewer into the cinematic space, leading to a person-environment interaction in the audience as well as in the narrative. Kennedy's structural analysis may be one method of understanding the interaction between self and space in *Badlands* and *Days of Heaven*, for it also presumes an act of voyeurism, of stitching together a flow of imagery into an aesthetic whole.

In order to explore more fully this notion of landscape-as-protagonist, I will concentrate on three key elements in *Badlands* and *Days of Heaven*: the fetishistic attention to nature's indifferent beauty in the midst of human mayhem; the expressive externalisation of private emotions; and the mythic meditation on the role of conflict, violence and death in nature. As I will demonstrate, the intensity of Malick's compositions casts nature as elegiac and opaque – by combining preoccupations with beauty, power and conflict within nature, he reflects back to us both 'the fundamental mysteriousness of individual motivation and the relationship of human ambition and achievement to the larger scheme of the universe' (Andrew 1999: 140).

Beauty

In his chapter on the elusiveness of film landscapes, Colin McArthur elucidates a key concept of social geography: 'Within those great historical oppositions which shaped the modern world a whole range of spaces can be identified: wildernesses; pastoral landscapes; agrarian landscapes; villages; rural towns; suburbs; inner cities; metropolises' (1997: 20). It is interesting to note the importance of such spaces in Malick's cinema – either as key action spaces or as far-off reference points ('the lights of Cheyenne') – and the way they impinge on the narrative. An application of McArthur's concept and the move from small-town Americana to the wide open plains is made explicit in Holly's opening voice-over in *Badlands*: 'Little did I realise that what began in the alleys and backways of this quiet town would end in the badlands of Montana.' Her words are a useful introduction – Raymond Williams' argument that the dichotomy of the urban and rural is one that 'fundamentally organises human existence' because the terms 'country' and 'city' stand for 'the experience of human communities' (1985: 1) further reinforces Malick's codifying of natural spaces. Traditional cultural configurations of the country and city were orthodox and strictly delineated: the country was codified as virtuous, imbued with a sense of community and shared purpose; conversely, the city was corrupting, the repository of individualism and a lack of community values. This Romantic attitude of privileging the countryside over the city is invoked repeatedly throughout early cinematic depictions of the two spaces, most explicitly in F. W. Murnau's *Sunrise* (1927) and *City Girl* (1928). Leaving the city for salvation in the countryside is also a recurrent pattern in American film noir: in *The Asphalt Jungle* (John Huston, 1950), Sterling Hayden's idea of happiness is owning a farm, whilst Burt Lancaster and Robert Mitchum (in *The Killers* (Robert Siodmak, 1946) and *Out of the Past* (Jacques Tourneur, 1947) respectively) have retired from lives of crime to the idyll of the country. The dichotomies between urban and rural are introduced at the outset of both *Badlands* and *Days of Heaven*. In the former, Fort Dupree is codified as isolated, claustrophobic, uneventful; in the latter, Bill, Abby and Linda flee the industrial blight of the city, all steel-grey colour schemes and grimy bleakness. What this escape from the urban crucible ultimately permits is an exploration of, and integration into, nature.

Sumptuously photographed – *Badlands* was shot by Brian Probyn, Tak Fujimoto and Stevan Larner, while Nestor Almendros's work on *Days of Heaven* won him an Academy Award[3] – each film contains renditions of nature and the landscape that are simultaneously passive and highly significant. In both, the cinematography fetishises nature to such an extent that the images threaten to engulf the narrative, turning the films into exercises in 'film painting'. Painterly elements run throughout: in *Badlands*, the employment office with its yellow and blue colour scheme recalls the static poignancy of Edward Hopper, as do the absurdly white clouds at the end of the film as Kit is about to be arrested. Pictorial imprimaturs are also evident in *Days of Heaven*. For Richard Combs, Malick and Almendros conjure 'pointillist-fashion, a beguiling landscape, both harsh and magical' (1979: 110), while contrasts in mood and landscape are established through the differing colour schemes – the final scenes of Bill fleeing justice are shot through a cold blue filter, emphasising the increasing sense of isolation and futility, and provide a stark opposition to the rich hues of the harvest and the farm.

In *Badlands*, nature is privileged and fetishised from the outset. The opening sequences offer a clue as to its eventual importance in the narrative – there are three static, empty shots of a suburban South Dakota town. On the soundtrack, birds sing and insects hum, and alongside the dappled light and stillness of the trees, Malick's widescreen framing shows nature as harmonious, at ease in the suburban back streets. Only with the arrival of the thundering dumpster truck is the spell broken – its mechanical and aural presence drowning out the songs of nature. Nature's most enduring presence is in the mid-section, where Holly and Kit take refuge in the forest, Tristan and Isolde-like with their network of tunnels and stolen food. The plants and trees are imbued with a strong, preternatural power – not only do they protect and hide the lovers but, as Holly suggests, the environment whispers to them, prefiguring Linda's memory in *Days of Heaven* that the wheatfields would 'go in my dreams'.

Basic daily rituals take place outdoors in both films. In *Badlands*, Holly and Kit live idyllically in the woods, and when they visit Cato the three eat outdoors. This scene is echoed in *Days of Heaven*, when the Farmer eats a meal with Bill, Abby and Linda in an isolated pavilion. The characters also sleep outdoors, either in a verdant forest or an ice-trimmed wheatfield, and Holly remarks that 'there wasn't a plant in the forest that didn't come in handy' – nature throughout Holly's and Kit's forest sojourn is codified as benevolent. Under the impassive eye of nature, Holly loses her virginity against a tree, while the scene where they play cards together next to a river bank seems to show how at ease they are in the presence of nature. Holly's attitude to nature is one of childlikeness – she refuses to pick flowers because they are 'so nice' and her need to idolise and capture nature's fleeting qualities is made explicit throughout. During the forest scene, there is a shot where the camera sweeps through the undergrowth and down a river. The juxtaposition of beauty and foreboding in this sequence highlights how nature is rendered as lyrical and passive yet can be charged with anticipation; the riverbank idyll sets up a narrative tension which points to the inevitability of Holly's father discovering the truth.[4] The sweeping camera movement recalls Jean Renoir, who uses similar techniques in *Une Partie de campagne* (1936) and *Le Déjeuner sur l'herbe* (1959) to highlight both the inherent beauty of his rural settings and also to explicitly link the human to their environment.

Importantly, there are several widescreen shots that accompany Holly's voice-over, for instance, 'Through desert and mesa, across endless miles of open range we made our headlong way steering by the telephone lines towards the mountains of Montana.' Conjuring images of National Geographic supplements, these ultra-photogenic shots are important structuring devices in the film, not least because they privilege the cinematography and give the audience time to contemplate the importance of the landscape in understanding the story. Placing the human protagonists within the widescreen frame, the subsequent dwarfing of their proportions by the natural surroundings is symbolic of their powerlessness against nature; the lack of human perspective and influence within the greater scheme of things. It also demonstrates how the scenery constantly changes for Holly and Kit during their journey, yet nature's monumentality remains unaltered. This is best exemplified by the Farmer's home on the prairie in *Days of Heaven*, which is positioned within the totality of the landscape, making explicit his isolation. Framing his landscape vistas more majestically through the use of widescreen also makes important statements about the futility of human intervention or impression on the landscape.

Nature does not simply pose for the camera, however, it has to be captured and aestheticised, and Malick's method for extrapolating the hidden power of nature is generally through the close-up. Béla Balázs (1992) has argued for an anthropomorphic poetics of film theory and a fetishisation of the close-up. The unlocking and capturing of an object's subconscious meaning espoused by Balázs continues a train of aesthetic thought that originated from Romanticism, summed up by William Blake's discovery of 'the cosmos in one grain of sand'. Balázs understood that the close-up had widened and deepened our vision of life, and although his concept of 'microphysiognomy' can be applied more directly to extreme close-ups of the human face (he made direct referral in his essay to Falconetti in Carl Dreyer's *La Passion de Jeanne d'Arc* [1928]), it can just as usefully apply to Malick's images of nature – for what makes any object expressive is the human expressions projected on them. Balázs also highlighted how close-ups show 'the fate of the dumb objects that live with you in your room and whose fate is bound up in your own' (1992: 261), and in this respect it is fitting that Malick's preferred technique of showing something is through the close-up, since it embodies a naturalist and humanist preoccupation with detail; not just the object itself, but also its relationship to, and power over, the human protagonist. The shots of the locusts gnawing on the wheat are prime examples of the way in which close-ups can magnify meaning and lend a deeper understanding of the power of nature. Seen in close-up, the locust gains in prominence. Alexander Sesonske has shown how close-ups of objects 'clarify and organise the space they reveal, and impose some order on our perceptions of the objects in it' (1980: 109). Such a technique becomes a major stylistic constituent in *Badlands*, and particularly *Days of Heaven*, as the director seeks to convey a clear image of the action space which contains his characters.

The films' rapturous portrait of the landscape is further enhanced by characters' experience of it through various point-of-view shots – Kit staring out transfixed at the mountains of Montana in the sunset, a look of sheer incomprehensibility on his face, Bill and Abby staring up at the moon. It is through this dynamic juxtaposition of image and point-of-view that the beauty of nature is cathected into both protagonist and spectator. Another stylistic technique to fetishise nature is the use of tableaux, interspersed throughout the film to heighten its formal qualities but also to remind us of the vastness and implacability of nature.

So in the final assessment, how can Malick's lush aestheticism be justified? Are we, as Gilbert Adair argued in his review of *The Thin Red Line*, 'bludgeoned by gorgeousness' (1999: 5),[5] or do we appreciate Malick's flow of imagery all the more because of the confluence between picturesque and picaresque? To consecrate nature means to capture it, to some extent place it, like a dead butterfly, under glass and examine it up close. As an audience, we are not dissimilar to Bill wandering around the house after the Farmer and Abby have left for their honeymoon. He stands and stares at frozen images of beauty – a monochrome photograph, two glasses, a half-full decanter. As with Malick's isolated renditions of nature, we stop and stare, transfixed by the awareness of a higher aesthetic power within the most ordinary of objects.

Power

Within the hyper-realism of nature in Malick's films lies something more mysterious, more metaphysical. Critics like Todd McCarthy may baulk at a perceived over-reliance on nature shots – 'More than once', McCarthy writes, 'one is made to recall the old saw about how, if a scene isn't cutting together, you cut to a seagull flying overhead' (2005), but such generalisations miss the point. Malick's renditions of nature are externalisations of inner feelings; the sense that somehow nature possesses an omnipotence and transcendence that is reflected in the human dramas taking place. In both films there is a sense of harmony in nature, of an equilibrium that is in direct opposition to the fractured and dysfunctional human concerns. Another crucial leitmotif is nature as uncompromising, possessing an arbitrariness with no fixed scheme. Inherent in Malick's landscape is a transcendent power that threatens to overwhelm human nature and reduce it to a mere constituent part of a wider pantheistic conception. The symbiosis within nature is reinforced and repeated throughout *Days of Heaven*. As the train passes through the Texas Panhandle, herds of buffalo (that most enduring animal symbol of native America) graze contentedly, while geese fly low over the horizon. In his analysis of the film, Robert Zaller argues that 'only animals seem to hold their ground; only the locusts seem able to contest it' (1999: 150). Linda tries to 'hold her ground', to attain a synthesis with nature as the film progresses – in one voice-over she tells us she would like to be a mud doctor, 'checking out the earth underneath'. Accompanied by a shot of her ear resting against the ground, it is a poignant attempt to frame her growing understanding of the natural environment along with Malick's own pantheistic world-view.

In *Badlands*, nature's implacability is evident in the scene when Holly's father throws the dead dog off the bridge and into the river. The audience has already seen this bridge, overlooking the spot near the tree where Holly lost her virginity, and the space has now been transformed into a negative one; the site of burial rather than love. Malick is also keen on reinforcing the insignificance of humanity in the face of nature. Richard Combs has written that 'the silences and absences of meaning in his characters' lives stand for all those things which are above and beneath their gaze' (1979: 111), so, for example, when Holly compares the various sounds in the forest as 'spirits whispering about all the things that were worrying them', Malick seems to set up a duality between human presence and a wider, more profound omnipresence within nature.

Arguably, Malick's films of the 1970s are highly experiential: the audience responds as much as the characters to the overall poetry, mood and lyricism, and the externalisation of nature is a fundamental way to convey inner states. In this respect, he adopts the same techniques and visual imprimaturs as the Impressionist painters – sweeping camera pans, a subtle use of colour, the aestheticisation of natural light and the human presence overwhelmed by nature's monumentality. He also uses animals and insects as Sphinx-like observers, most explicitly in *Days of Heaven*, when personal and professional tragedy is symbolised by the locusts. Here, the film is pantheistic, finding motivation and inspiration in nature itself, where people are only slightly more complex than pheasants, wheat and locusts, but just as much a part of the environment. Zaller concludes that 'recurrent images – of flames, of animals and insect life, of fields, ponds and rivers – not only presage events, but create their own cyclical undertow' (1999: 150).

The use of a time-lapse shot of growing wheat is key here, for it lends an extra layer of texture to the whole narrative. On the surface, the shot simply signals the cyclicity of nature and the never-ending harvest pattern, but the sequence also accompanies the emotional growth of Abby and the Farmer and their subsequent, albeit fragile, happiness. It is only when Bill returns that this spell is broken – nature turns in on itself and destroys itself through human intervention; Malick cuts to shots of the wind rustling through the wheat, of horses neighing and the first appearance of the locusts in the Farmer's house. This extended scene culminates in the destruction of the fields by fire – an element which has been identified with Bill since the opening scene in the furnace – and reinforces Ding-Dong's warning that one day 'the whole earth is going up in flame'. The locust plague and fire acts as an objective co-relative for the Farmer's realisation of the true nature of Abby and Bill's relationship, an externalisation of inner emotions refracted through nature.

In another scene, when Bill and Abby lie together in the fields one night, Malick's camera shifts from a dreamy contemplation of the clouds above to a brief shot in which we see a glass they have discarded sinking through water, coming to rest amid the flora and fauna of the riverbed. This brief sequence may be symbolic of the deterioration of their relationship or the pollution of nature by human presence, but it showcases Malick's detached camera style and indicates the impassivity of nature, in which individual motivation stands for nothing.

Akin to the films' settings, the central characters are shown poised at economic and emotional borderlands. In *Badlands*, Holly and Kit are like cinematic heroes of the West, seeking to forge a new identity. Yet it is almost as if nature stops them, its omnipotence precluding the possibility of human intervention or transcendence. The 'mountains of Saskatchewan' are forever on the horizon, unattainable objects. The open-ended finale of *Days of Heaven* suggests a cyclicity in human nature that resonates with nature. Linda walks along the railway tracks with her new friend, signifying endless possibilities and multiple narratives. That Abby leaves on a train full of soldiers off to war suggests a further way in which humanity continues to attempt to dominate the landscape, this time through geographical conflict and war with the natural elements. The spectator, meanwhile, is sure in the knowledge that the same harvest cycle will recur again in the Panhandle for years to come – the never-ending birth-death-rebirth triangle of nature, unaffected by human tragedy.

Although 'this war at the heart of nature' is most fully realised in *The Thin Red Line*, the war in nature in *Badlands* and *Days of Heaven* is simply a displacement of the very human clashes that are taking place in the narrative – the conflicts are essentially between a *ménage à trois* (Kit, Holly and her father in *Badlands*, Bill, Abby and the Farmer in *Days of Heaven*). In the latter, there is a sequence where the two men go out pheasant shooting, and a triangular power matrix is established: the Farmer shoots the pheasant while Bill nearly attempts to shoot the Farmer. Here nature and humanity are inextricably bound up in conflict and power struggle. *Days of Heaven* is predicated on the complications brought by humans to the natural world, and especially by those who exercise control over it, hence the setting on a farm. Given its Rousseauesque subject matter and Malick's metaphysical preoccupations, the human war with nature is constantly being fought throughout the film. At the outset, it is a conflict won by the human – Linda nonchalantly plucks a dead chicken, while the endless drone of the threshing machine symbolises the never-ending battle between nature and technology. Yet the parameters shift as the film develops, and the emergence of the relationship between Bill and Abby coupled with the deteriorating health of the Farmer signal a seismic shift in the balance of power – the locusts and the fire, both Biblical in their appearance and vengeance, reclaim the initiative and exert their own dominance over the environment. When Linda tells us how, after the Farmer discovers the truth behind Bill and Abby's relationship, she thought 'the Devil was on the farm', she encapsulates the conflict between primal forces that are mirrored in the protagonists' struggles and humankind's contamination of natural beauty. 'Look at those vines, the way they twine around the trees, swallowing everything', instructs Lt Colonel Tall in *The Thin Red Line*. This proves an apt summation of Malick's relationship with and representation of nature in *Badlands* and *Days of Heaven*. In both films nature is simultaneously passive and active, beautiful and threatening, whilst its sheer totality and 'there-ness' is a key structuring external metaphor for the protagonists' interior dilemmas and conflicts.[6]

It is interesting to note that in Malick's films we never know exactly where we are. The landscape provides us with recognisable co-ordinates, but we are rarely given exact spatial specificity. This lack of a precise anchoring point corroborates his mythic undertaking – place in itself is not important but rather the effect that place has on a certain group of individuals. The very human dramas unfolding in both landscapes attain an even greater poignancy and reverberation when one realises that they are occurring against the backdrop of a passive landscape, one that is simultaneously detached from, and vital to, the development of relationships, power struggles and co-existence with nature. That the landscapes in *Badlands* and *Days of Heaven* are recognisable renditions of Americana (small-town life and the open road in the former, the vast open plains of the Texas Panhandle in the latter), reinforces the notion that Malick's fascination with nature and landscape stems not just from his metaphysical view of nature but also from wanting to examine the way in which key iconographic images of the American environment can serve a narrative and emotional purpose.

Watching Malick's renditions of landscape and nature is experiential – the audience responds to its overall lyricism. This is a key point because the audience is constantly in danger of being overwhelmed by the power of the images. When David Thomson wrote that *Badlands* balanced 'the externals of landscape and violence with their imaginative resonances' (1994: 470–1), he also observed how in *Days of Heaven* the landscape had been diluted by a 'sentimental, decorous spaciousness', suggesting that Malick's fetishisation of nature can only be completely successful if he combines the lyricism and beauty of nature with the very human concerns of the narrative. To dismiss *Days of Heaven* so summarily is unfair, for it is precisely the interconnection between the sentimental and the decorous that lends the film such a transcendence. Far from being submerged by a random flow of images, the spectator is enveloped inside a combination of epic painting and pastoral poem.

Malick's cinema continues a preoccupation with the (American) landscape and surroundings which resonates throughout the decade, whether in psychological study (*Taxi Driver* [Martin Scorsese, 1976]), horror (*Jaws* [Steven Spielberg, 1975]) or political thriller (*The Parallax View* [Alan J. Pakula, 1974]). All of these films rhapsodise the shape and symbolism of the American landscape, and similarly, Malick's pictorial strategies function as aesthetic exercise and important cultural procedure. As far as the road movie is concerned, *Badlands* defamiliarises and critiques its familiar generic co-ordinates – the film's most audacious stroke was to evoke pastoral Americana with a beauty and lyricism that counteracted the violent story he was telling, while in *Days of Heaven*, America has never looked so simultaneously ugly and beautiful, so surreal and yet true-to-life.

Myths reverberate beneath the surface, yet Malick never privileges them over ordinary contemporary existence. The picturesque idyll in *Badlands* is undermined when Holly looks at a selection of images using her father's Stereopticon. The initial allure of the forest quickly wears off and she wishes she 'could fall asleep and be taken off to some magical land'. The images have triggered different feelings towards the environment in her – she does not want to live 'like an animal' but in a house like the Rich Man's – and Malick seems to be suggesting that landscape devoid of any wider personal implications can never fully replace nature in harmony with human satisfaction and fulfilment.

Having demonstrated the extent to which visual ambience enhances a film's emotional dimensions, we can see how both *Badlands* and *Days of Heaven* embody an organic, pantheistic and sublime conception of nature and the environment. The confluence of nature and human interaction are forever fraught with tension. Through a series of widescreen shots, close-ups and point-of-view shots, Malick undoubtedly 'enjoys the scenery' yet never allows such vistas to obscure his thematic concerns. In both films the consecration of the landscape affirms the promise of wide open spaces to be explored and controlled and the audience, like the characters, are invited to navigate their way through the landscape, to select and isolate those symbolic or pictorial renditions that add extra significance to Malick's narrative. When Tall tells Staros in *The Thin Red Line* that 'nature's cruel' he is embodying a world-view that accepts the transfiguring power of nature but also underscores the arbitrariness of landscape. Whether landscape-as-protagonist means a pastoral setting of violent conflict, the ineffable promise of wide vistas or the recurring images of animal and insect life, Malick undoubtedly fashions a cinematic poem of the American landscape in which human figures are part of a grander vision of the spirit. He achieves a rare lyrical intensity coupled with an intuitive understanding of the American landscape, and within these established parameters, places his characters into the space, and watches them interact, successfully or unsuccessfully, with the myths, meanings and meanderings of the landscape.

Notes

1 As Robert Silberman writes in his chapter in this collection, 'It is in the visuals of the landscape … that Malick is able to express his vision of the world as paradise and paradise lost'.
2 For example, the connection between images of the landscape and the construction of national identity is axiomatic, and has been an enduring function of cinema since its inception.
3 The award was all the more remarkable as Almendros was slowly going blind at the time. Cinematographer Haskell Wexler also contributed.
4 This shot is virtually repeated in *The Thin Red Line* when the camera snakes through the thick, verdant grass of the hillside prior to C-Company's attack on the Japanese outpost.
5 Adair goes on to add, 'If there were an Oscar for Best Foliage, *The Thin Red Line* would be a shoo-in…' (1999: 5).
6 In his essay on *The Thin Red Line*, Simon Critchley argues that Malick views nature as 'a kind of fatum … an ineluctable power'. He concludes that Malick's central concern in his films is the 'nevertheless of nature'. It is this indifference of nature to human purpose that corroborates Malick's notion of a broadly naturalistic conception of nature. See Critchley 2002.

References

Adair, Gibert (1999) 'The Thin Red Line', *Independent on Sunday*, 28 February, 5.
Andrew, Geoff (1999) *Directors A–Z: A Concise Guide to the Art of 250 Great Filmmakers*. London: Prion Books.
Balázs, Bèla (1952) *Theory of the Film: Character and Growth of a New Art*, trans. Edith Bone. London: Dennis Dobson.
_____ (1992) [1945] 'The Close-Up', in Gerald Mast, Marshall Cohen & Leo Braudy (eds) *Film Theory and Criticism: Introductory Readings*, fourth edition. New York: Oxford University Press, 260–7.
Biskind, Peter (1998) *Easy Riders, Raging Bulls*. London: Bloomsbury.
Combs, Richard (1979) 'The Eyes of Texas', *Sight and Sound*, 48, 2, 110–11.
Critchley, Simon (2002) 'Calm: On Terrence Malick's *The Thin Red Line*', Film-Philosophy, 6, 48. Available at: http://www.film-philosohy.com/vol6-2002/n48critchley [Accessed: 13 February 2007]
Henderson, Brian (1983) 'Exploring *Badlands*', Wide Angle, 5, 4, 38–51.

Kennedy, Christina B. (1994) 'The Myth of Heroism: Man and Desert in Lawrence of Arabia', in Stuart C. Aitken & Leo E. Zonn (eds) *Place, Power, Situation, and Spectacle*. Maryland & London: Rowmann & Littlefield, Lanham, 161–79.

McArthur, Colin (1997) 'Chinese Boxes and Russian Dolls: Tracking the Elusive Cinematic City', in David B. Clarke (ed.) *The Cinematic City*. New York & London: Routledge, 19–45.

McCarthy, Todd (2005) '*The New World*', available at: http://www.variety.com/award-central_review/VE1117929092.html?nav=reviews?nid=2848 [Accessed 13 February 2007]

McConnell, Frank D. (1979) *Storytelling and Mythmaking: Images from Film and Literature*. New York: Oxford University Press.

Sesonske, Alexander (1980) *Jean Renoir: The French Films, 1924–1939*. London & Cambridge, Mass: Harvard University Press.

Sitney, P. Adams (1993) 'Landscape in the Cinema: The Rhythms of the World and the Cinema', in Salim Kemal & Ivan Gaskell (eds) *Landscape, Natural Beauty and the Arts*. Cambridge: Cambridge University Press, 103–26.

Thomson, David (1994) *A Biographical Dictionary of Film*. London: André Deutsch.

Williams, Raymond (1985) [1973] *The Country and The City*, second edition. London: The Hogarth Press.

Zaller, Robert (1999) 'Raising the Seventies: The Early Films of Terrence Malick', *Boulevard*, 15, 1–2, 141–55.

CHAPTER SEVEN

Innocents Abroad: The Young Woman's Voice in Badlands and Days of Heaven, with an Afterword on The New World

Anne Latto

Among the most striking features of *Badlands* (1973) and *Days of Heaven* (1978) is Terrence Malick's decision to use young female narrators. Voice-over is a familiar convention of Hollywood movies but the voice is almost always male. In the infrequent case of female voice-over, the narrator tends to be adult.[1] Employing a child's or a young person's voice-over raises questions of point of view more acutely than the familiar adult voice – the possible limitations of the narrator's experience, the reliability of their judgements.

If children's and young person's voices are rare in Hollywood narration, they are more central to American fiction, and the notion of the 'innocent abroad'[2] points to its literary antecedents. Malick was writing out of a rich literary tradition of first-person narrative. Huck Finn in Mark Twain's *Adventures of Huckleberry Finn* and Holden Caulfield in J. D. Salinger's *The Catcher in the Rye* exemplify the traditions of the colloquial voice heard in the male child and adolescent. Female voices are rarer, but in *What Maisie Knew*, Henry James uses the female child's voice, not in a first-person narrative but as his third-person centre of consciousness. These literary precedents are significant for several reasons: the 'innocent' voice, rooted in the idea of the child's innate moral sense; marginality as a position from which to comment on the adult world; and the use of the colloquial idiom.

In each case, Malick inflects these for his own purposes. When interviewed about the influences on *Badlands*, he cited a number of popular children's stories, among them *Tom Sawyer* and *Huckleberry Finn,* the latter 'involving an innocent in a drama over his head'. He admitted that although 'I didn't actually think about those books before I did the script it's obvious to me now', and described Holly, like Huck, as an 'innocent abroad' (in Walker 1975: 82). The term could also apply to Linda as both are young, leave home and relate their stories of being 'abroad' in the first person. But neither, of course, is male. How one interprets 'innocence' in the context of these films will form the chief discussion of this essay; intricately bound up with this will be issues of gender and of point of view.

Gender

Within the traditions of Hollywood cinema the child or young woman speaks from what is generally a marginal social position, a location outside the dominant, usually male, discourse. Malick's decision takes on an additional resonance in the context of the 1970s as the womens' movement gained increasing cultural significance. In 1970, when Malick was studying at the American Film Institute, four seminal books about the position of women in society were published.[3] These exemplified Simone de Beauvoir's contention that women were socialised into playing a passive role, pointing out that, 'the passivity that is the essential characteristic of the "feminine" woman is a trait … imposed on her by her teachers and by society' (1949: 307). In one of those four books, *The Dialectic of Sex*, Shulamith Firestone argued that children were also affected by this attitude towards women: that the nature of the bond between the woman and the child 'is no more than shared oppression' (1970: 73).

The voices in *Badlands* and *Days of Heaven* are dissimilar. During the events of the film, Holly (Sissy Spacek) is a fifteen-year-old, but she narrates from an unspecified future date after her marriage, in a style that suggests a retrospective, written account. Linda (Linda Manz) is considerably younger than Holly and the issues of gender and sexuality are correspondingly articulated differently in the two films. Her narration is fragmented, colloquial and immediate, suggesting a more spontaneous, unreflective response. However, both narrate a story in which men are the protagonists, the major narrative agents. The stories would conceivably be told in more orthodox ways, placing the man at the centre of events and of narrative focus, but Malick reverses conventional narrative precedence. His narrative method de-centres the male protagonist and destabilises the familiar conventions of a narrative world controlled by men. In this respect, the films correspond to the tendencies outlined by Thomas Elsaesser writing about the 'unmotivated hero', of whose journey he notes: 'the off-hand way it is usually introduced specifically neutralises goal-directedness' (1975: 15). He sees the violence often displayed in such films of the 1970s as 'the defensive gesture of the self-alienated individual in a society he does not understand and over which he has no control' (1975: 15). So the men remain active, but they are viewed obliquely, via characters whose voices would be traditionally marginalised or suppressed.

Woman's voice in film theory denotes not only the physical voice of the woman but her overall identity. There is no direct evidence of Malick's reading of feminist literature but his creation of Holly illustrates de Beauvoir's concept of Woman as a cultural construction. It is useful to draw on more recent feminist theories that pursue this concept, arguing that 'woman is a social construct, internalised and reinforced by psychic processes' (van Lenning, Maas & Leeks 2001: 93). Judith Butler denies essentialism, maintaining that 'gender reality is created through sustained social performances' (1990: 141). She asserts that such performances create the illusion of a gendered core in which 'the political regulations and disciplinary practices ... are effectively displaced from view ... preclud[ing] an analysis of the political constitution of the gendered subject' (1990: 136). Like any performance, it is 'the ability to compel belief, to produce the naturalized effect [which] is the result of an embodiment of norms ... that remains the standard that regulates the performance' (Butler 1993: 129).

Malick departs from the classic cinema's presentation of female characters: Holly and Linda are neither stereotypically glamorous adult women nor well-known stars, but rather, respectively, a plain adolescent and a child, both played by relatively unknown actors. Arguably, Holly can be defined as already socialised into performing as a middle-class young female of the 1950s. Even her language is a performance, drawing on romance story clichés, and as the film progresses she becomes increasingly influenced by the male discourse. Linda, a working-class, street-wise child from the ghetto, does not appear to have been so constrained to embody accepted social norms of feminine behaviour. Her gender identity is in the making, her rough voice (heard before we see her) hardly decipherable as either male or female. Improvised, unlike Holly's, her voice-over suggests an oral narrative rather than a scripted one. She exemplifies Butler's concept of the fluidity of the category of woman, of 'the inherent instability of that construction' (1990: 28).

Point of View

Classical Hollywood movies favour identification with the protagonist and one way in which this can be achieved is by use of the voice-over, which anchors and controls a key aspect of our access to the narrative world. In the case of a homo-diegetic narrator, the voice-over often conveys authenticity ('I was there and this is what happened') so we are inclined to believe what we hear and see. It is only if the images contradict what is reported or if the character appears to be an unreliable witness of events that we question the related story and its teller. As Douglas Pye comments, 'visual narration is not to be identified with the verbal narrator's memory or experience [so that] the inferences we draw from the visual image may or may not accord with what the narrator says' (2000: 10). Malick's narrators offer, in differing ways, obviously partial and limited views and/or attitudes.

Murray Smith provides a number of concepts that can usefully guide an analysis of the ways in which our point of view of the narrators and their world is organised. He maintains that 'character structures are the major way by which narrative texts solicit our assent for particular values, practices and ideology' (1995: 4) and suggests three stages of the identification process. In the first, *recognition*, we make assumptions and have expectations about the character based on the recognition of certain stereotypic traits. This is 'rapid and phenomenologically "automatic"' but some films can problematise the process and 'undercut and retard recognition' (1995: 82–3). The second stage Smith terms *alignment*, in which there is access to a greater degree of knowledge of the actions of the character(s) and, as a separate function, to their internal state. The third stage, *allegiance*, is closer to what we usually refer to as identification, having 'both cognitive and affective dimensions' (1995: 84). At this stage, our knowledge of and emotional reaction to the character causes us to evaluate them morally and rank them accordingly 'in a system of preference' (ibid.).

Holly and Linda are recognisable as types but the film it seems is initially reluctant to focus on them. The camera barely rests on Holly before drawing back so that her image in engulfed by the enormous dog she is stroking. This, together with the dimly lit room that denies us a clear view of her, already implies that the visual and verbal levels of narration will offer separate and even conflicting perspectives. The film gives us access to her actions and, selectively, to her thoughts (though we do not hear those regarding her father's murder), but both seem to be governed largely by Kit, thus undercutting our trust in her. Her expressionless tone of voice also distances the spectator and contributes to a detached view of Holly. These factors, together with her moral vacuity, prevent an affective identification or allegiance to her. *Days of Heaven* withholds an image of Linda until the end of the first sequence when we see her briefly: a child working in a sweatshop. We recognise her type, and as the film progresses align ourselves to her, following her physical journey and having some access to her thoughts. Even though her moral position is at times ambiguous we feel more inclined, perhaps because of her age, situation and empathetic attitude towards others, to identify with her as she struggles to make sense of the world.

Holly

Holly's voice is heard almost immediately after the first visual image of her is shown. It is an unsophisticated voice apparently reading from a text originating from a time after the diegetic events. The next shot of her is as an adolescent girl on the lawn outside a middle-class home, twirling a baton in a typically female-orientated pursuit to support a male team. She is thus placed within her society – one that marginalises the female, giving them little scope to develop other than in acquiescence to the hegemony of male structures.

The 1950s were an era of oppressive conformity especially for young adolescent women whose social world is aptly described by the female protagonist in Erica Jong's novel *Fear of Flying*.

> Growing up in America. What a liability! You grew up with your ears full of cosmetic ads, love songs, advice columns, whoreoscopes, Hollywood gossip, and moral dilemmas on the level of TV soap operas … and what all the ads seemed to imply was that … you would meet a beautiful, powerful, potent and rich man who would satisfy every longing. (1974: 17)

Holly is aware of popular movies: she is shown reading a magazine about Hollywood celebrities and comments that Kit is 'handsomer than anyone I'd ever seen – he looked just like James Dean'. Such details are symptomatic, however, of a sensibility permeated by the culture Jong evokes. The impression we have is of the stereotypic female role, of Holly playing the part of the loyal 'wife', of standing by her man: 'He needed me now more than ever' she states as they travel across the badlands. Within the confines of the narrative, Holly's relationship with Kit has allowed for no element of self-assertion. Although she is pleased to learn how to handle a gun it is a skill that a man has taught her. The film empowers the female voice to deliver her story, but the narrative is driven completely by the male protagonist, Kit. It is her very language that he dominates, changing her name (to cover their pursuit) to that of Priscilla, a name with derogatory feminine connotations. Even after she has acknowledged his 'trigger-happy' tendencies, she immediately acquiesces to Kit's suggestion that 'solitude' was a more appropriate word than 'loneliness' – 'because it meant more exactly what I wanted to say'. Her willingness to passively mirror the male discourse and even adopt their script becomes a performance:

> Caught in the specular logic of patriarchy woman can choose either to remain silent … or to *enact* the specular representation of herself as a lesser male. (Moi 1985: 135)

Holly chooses silence: as she becomes disillusioned with Kit she says she 'stopped paying attention to him … and spelt out entire sentences on the roof of my mouth where nobody could read them', indicating her desire to hide her growing independence of him and find her own voice rather than mimicking the male. Her final refusal to accompany him any further, albeit delivered in a frightened tone as she cowers behind the oil truck, shows her daring at last to assert herself. Malick's construction of her character implies that identity is constituted, as Butler argues, by 'acts, gestures, enactments [that] are *performative* in the sense that the essence or identity that they otherwise purport to express are *fabrications*, manufactured and sustained through corporeal signs and other discursive means' (1990: 136). Thus no authentic identity is accessible.

Some writers have commented that Holly's attitudes and clichés mirror the pulp magazines of the day[4] but Malick pointed out that 'her kind of cliché didn't begin with pulp magazines [but] exists in *Nancy Drew*[5] and *Tom* Sawyer' and is 'the mark … of the innocent abroad' (in Walker 1975: 82). He suggests that, in trying to reach for what is most personal in her experiences, she could 'only come up with what's most public' (ibid.). Holly's language attests to her internalisation of attitudes from popular culture: her narration is full of clichés, such as 'I sensed that my destiny now lay with Kit', 'each lived for the precious hours when he or she could be with the other' and 'we had our bad moments like any couple'. The impression is of a culture constituted by fragments of narrative, image and social role derived largely from popular media, but in which the magnetic field of traditional morality, the cornerstone of American ideology, has been switched off.

One effect of these clichés is to distance the spectator: we align ourselves with her in following her actions and having some access to her thoughts, but such clichés signal her immaturity and lead us to question the reliability of her statements. There is a certain sense of irony in some of these grand phrases. In Seymour Chatman's (1978) terms, she is an unreliable narrator; it is the narrating agency taking an ironic stance with regard to the character.

At the same time, in a crucial departure from the innate moral sense of Huck Finn, which critically focuses Twain's view of American society, Holly exhibits a lack of any moral sense. Brian Henderson notes that not only is her narration 'unreliable by virtue of her youth and naïveté, [but] by her inability to grasp the nature of what she describes and by virtue of her faulty moral sense' (1983: 41). We wonder at her passive acceptance of her father's murder as the film only shows Holly shedding a few tears. Has the film withheld information as Malick implies by his comment, 'She might have cried buckets of tears, but she wouldn't think of telling *you* about it'? (in Walker 1975: 82). We question her acceptance of Kit's explanation that it was legitimate to kill bounty hunters but although she tells us that he feels bad after these murders the film simply shows him surveying the forest site dispassionately before leaving. Such cognitive restriction leads us to assume a moral vacuity in Holly, further adding to our distrust of her perception of events. Later, when she makes small talk with the dying Cato (Raymond Bieri), her complete lack of sensitivity would appear as callous. We now might hesitate to call her innocent and legitimately ask whether Holly is simply an 'innocent in a drama over her head', as Malick stated, or if the film creates the impression of someone completely amoral? However, Malick applies no pressure on the spectator to view the character negatively other than through the irony of her words in relationship to the events she observes.

As a 'fairytale or romance' the film appears to come to a satisfactory closure with Holly, like the traditional storyteller, narrating how it ended 'happily ever after' with her marriage to the son of her lawyer. Yet this 'retreat into middle-class respectability' (Kinder 1974: 7) carries an ironic twist as we realise that Holly is merely moving from law breaker to law upholder, from rebel to conformist without questioning her experiences, and as Kinder says, 'realising Kit's fantasy of joining the law' (ibid.).

Holly's voice, as indicative of her female identity, has exemplified Kaja Silverman's thesis of the voice as an 'acoustic mirror' first learnt from the mother whose voice 'is the acoustic mirror in which it first hears "itself"' (1988: 100). But this is a voice already socialised into the male discourse. Holly exemplifies that voice, which is increasingly augmented by her father and then Kit. She rebels against her father's strictness in an effort to sustain Kit's attention but continues to embody the current norms and perform the social constructions of the feminine. These appear as natural manifestations but as Butler notes, 'the deconstruction of identity … establishes as political the very terms through which identity is articulated' (1990: 148). Holly represents an ironic comment on the 1950s 'innocent abroad', whose moral vacuity is to be interpreted with knowledge of the overwhelming pressures on women to conform to male expectations of the female stereotype.

The effect of her voice-over seems almost the opposite of Twain's radical invention of Huck as his novel's moral centre. Giving voice to a marginal, adolescent female character in *Badlands* carries little if any liberating force. Holly's narration displaces male control of the narrative but the woman's voice remains trapped within the performance of a factitious femininity.

Holly in *Badlands*: amoral or 'an innocent in a drama over her head'?

Linda

Days of Heaven opens with a montage of early twentieth-century sepia photographs depicting the poverty of life in an industrial inner city. The first shots are of a dark looming factory, of women scavenging in a slagheap, and scenes of a young foundry worker attacking the foreman. It is only then that a strange, cracked voice-over speaks, 'Me and my brother – it used to be me and my brother – we used to do things together – we used to have fun.' We presume it belongs to the man's younger sibling. When the film dissolves to show a young girl making artificial flowers we are still unsure of her identity until, after an intervening scene, she asks, 'What else do I get to do today?' and we match the voice to the face. Only then we might remember her face gazing directly at the camera in the final sepia photograph of the credit sequence. This would, retrospectively, emphasise her role as part of the group of marginalised and poverty-stricken working-class people escaping from the city, perhaps hoping to find some 'days of heaven' in the wheatfields of Texas.[6]

This marginalisation is emphasised in the opening scenes in the mill and sweat-shop, inferring that the film will explore the relationship of authority and the struggle of the individual within the power structure. Linda is triply oppressed – by class, by age and by gender. She sits on the margin of this struggle, observing and commenting, or not, as she chooses. Through her fragmentary and partial commentary, the specta-tor is placed in relationship to a world that seems strange and inexplicable, her words often working 'as a counterpoint to the romance story and in contrast to the visual track' (Zucker 2000: 7). She might exemplify the elusive figure of the 'enigmatic child [who] is rarely found centre stage but remains a peripheral figure' (Kuhn 1982: 61).

Linda's first words about her brother coincide with, but do not refer to, the event in the mill that she could not have witnessed. The spectator shares the narrative present in the visuals, but the verbal narrative speaks from a distance in some unspecified future. As she travels southwards, her voice-over relates an apocalyptic vision of the whole world going up in flames. This is not told directly by the character Ding-Dong, but is filtered through Linda's memory of his telling. Simultaneously, the film presents images of the journey unrelated to Linda's narration – some from her visual point of view on the train, others simply placing the narrative spatially and temporally. Are we to believe Linda's version or is her child status an indication of her gullibility and therefore unreliability as a narrator? It is not until much later in the film that the vision is revealed as prophetic when the wheatfields go up in flames. Do we then revise our estimation of Linda or regard it as merely a strange coincidence? Seen through a child's eyes, the film presents a world that is enigmatic and ambiguous, full of mystery and incapable of rational explanation. As Malick intended, he wanted her voice to convey 'an innocent, fairytale ambience' similar to the voice in Henry James's novel *What Maisie Knew* (Combs 1987: 84).

It is perhaps Linda's use of the vernacular that reminds us of Huck Finn and the untutored innocence of the young. Like Huck, whom Peter Messent notes is similar to Bakhtin's 'radical character' (1990: 422, n.46), Linda is the narrator whose seeming lack of comprehension makes the social conventions and appearances of the world seem strange. As an anonymous worker she sees that if you did not work hard, 'they'd ship you right out … they can always get someone else', but after Abby marries the Farmer she comments that they are 'living like kings … I'm telling you, the rich got it figured out'. The acuity of Linda's observation is a recurring feature, one that undercuts our common view of the child as an immature adult. Later, however, we have cause to doubt her morality. As the Farmer's condition is not deteriorating, she assumes that the doctor must have given him some restorative medicine, one which she could have 'put … in a ditch. Like they do to a horse. They shoot it right away.' Is this an innocent childish wish to alleviate the farmer's suffering as one does for an animal, or a desire to hasten his death so that Abby can lay claim to the farm, or simply an absence of moral sense? She does not act on it and we remember that earlier she said of the farmer who 'knew he was goin' to die', that 'you only lie in the sun once and that's my opinion – as long as you're around you should have it nice'. The film gives us no answer to these conflicting views of Linda. As Joan McGettigan observes, 'we must decide for ourselves who the guilty parties are in the diegetic world we are watching – and hearing' (2001: 42).

In Douglas Jefferson's Introduction to 'What Maisie Knew', he remarks of Maisie that 'her words often have the freshness of a revelation, coming from processes of thought to which we have had no access' (1966: xvii). Linda's thoughts often puzzle the adult viewer, causing us to wonder from what source they spring. Apparently Linda Manz was 'found by talent scouts hanging about in laundromats' and 'many of her feelings about her own life and experiences found their way into the voice-over'

Linda Manz on the set of *Days of Heaven*, playing a character oppressed by class, age and gender

(Combs 1987: 84). This may account for the spontaneous quality and improvisatory nature of her narration that communicates a sense of immediacy to which the spectator warms. It also suggests that the film gives us direct access to a female consciousness, though it is impossible to separate Malick's written script from Manz's improvisations. Unlike Holly, Linda's innocence seems unhampered by formal education or dominant authoritative opinions, and although the above instance appears ambiguous, she does seem to have a sense of the complexity of moral issues. Her evaluations of others often differ from those presented by the visual images or expressed by other characters. Although the Farmer represents the capitalist landowner that Bill believes simply exploits the workers, she comments, 'there wasn't no harm in him – you give him a flower he'd keep it forever'; he may be dying, but he was not 'squawking' about it. Yet the images do show the Farmer as the archetypal landowner, ordering the harvesting as he rides amongst his sweating labourers, going some way to negate Linda's child-like view of him. In coming to terms with her brother's unintentional killing of the Farmer, she notes that 'nobody's perfect – there never was a perfect person. You just got half-devil, half-angel in you'. Meanwhile, the visual image shows Bill selling Abby's jewellery to aid their escape, appropriating the results of the Farmer's profits, to which, ironically, Bill and Abby have contributed through their labour. Combining both innocence and experience, Linda's words are articulated through a voice 'by turns innocent, hard-bitten, foreboding, ironic' (Donougho 1985: 18).

Linda's narration is not the only aspect of her presentation that puzzles the spectator. As noted above, at the opening of the film we are unsure whether the voice-over belongs to a boy or a girl. The first image confirms her gender and child status – both underlining her marginality and denying objectification sexually. Although she is dressed as a female, we have no sense of the feminine as a dominating factor in her life. Linda follows her brother to the wheatfields but does not appear to be over-ruled by him as Holly is by both her father and Kit. Nor does there seem to be any previously socially conditioned sieve through which her observations have passed. Being small and referred to as 'Little Sister' (and at the end placed – incongruously – in a school for young ladies) suggests that she is probably pre-pubescent, so we might assume that her lack of awareness of how to perform any expected gender role is because her sexuality is still unawakened. This, of course, presumes that she will be orientated to heterosexuality, though the ending of the film, signalling an assertive independence in her rejection of the young ladies' academy, suggests that, at the least, her gender identity is fluid. Although biologically female, it is possible to see how Linda thus exemplifies 'the radical instability of the category [of woman]' of which Butler writes (1990: 142). There is little evidence of her 'performing' a specifically gendered role.

Categorising Linda is problematic: we are given little access to her previous life and this cognitive restriction, together with Linda's disjointed and dispersed commentary and her marginalised role in the action, hardly encourages the spectator to identify with her in Murray Smith's terms. We *recognise* her type, *align* ourselves with her situation and are even given access to her thoughts, but by placing her on the outskirts of the narrative, rarely even focusing on her directly, the spectator is deflected from full identification or *allegiance*. Yet Linda's quirky personality, her off-beat observations and her empathy with others intrigue us. Her uneducated speech, full of grammatical errors, still engages the listener in its direct approach. With reference to Bill's pretence that Abby is his sister rather than lover, she comments, 'My brother didn't want nobody to know – you know how people are – you tell 'em something they start talking.' The assumption that the speaker and listener share some basic human observations forms a link between spectator and character. In contrast to Holly, who is intent on telling her story, Linda's role is that of a commentator of the events she witnesses and an interpreter of the characters' feelings. She is the mediator between spectator and story, leading us through it as best she can.

Vlada Petric maintains that Malick's film 'intentionally detaches the audience from the story and the characters' destinies' (1978: 40–1). By doing so, we are pressed into viewing the characters as representative of a class of people who long for a place of happiness in which their dreams would come true. Robert C. Cumbow perceives Abby (Linda's 'sister') as presenting a 'young America, walking the narrow path between an impulsive immigrant class and a complacent, powerful ruling class' (1979: 43). That Linda is part of this class is undeniable, but her gender cannot be ignored. During the final shots, we see Linda, like Huck, 'light[ing] out for the Territory' (Twain 1995: 265). However, she speaks in the past tense about her companion, 'hoping things'ud work out for her', indicating that she did not accompany her but giving us no information about her own present position. Enigmatic to the last and denying a traditional closure, the final image is one of Linda continuing her picaresque travels into an unknown future.

Twain's use of the term 'innocent' referred to himself as an adult male, ignorant of and unschooled in European culture, venturing abroad hoping to be enlightened. In *The Adventures of Huckleberry Finn*, he dramatised this vision of innocence in terms of childhood. Malick creates an analogy, but rather than use a boy chooses instead to portray young girls each of whom, like Huck, leave home and become 'caught up in a drama over his or her head'. By describing them as innocent, Malick implies that he regards them as naïve, guileless, as yet untainted by the world.

The films' representations of these characters, however, are more complex than he suggests. Holly loses whatever innocence she may have had: she lacks the moral courage to condemn her father's murder and in preferring to accompany Kit 'abroad' becomes implicated in his crimes. The effect of her narration in the context of the film leaves us in no doubt as to Malick's intention to uncover her inner emptiness. Her last words – that she got off with probation 'and a lot of nasty looks' – indicate that she takes no responsibility for her acquiescence in his crimes: for her there has been no enlightenment.

The representation of Linda is altogether more problematic. She seems guileless and carefree, roaming the streets with her brother, yet hardly ignorant of people's suffering. When Bill murders the Farmer, albeit in self-defence, she does not betray him. Like Huck's decision not to betray Jim, she moves from a state of innocence to one of experience, but is more willing than Holly to implicate herself in his crime.

Malick departs from the classical cinematic approaches in his presentation of the female characters: they are neither the glamorous star, the femme fatale nor the cute child. Of their gender role, the films offer marked contrasts. In Holly, we see the effect of a rigid conformity on the female adolescent, 'of the cultural operations of gendered oppression' (Butler 1990: 13) that result in a socialised performance of the required role that passes as 'natural'. In Linda, the role is not yet so fixed; by casting a female actor and presenting her ambiguously, the spectator is led to question the concept of 'the category of women as a coherent and stable subject' (Butler 1990: 5). Linda exemplifies the fluid nature of the gender role in the developing child.

Through a contextual reading of their class status and their period, we can see the pressures that were brought to bear on Holly and Linda in the socialisation process that produced their marginalisation. In the disjunction between the image and their voice-over, *Badlands* and *Days of Heaven* convey an ironic stance and in so doing, the audience questions their reliability; as the films refuse the usual mechanisms of identification, they can ultimately be viewed not as 'innocents abroad' but as inevitably caught up in and formed by their respective worlds.

Afterword: Pocahontas and The New World

The New World (2005) confirms, if confirmation were needed, that the use of voice-over makes storytelling a major subject of Malick's films. After *The Thin Red Line* that is dominated by male voices, Malick returns to a central female voice, although this film sets the woman's voice in relation to two, more often heard, male voices. Though ostensibly a 'princess', Pocahontas (Q'Orianka Kilcher) is, by virtue of her age and gender an innocent, and within the patriarchal structure of her tribe, a marginalised figure. Similar to Holly and Linda in that respect, as a narrator she differs from them as she barely comments on the action and her voice-over perspective is absent for long stretches of the film. But it is her story that the film follows.

The film opens with wavering reflections of clouds on water that changes to a low-angled shot of a figure whose arms are out stretched to the sky. Over these a young female voice-over is heard: 'Come spirit, help us tell the story of our land. You are our Mother, we the fields of corn. We rise out of you'. Her invocation suggests a wish to be a conduit for the spirit to relate the 'story', while the fluctuating reflections invite us to expect that the account will be an uncertain reconstruction of the legend. Soon after, she is shown watching the arrival of the English ships and placed within her society we recognise her, in Murray Smith's terms, as a young Native girl. But, as others in her tribe are speaking in their own language, we may question why her narration was not in her native tongue. Amy Taubin finds it difficult to 'overlook the colonialist implication of making English the default language … for Pocahontas' voice-overs' (2006: 44) but, as in *The Thin Red Line*, the film seems to use the device of re-telling the story after the narrator's death, in this case after a time when Pocahontas has acquired English. Nevertheless, this remains a problem. Again, as in his previous films, Malick plays complex games with the status of voice-over (where and when does the voice speak from; are we hearing verbalised text or thought?): Malick increasingly exploits the potential for these kinds of indeterminacy.

Though the disjunction between voice and image is not an issue in this film, there is still reason to doubt the narrator's reliability. When John Smith (Colin Farrell) strays onto the tribal lands and is allowed to stay, he and Pocahontas fall in love and in her eyes he seems 'a god'. However, as the film has depicted Smith arriving in chains and threatened with hanging for 'mutinous remarks' we suspect, if only because of her naiveté, that as a narrator she may be termed a 'fallible filter' (Chatman 1978: 149). Nevertheless, with greater access to her subjectivity, the spectator has now begun to align with her.

But Pocahontas is not depicted as a passive victim of her tribal mores but one who is willing to contest its values. When Smith is captured she impulsively throws herself upon him and saves him from impending death thus defying her father, the Chief, and later, after Smith has been sent back to the colony, she not only takes the starving settlers food but gives them maize seeds. Is it her limited perspective that prevents her from seeing this as an act of betrayal that will ensure the invaders' stay? From the English point of view it is an act of compassion but the spectator may now question whether her innocence could be seen as 'not … of direct static contrast [between Innocence and Experience] but of shifting tensions' (Johnson & Grant 1979: 16). The film questions the nature of innocence by asking from whose perspective we judge it.

Banished from the tribe and taken in by the English, Pocahontas finds herself 'abroad' in an alien environment. In order to survive she has to adopt and learn to perform the roles required of her: divested of her native garb, she is put in European dress, baptised and given a new name. She reveals her reliance on a male figure when she acknowledges that Smith's absence on a mission 'has killed the god in me', suggesting that he has displaced her Mother spirit on whom she relied. After being told of Smith's alleged death, she is shown in utter despair and traverses, as in an archetypal fairytale, the dark forest of the night, seeming to lose all sense of self. Allegiance to her character begins to form when, empathising with a man in the stocks, she takes him water: her moral universe is shown to be a deeply humane one.

When John Rolfe (Christian Bale) arrives from England he is presented not as an Elsaesser unmotivated hero but one matching Pocahontas in understanding. With his encouragement she takes on the role of instructing the colonists in tobacco cultivation and begins to revive in the warmth of his attentions. Again, her words betray her transference of dependence onto a male figure: 'He is like a tree – he shelters me, I lie in his shade'. But in an extraordinary moment after overhearing that Smith is still alive and that she has been betrayed, she explains to Rolfe (whom she has married) that she can no longer be his wife as she is already 'married'. Her innate morality, like Huck Finn's, impels her to reveal her relationship with Smith.

Finally, Pocahontas accompanies Rolfe to England, now literally travelling 'abroad'. There, clothed in elaborate Stuart costume, she takes on the role of being presented at Court and the film depicts 'the strangeness of its rituals through her eyes' (Taubin 2006: 45). Eyed by the nobility who are dressed in equally elaborate attire, the sequence clearly demonstrates the concept of performance as Pocahontas again shows she is able to enact whatever role is required of her, regardless of clothes or name. After, while playing with her son in the gardens of Hampton Court, she addresses her spirit Mother with the words, 'Mother: now I know where you live.' I find this an enigmatic statement but one that suggests that she has now forged an identity that is inviolable and that neither resides in the roles she plays nor the environment she inhabits. As Luce Irigaray writes, 'To play with mimesis is thus, for a woman, to try to recover the place of her exploitation by discourse, without allowing herself to be simply reduced to it' (1985: 76). Though her gender is not contested, Butler's performance trope is again illustrated in this character who, unlike Holly, is able to resist societal pressures to conform and can mould her own identity.

* The author would like to thank Douglas Pye (University of Reading) for his advice and encouragement in the preparation of this chapter.

Notes

1   *Citizen Kane* (Orson Welles, 1941) and *Double Indemnity* (Billy Wilder, 1944) are early seminal examples of the use of the male voice-over. But even the female voice-over has seldom been that of a young girl: *Mildred Pierce* (Michael Curtiz, 1945), *Letter to an Unknown Woman* (Max Ophuls, 1948), *All About Eve* (Joseph L. Mankiewicz, 1950) and *Hiroshima Mon Armour* (Alain Resnais, 1959) all use the mature woman's voice. See Kozloff 1988.

2   This was how Twain conceived of himself and his fellow Americans as they toured Europe in 1867 and gave the title to the book about his travels: *The Innocents Abroad*, published in 1869.

3   Germaine Greer's *The Female Eunuch*, Shulamith Firestone's *The Dialectic of Sex*, Kate Millett's *Sexual Politics* and Eva Figes' *Patriarchal Attitudes* were all published in 1970.

4   See Buckley (1974: 245).

5   Nancy Drew was the young amateur detective character in novels by Carolyn Keene. These were popular with young people and were published under the over-

all titles of *A Nancy Drew Mystery Story*. Published in the 1940s in New York by Grosset & Dunlap.

6   Malick and his cameraman Nestor Almendros chose these photographs 'thereby setting the mood and sense of the period for the picture' (Almendros 1979: 564). Chaplin's film *The Immigrants* (1917), a clip of which is shown in the Texas farm sequence, is an ironic comment on the immigrants' hope of realising the American Dream and *Days of Heaven* confirms that for some this hope did not always materialise.

References

Almendros, Nestor (1979) 'Photographing *Days of Heaven*', *American Cinematographer*, 60, 6, 562–630.

Buckley, Michael (1974) '*Badlands*', *Sight and Sound*, 25, 245.

Butler, Judith (1990) *Gender Trouble: Feminism and the Subversion of Identity*. New York & London: Routledge.

_____ (1993) *Bodies That Matter*. New York & London: Routledge.

Chatman, Seymour (1978) *Coming to Terms*. Ithaca & London: Cornell University Press.

Combs, Richard (1978) '*Days of Heaven*', *Sight and Sound*, 47, 84.

Cumbow, Robert C. (1979) '*Days of Heaven*', *Movietone News*, 41–3, 60–1.

De Beauvoir, Simone (1973) [1949] *The Second Sex*, trans. E. M. Parshley, New York: Vintage.

Donougho, Martin (1985) 'West of Eden: Terrence Malick's *Days of Heaven*', *Postscript*, 5, 1, 17–30.

Elsaesser, Thomas (1975) 'The Pathos of Failure: American Films in the 70s. Notes on the unmotivated hero', *Monogram*, 6, 13–19.

Firestone, Shulamith (1970) *The Dialectic of Sex*. England: Paladin.

Graff, Gerald & James Phelan (eds) (1995) *Adventures of Huckleberry Finn*. Boston: Bedford Books of St. Martin's Press.

Henderson, Brian (1983) 'Exploring *Badlands*', *Wide Angle*, 5, 38–51.

Irigaray, Luce (1985) 'The Power of Discourse', in *This Sex Which Is Not One*, trans. Catherine Porter with Carolyn Burke. Ithaca: Cornell University Press.

James, Henry (1966) [1897] *What Maisie Knew*. Oxford: Oxford University Press.

Jefferson, Douglas (1966) 'Introduction', Henry James, *What Maisie Knew*. Oxford: Oxford University Press, i–xxi.

Johnson, Mary Lynn & John E. Grant (eds) (1979) *Blake's Poetry and Designs*. New York and London: W.W. Norton and Company.

Kinder, Marsha (1974) 'The Return of the Outlaw', *Film Quarterly*, 27, 4, 2–10.

Kozloff, Sarah (1988) *Invisible Storytellers: Voice-Over Narration in American Fiction Film*. Berkeley: University of California Press.

Kuhn, Annette (1989) *The Power of the Image: Essays of Representation and Sexuality*. London: Routledge & Kegan Paul.

Kuhn, Raymond (1982) *Corruption in Paradise: The Child in Western Literature*. Hanover & London: University Press of New England.

McGettigan, Joan (2001) 'Interpreting a Man's World: Female Voices in *Badlands* and *Days of Heaven*', *Journal of Film and Video*, 52, 4, 33–43.

Messent, Peter (1990) *New Readings of the American Novel*. London: Macmillan.

Moi, Toril (1985) *Sexual, Textual Politics: Feminist Literary Theory*. London: Routledge.

Petric, Vlada (1978) 'Days of Heaven', *Film Quarterly*, 32, 37–45.

Pye, Douglas (2000) 'Movies and Point of View', *Movies*, 36, 1–34.

Salinger, J. D. (1951) *The Catcher in the Rye*. England: Penguin.

Silverman, Kaja (1988) *The Acoustic Mirror*. Bloomington & Indianapolis: Indiana University Press.

Smith, Murray (1995) *Engaging Characters*. Oxford: Clarendon Press.

Taubin, Amy (2006) 'Birth of a Nation', *Sight and Sound*, 2, 44–6.

Twain, Mark (1966) [1869] *The Innocents Abroad*. New York: New American Library.

_____ (1995) [1884] *Adventures of Huckleberry Finn*, in Graff & Phelan (eds) (1995) *Adventures of Huckleberry Finn*. Boston: Bedford Books of St. Martin's Press.

Van Lenning, Alkeline, Saskia Maas & Wendy Leeks (2001) 'Is Womanliness Nothing But a Masquerade?', in Efrat Tseëlon (ed.) *Masquerade and Identities*. London & New York: Routledge, 83–100.

Walker, Beverly (1975) 'Malick on *Badlands*', *Sight and Sound*, 44, 2, 82–3.

Zucker, Carole (2000) '"God Don't Even Hear You", or Paradise Lost: Terrence Malick's *Days of Heaven*', *Literature/Film Quarterly*, 29, 1, 1–9.

CHAPTER EIGHT

Listening to the Aquarium: The Symbolic Use of Music in Days of Heaven

Richard Power

Terrence Malick's *Days of Heaven* (1978) is perhaps best known for Nestor Almendros and Haskell Wexler's cinematography, and for Malick's use of visual images to amplify his themes and narratives. The film earned Almendros an Academy Award, and *Visions of Light* (1992), a documentary on the art of cinematography, devoted an entire section to it, drawing attention to its location photography and use of the 'magic hour'. Almendros is interviewed in the documentary and, while discussing his experience of filming *Days of Heaven*, states that Malick

> told me it would be a very visual movie. He said that the film will be a visual film, that the story would be told through visuals. Very few people really want to give that priority to the image. Usually directors give the priority to the actors and to the story, but here the story was told really through images.

While the images may indeed be strikingly beautiful, its sounds are equally intriguing. If one were to rearrange Almendros' quote, replacing the word 'visual' with 'sonic', 'visuals' and 'images' with 'sound', and 'image' with 'soundtrack', the statement could still apply.

There are many ways in which Malick uses the soundtrack of *Days of Heaven* to tell his story, adding a depth of meaning that few films possess. Linda's voice-over, for instance, not only provides syntactical narration, but also allows us to understand the narrator's experience in ways that cannot be accomplished visually – from her accent and grammar, which firmly identify her as a member of the uneducated working class, through to her specific inflections and scattered subject-matters, suggestive of a child in the complex process of becoming an adult. Several sound effects also function symbolically and are combined with the film's images in a quasi-musical fashion. For example, the sound of the fires at the steel mill drowns out the shouted words between Bill and the foreman, becoming a different mode of expression for Bill's rage. The sound of the windmill on top of the Farmer's house, which is initially symbolic of his wealth and status, towards the end of the film has increased in volume; when the Farmer realises that his wife Abby and Bill might be lovers, the windmill begins to sound the same as the fires of the mill, now signifying the Farmer's rage.

But it is *Days of Heaven*'s music, as rich and expressive as the film's other sonic detail, which will be the main focus here. Consisting of three distinct elements – the pre-composed classical-style piece *The Aquarium*, written by Camille Saint-Saëns, several examples of folk music and a score composed specifically for the film by Ennio Morricone – it crucially signifies class and emotion, amongst other central themes.

These first two elements of the music work in conjunction to underline the differences in class that are important elements of the story. Because of its status as 'classical' music, *The Aquarium* is associated with a privileged upper class, one that has the time, education and means to attend the concert hall. Folk music, on the other hand, is the music of the working class, based upon oral tradition and simple enough to be performed by non-professionals. The difference between these two approaches to making music embodies the class conflict that propels the film's plot. All of his life Bill has had to work at difficult, menial jobs, and has little to show for it. He wants desperately to make a better life for himself, his lover Abby and his sister. After losing his temper and attacking the foreman, the three of them flee by train to the Texas Panhandle where they find work on a farm. When Bill discovers that the Farmer is terminally ill and also in love with Abby, he dreams of inheriting the farm and finally achieving the wealth and easy life he has been longing for.

Abby's own aspirations towards a better life are also demonstrated musically. Late in the film, after she has married the Farmer, we see her dancing on the porch to a recording of classical piano music. Recordings were still luxury items in 1917, the year this scene takes place, but they were already beginning to make music available to a wider number of people. They also allowed non-musicians the opportunity to enjoy music intended for the concert hall within their own homes. While Bill is interested in raising his social status so that he can have money and stop working, we see here that Abby seems more interested in the intellectual pursuits that leisure time enables.

The Aquarium was composed in 1886 as part of Saint-Saëns' orchestral suite *The Carnival of Animals*, a collection of short pieces designed to portray zoological scenes. It is different from the majority of his compositions; primarily classic in style and concentrating on form and craftsmanship rather than expression, his favourite orchestral genres were the symphony and concerto. *The Carnival of Animals*, however, can best be described as a series of character pieces, a form made popular by nineteenth-century Romantic composers such as Schumann and Chopin. These were short, descriptive pieces designed to express a certain mood or portray a particular scene. *The Aquarium*, for example, is supposed to convey the image of life within an aquarium as it floats slowly along. It accomplishes this through long, melodic lines that gently rise and fall in a wave-like pattern, and with slowly changing harmonies that convey a languid, relaxed feel. Most of the rhythmic principles of the melody are appropriately long and of consistent values, although quick arpeggiated figures are played over these by the pianos, suggesting reflections of light upon the water's surface. The work's unusual orchestration, for two pianos, celesta and chamber orchestra, gives the piece an exotic sound and is suggestive of an aquatic world.

Filmmakers have often used classical music, but Malick's use of *The Aquarium* in *Days of Heaven* provides much more than just an attractive background to the images. Here the work's title and its essence as a character piece provide metaphoric opportunities. The concept of aquariums is suggested throughout, as if the film itself were a kind of character piece. When Saint-Saëns wrote the work, he was captivated by the romance of the aquarium, by its similarity to the sea itself, and by the fascination that viewing one can hold. Although Malick seems interested in this vision to some extent, he is drawn far more to the idea of an aquarium as an artificial environment.

There are several instances throughout the film when the idea of an aquarium is used symbolically, even when the piece of music itself is not being played. The wheatfields remind us of ocean waves, and form the Farmer's aquarium; the 'aquatic' life, in this case, is made up of the workers from whom the Farmer always stays distant, observing from afar. Once the Farmer has married Abby and the harvest season is over, we often see the main characters playing in the fields, the Farmer has now a participant himself. The four are living out their days of heaven, but the metaphor of the aquarium suggests that they are living in an artificial world and not a real one.

One scene in particular emphasises the comparison of the wheatfield with water, and simultaneously foreshadows the flight of Bill, Abby and Linda following the disaster that ends their artificial world. Bill has already left the farm because he realises that Abby loves the Farmer more than him, and in a montage that shows us the Farmer and Abby's happiness together, we see a shot from above of the outline of a small boat made in the field with stones. The Farmer explains to Abby where certain parts of the boat would be, as if he plans to build one for her in the future. After Bill kills the Farmer he, Abby and Linda find themselves on a real boat as they escape from the farm by river. Linda remarks in a voice-over that 'nobody's perfect, there was never a perfect person around. You just got half-devil and half-angel in you', suggesting not only that everyone has a multitude of potentialities, but that how one views what happens in the world depends upon one's perspective. The characters are objects within an aquarium once again, creating their own world for themselves, viewed this time by people along the riverbanks. Yet Linda is still an observer herself, studying the landscape and speculating upon what those same people might be doing.

The Aquarium is played only three times during the film, and its association with the upper class adds considerable meaning to these scenes. We hear it first during the opening credits, accompanying sepia-toned photographs of turn-of-the-century urban, working-class life. As the very first sound we hear, its importance is emphasised, preparing us also for the melodic references that will occur throughout the film in Morricone's music. It casts a romantic glow upon these particular images, while its associations with the social and leisure qualities of classical music contrast with the poverty and labour depicted in the photographs. *The Aquarium* closes with a chord held very softly by the strings. As the opening credits end we hear the chord fade into the sound of steam from the steel mill, in such a way that the two sounds seem identical. It is an effective transition from the still photos into the first motion-picture scene, but the resemblance between the two sounds suggests that what we hear from the mill is a continuation of Saint-Saëns' aquatic character piece; the entire film is an extension of the music.

The second scene to feature *The Aquarium* occurs much later, 51 minutes into the film, and more clearly alludes to the aquarium metaphor. President Wilson's whistle-stop tour passes through the Farmer's land and the Farmer, Abby, Bill and Linda watch and wave as it goes by. It is dusk, and because the President's coach is lit brightly from within we can see the shadows of its inhabitants, as well as the luxury of its decoration. The car gives the impression of being an aquarium itself, allowing the viewers to glimpse a style of life to which they are unaccustomed. For the three companions from Chicago, in particular, that world of privilege and luxury is an alien one. When they travelled to the farm by train, they had to ride on the top of freight cars, along with dozens of other workers. While their lives may be better now that they are the Farmer's guests, and they dress in the fancy clothes provided for them, the opulence of the train – and the fact that its riders do not stop to converse with them – emphasises the fact that they have not reached the highest social stratum.

Near the end of the film, after Bill has been killed, Abby enrolls Linda in a boarding school. As they enter, the same music that Abby danced to earlier on the porch of the farmhouse is heard coming from a player piano as an accompaniment to the students' ballet practice. Like the phonograph from the earlier scene, the player piano was a recent invention, an industrial-age product that brought classical music to a wider public. Abby is trying to provide Linda with the cultured life that she wanted for herself, and she is doing so with the money of the now-deceased Farmer. This sort of life is not for Linda, however, and with the help of a friend she decides to escape. It is at this point that we hear *The Aquarium* for the third and final time. Ending the film with the same music with which it began is of course an effective means of closure, but it also serves to remind us of the various ideas which this specific music has previously signified. Importantly, *The Aquarium* is here played in conjunction with images of adventure and working-class life, as it was during the opening credits. Linda has rejected her chance for an upper-class life, deciding instead to continue 'looking for things, searching for things, going on adventures'.

Working-class life is more obviously signified sonically by folk music, the first example of which comes soon after the opening credits. Bill, Abby and Linda are fleeing Chicago, travelling by train along with the other migrant workers, and over this action we hear guitarist Leo Kottke performing a piece entitled *Enderlin*. While *The Aquarium* accompanied the still, black and white images of the working class in an elegiac, romantic fashion reflective of what an observer outside class might find interesting, *Enderlin* accompanies colour and movement, the lives of these people as they see themselves, as they really are. The lively character of the music also signals their hope and sense of adventure as they travel to a new life; significantly, *Enderlin* is heard once more much later in the film, as Bill, Abby and Linda are forced to escape again because of Bill's anger.

Like *The Aquarium*, *Enderlin* is non-diegetic sound, sound that accompanies the image but which takes place outside the time and space of the action (Chion 1994: 80). Once the characters arrive at the farm, however, there are two important examples of folk music being used diegetically. After the final day of harvesting, one of the workers is playing a jig on a harmonica, while Linda and another man tap dance. Shortly thereafter, all of the workers enjoy an evening dance in front of a bonfire, to celebrate the end of the harvest. A fiddler, played by musician Doug Kershaw, performs a Cajun tune titled *Swamp Dance*. In both scenes workers are shown entertaining themselves with their own music, drawing further attention to the class dichotomy. Bill is not seen enjoying the music in either of the scenes, whereas Linda, for whom social standing is unimportant, dances enthusiastically to the harmonica music and smiles at Kershaw's playing. During Kershaw's performance even the Farmer – who is the closest he has been with his workers, participating in their celebration rather than observing them – enjoys the music.

Within this segment featuring Kershaw, the image of hell is unmistakably suggested as the workers dance wildly before the flames. The Devil himself has appeared in folklore for centuries as a fiddler, seducing his victims with his playing: 'While the Devil plays all instruments equally well, he seems to prefer the violin. He was said in the Middle Ages to own a violin with which he could set whole cities, grandparents and grandchildren, men and women, girls and boys, to dancing, dancing until they fell dead from sheer exhaustion' (Rudwin 1931: 256). We are reminded of this association again immediately after the Farmer fatefully marries Abby, and another fiddler is shown playing behind the procession.

At the end of the dance, just after Abby tells the Farmer that she will stay on the farm, a remarkable transition to the following scene is accomplished sonically. As the music fades, Kershaw issues a final yell, which is then superimposed over the scream of a whistle so that the two sound identical. The whistle comes from a train, which the workers board to leave the farm. The whistle symbolises the end of the harvest season and the beginning of the days of heaven for the four main characters. The association of the whistle with the fiddler's voice, however, suggests that the subsequent turn of events has been brought on by the Devil. A year later, after the workers have returned for the next harvest, a plague of locusts attacks the farm. The workers light bonfires to destroy the insects, but the Farmer decides to set the fields on fire, having realised Bill and Abby's deception. This destruction is very clearly foreshadowed by the earlier bonfire scene, linking the Devil's seductive fiddling as having led to the final disaster.

As discussed, the very different sounds of *The Aquarium* and the folk music work together to articulate the opposite worlds of the Farmer and the other three central characters. Ennio Morricone's score, the film's third major musical element, although sonically similar to *The Aquarium*, functions to express precise narrative content rather than broad thematics. The most obvious link between *The Aquarium* and the score is Morricone's use of melodic themes from Saint-Saëns' piece. Although varied, they retain enough of their identity to still be recognisable. In addition, the orchestration of the two works is very similar: Morricone retains the prominence of the piano and flute in addition to the strings. Indeed, the similarities are close enough that some viewers might not initially be aware that *Days of Heaven*'s orchestral music is written by two different composers from different centuries.

When analysing a film's music, it can be helpful to refer to the soundtrack recording that breaks the music up into classifiable units, and often presents the music more clearly by excising extraneous sounds. Due to the wide diversity of Morricone's music, and its extensive use within the film, I will refer to the titles of the selections as they appear on the soundtrack album released by Pacific Arts. It includes nine separate pieces composed by Morricone: 'Harvest', 'Threshing', 'Happiness', 'The Honeymoon', 'The Return', 'The Chase', 'The Fire', 'Ashes and Dust' and 'Days of Heaven'. There is some additional, minor music in the film that is not included on the album, and 'The Chase' does not appear in the finished version of the film. The placing of the selections and their emphasis within the film vary widely. Some serve as short, incidental pieces used to lightly underscore the emotion of a scene, while others are longer and provide important narrative information through associations with different sections of the film. While all deserve discussion, I will focus here on four selections that develop our understanding of the characters and their relationships to one another. Each is played more than once during the film, and comparing the differences between corresponding scenes reveals important subtext.

'Harvest' is a particularly rich selection. It is the first of Morricone's pieces in the film, and opens with a melody that is very similar to *The Aquarium*'s main theme. It occurs five times during the film, and on each occasion accompanies particular events in the story that are the result of Bill's desire to have a better life, but ultimately lead to his death. The first, for example, is the beginning of the year's harvest, as well as the beginning of Bill, Abby and Linda's lives on the farm. We also hear it when the Farmer first takes notice of and asks about Abby, when Bill, Abby and Linda begin their new period as the Farmer's guests, during the wedding, and, finally, after Bill is shot and killed.

'Happiness' is played twice in the film, linking two montages that are almost identical in subject matter, but also differ because of the manner in which the characters' relationships have evolved. The music begins after Abby and the Farmer leave Bill and Linda behind to go on their honeymoon. It plays during the honeymoon, and then as the four of them are back on the farm, enjoying themselves in the river. Linda says in voice-over, 'I mean, we were just all of a sudden living like kings … I'm tellin' you, the rich have it figured out.' Before 'Happiness' is played for the second time someone again leaves the farm, this time Bill, who finds it is too difficult to witness the love growing between Abby and the Farmer. The following montage shows the three remaining characters enjoying their lives on the farm, as happy as they had been in the earlier sequence; the fact that Bill is gone, however, signals that he no longer has a place on the farm within the world of happiness that the others have discovered.

The music in these scenes is a beautifully romantic passage, crescendoing to an emotionally moving section that is distantly related to the main theme from *The Aquarium*. The music encourages the audience to empathise with the characters here and also emphasises the montages' similarities; moreover, it reveals that the days of

The Farmer's house in *Days of Heaven*, emblematic of the life Bill has pursued in his dreams

heaven on the farm are not dependent upon Bill, despite his instigation. The happiness is now the result of the marriage between the Farmer and Abby, and their love for one another.

Like 'Happiness', 'The Honeymoon' follows two unaccompanied scenes in which people leave the farm. In the first, the Farmer and Abby leave for their honeymoon, and the Farmer tells Bill he can live in the house while they are away. The music begins as Bill enters the house and explores its contents, an expression of awe and wonder growing on his face as he discovers for the first time the kind of life he has been pursuing in his dreams. Well suited to the reverential nature of the scene, the theme is slow and quiet, played only on strings. Later, before the piece's second appearance, the Farmer's foreman drives away from the house, exiled because of his mistrust of the visitors. 'The Honeymoon' begins as Abby and the Farmer prepare for bed. The Farmer tells Abby how much she means to him, saying that, 'sometimes it's like you're right inside of me, you know, like I can hear your voice and feel your breath and everything'. During both scenes characters are shown encountering their greatest desires: for Bill, this is wealth, and the easy, comfortable life that it provides; for the Farmer, however, it is the discovery of his soulmate. Aspects of their lives that they felt were missing, their similar reactions to experiencing them are underscored by the identical music.

'The Return' is played three times, first appearing when the Farmer initially notices Abby. In a voice-over Linda says, 'This Farmer, he didn't know when he first saw her, or what it was about her that caught his eye. Maybe it was the way the wind blew through her hair.' It plays again when Bill and Abby are lying in the fields and Bill tells her, 'I remember the first time I saw you, I'd never seen hair black as yours.' The parallel between these two views reveals the similarities between Bill and the Farmer, through their love for her, a similarity that is also evident in the way they wear their hair, and their often-identical fashion of dressing. Indeed, they are enough alike that Abby falls in love with them both. The third scene that uses 'The Return' most obviously reflects its title: Bill has come back to the farm following his exodus, and the music begins as he watches Abby practicing dance steps on the porch. He reunites with Linda and the Farmer, and as he examines their current lives together he realises that by leaving the farm he has lost her forever. He tells Abby, 'I didn't know what I had with you ... I got nobody to blame but myself.'

The longest piece from the score is titled 'The Fire'. Played only once, it accompanies the climactic section in which the locust plague strikes the farm, the workers fight to stop it, and finally the Farmer destroys the fields by igniting them. The music here, more so than in the rest of the film, is designed to closely match the events taking place. It can be divided into four distinct sections, and follows the crescendo of images that portray the rising action of the tragedy. The music begins, very softly, as Bill notices the locusts in the field. It does not consist of melody and accompaniment as it has up to this point, but of a low atmospheric rumble in the strings, gradually climbing in pitch along with occasional percussion. The entrance is soft enough that we hardly notice its appearance; by the time we become truly conscious of it, we realise that it has been present for some time, as has the gathering of the locusts. Furthermore, the sound of the strings' tremolos, an effect in which the players alternately bow a note back and forth as quickly as possible, matches the locusts' chirping.

A true melody emerges as the workers fight the invaders. The second section of the music, it marks the realisation of events and the enormity of what is at stake. The melody continues as the workers throw the gathered locusts onto the bonfires, and a new melody enters as the Farmer attacks Bill. This third section of music is more dissonant and further increases the tension. The fourth section begins as the fire takes over the farm. The music here is a slight variation of that in the second section. Earlier it accompanied the realisation that the locusts could destroy the farm, and now it accompanies Bill and Abby's realisation that the Farmer is aware of their lies. Once the music ends, the battle with the fire continues, and for another 80 seconds we hear the sounds of the flames, workers, tractors and fleeing animals. The continuation of these sounds without the previously extended musical accompaniment drives home the fact that natural forces have overcome the people.

Near the beginning of the film, as the migrant workers travelled to the farm, Linda spoke in a voice-over, the content of which has particular significance here, when the farm becomes wrapped in fire:

I met this guy named Ding-Dong. He told me the whole earth is goin' up in flames. Flames will come out of here and there and they'll just rise up. The mountains are gonna go up in big flames, the water's gonna rise in flames. There's gonna be creatures runnin' every which way, some of them burnt, half their wings burnin', and people are gonna be screamin' and hollerin' for help. See, the people that have been good, they're gonna go to heaven and escape all that fire, but if you've been bad, God don't even hear ya, he don't even hear ya talkin'.

Although this brief passage reveals much about Linda's knowledge and beliefs, it also sets the tone for the rest of the film, providing a mythological sweep and background. Her apocalyptic vision takes on new meaning when we see the fiddler associated with the Devil, when she later states 'I think the Devil was on the farm', and most definitively after the farm is destroyed by flames. It raises more questions than it answers, however, because the wrath of God as predicted by Ding-Dong is not fully realised by the film's climax. Abby and Linda manage to escape the farm's destruction, yet Abby is as guilty of deceit as Bill had been, with the only exception that she has been more conscious of that guilt. The Farmer also dies, and was himself directly responsible for the fire, but it is questionable whether he has 'been bad'. Perhaps Linda would conclude that the Farmer has gone on to heaven after death, but if so, what is she to think about her brother's fate?

Linda's voice-over throughout the film is in many respects a musical theme itself. Setting aside the semantic content of her statements, we are left with a series of interesting sounds that compel us to listen to her. Indeed, it is the quality of Linda's voice that makes her narration one of the most commented upon elements of the film. The voice-overs of most films have a self-conscious narrative style that make them sound as if they are being read, but Linda's is extraordinarily natural and conversational. It invites us to trust her, and allows us to observe as she processes her own feelings about events. She constantly studies everything around her, taking mental notes; interestingly, the events that lead to her brother's death seem to have as much significance for her as others that might seem less important. Everything that happens on the farm is new to her, and therefore shapes the views she will have as an adult.

While the story of *Days of Heaven* is focused on the love triangle between the three adults, the narrative is ultimately Linda's; because she has been narrating events, we realise that the world we have been witnessing belongs to her. In that sense, one can view *Days of Heaven* as an aquarium of experience, one that reflects the thoughts and beliefs of its creator. Filled with ambiguous messages, manifest in Linda's aquarium is the ambiguity that children encounter as they try to discern the world based upon what they see and hear. Significantly, our first image of her is in a sepia-toned photograph during the opening credits, and the manner in which Malick subsequently fades in the noise of the steel mill from the final chord of *The Aquarium* suggests that the sounds throughout the film are a continuation of that piece. *Days of Heaven* can thus be interpreted as a sort of 'character piece' itself, portraying past events as reconstructed by Linda.

References

Chion, Michel (1994) *Audio-Vision: Sound on Screen*, ed. and trans. Claudia Gorbman. New York: Columbia University Press.
Days of Heaven: The Original Soundtrack from the Motion Picture (1978). Carmel, California, Pacific Arts Corp., Inc. [phonograph recording]
Rudwin, Maximillian (1931) *The Devil in Legend and Literature*. Chicago: Open Court.
Visions of Light: The Art of Cinematography (1992) Directed by Todd McCarthy. Los Angeles, The American Film Institute. [Film, DVD]

CHAPTER NINE

Sound as Music in the Films of Terrence Malick

James Wierzbicki

In an article on the aesthetic impact of Hollywood's gradual adaptation of the so-called Dolby system of high-fidelity, four-channel stereophonic sound, Charles Schreger (1985) focuses his attention primarily on the work of Robert Altman, but deals in passing with a dozen other directors who in the late 1970s seemed interested in exploring the potential of the new Dolby technology.[1] *Days of Heaven* (1978) receives three mentions, the first of which notes only that the soundtrack teems with cricket noises and the second that the narrator's thick Chicago accent might well be unintelligible were it not for the sonic clarity afforded by the Dolby technology. The third reference is slightly longer, balancing a few quibbles against a strikingly bold evaluation. Schreger points out that Terrence Malick's film features an occasional moment in which voice and lips are out of synchronisation, and that the cross-fade of the airplane roar is noticeably abrupt; nevertheless, he asserts with confidence, 'there's no more intelligent use of sound than in *Days of Heaven*' (1985: 352).

It is impossible to establish whether or not *Days of Heaven* in its day truly represented the highest level of film-sound intelligence. It can safely be granted, however, that the use of sound in Malick's films is at the very least intelligent to an extent. With that as a starting point, this essay will analyse his first three works, focusing in the main on *Days of Heaven*, and argue that the play of sound effects exhibits a particular kind of intelligence. In the latter two films, the sonic material is often utilised in a way that goes far beyond the standard needs of filmic narrative, and in *Days of Heaven* particularly, the soundtrack bears the mark of a strong compositional hand – at certain key moments of the film, Malick's use of sound is demonstrably *musical*.

The seed of this idea is my experience upon re-viewing *Days of Heaven* almost two decades after its release. Closer attention paid to the stills on the back of the video at the store might have informed me that once upon a time I had indeed watched this film. In fact, the moment of recognition came only after the tape had been playing for a while; and it was primarily a case not of *déjà vu* but, rather, of *déjà entendu*.

Although the undulating music that for more than two minutes accompanies the opening sequence of credits and sepia-toned photographs was certainly familiar, I recognised it only as a lushly orchestrated version of *The Aquarium*, a portion of Camille Saint-Saëns' *The Carnival of Animals*, not as theme music for a film. But as the imagery turned colourful and animated, and as the concluding orchestral gestures dissolved into a steady babble (a trickling urban stream) punctuated by sporadic clinks (scrap metal tossed into buckets), I sensed that I had *heard* this film before. An aural memory having been jogged, I had a strong suspicion that the gentle streamside sounds were but a prelude to something much more forceful; only when the scene shifted to the steel mill did the visual elements of *Days of Heaven* begin to seem familiar, yet it was primarily with the jump cut's loud and rhythmic thumps – not its images of fisticuffs amidst the glow of molten steel – that I felt vindicated. There was vindication, too, as the crescendo of hisses, clangs and screeches climaxed with the dull thud of the murderous blow to the foreman's head.

Upon reflection, that these tingles of pleasure should be at odds with the anxious content of the film's narrative seemed only mildly interesting; the 'positive' release of sonic tension embodied in the thud coincides precisely with the 'negative' action that impels the film's protagonists to run away, but emotionally asynchronous devices of this sort have been common to film since the 1930s. On the other hand, it seemed highly interesting that my aesthetic response to this episode – beginning with the streamside idyll and ending with the fade-in on the image of the narrator – was so akin to an experience I tend to associate not with the movie theatre but with the concert hall. I realised that I had been caught up by sonic stimuli whose pattern of stasis, tension and eventual relaxation – whose dynamic juxtaposition of consonance and dissonance – not only bore an oblique relationship to the emotional content of the film's narrative but beautifully fit the phenomenological model for musical expressivity (Meyer 1956; Kerman 1994).

Different people, of course, absorb a film's myriad elements with differently tuned sensors, and it would be solipsistic to argue that any particular weighting of the scene's aural, visual, textual and narrative components should be considered universal. Nevertheless, it seems that for this listener the opening episode of *Days of Heaven* on more than one occasion provoked a meaningful musical experience. And the musical experience in question was effected by a soundtrack whose material for the relevant 90 seconds contains nothing but diegetic noise.

Most of the noise heard in films serves no purpose other than to make on-screen action seem more realistic. Seldom is this noise in fact real. As the French sound theorist

Michel Chion reminds us, 'sound that rings true for the spectator and sound that *is* true are two different things', and we tend to measure the truth of cinematic sound not against 'our hypothetical lived experience' but against the 'codes established by cinema itself' (1994: 107). By adding the equivalent of a third dimension to an otherwise two-dimensional image, quotidian film sound contributes to the image's credibility.

Raymond Bellour (1975) classified such quasi-realistic sound as 'motivated noise' (because it is motivated, or necessitated, by the scenic circumstances), and he made the important distinction between this and what he called 'arbitrary noise'. His terminology is unfortunate, for 'arbitrary noise' is invariably the result of conscious decisions on the part of the filmmaker. But Bellour's point is nonetheless telling. Cleverly used, he says, 'arbitrary noise ... can go so far as to serve as a [musical] score, then escaping all translatability since it is not even codified as the musical score is' (1975: 23–4).

The film score – codified almost from its earliest days to represent certain emotional states by means of specific melodic, harmonic and rhythmic gestures – can contribute a great deal to the artwork of which it is a component.[2] Holding to its well-established system of symbols, the score can parallel the dramatic flow of a scene or deliberately run counter to that flow, and it can identify the presence – on-screen or not – of certain 'entities' crucial to the film's narrative. As a structural tool, the film score can define the limits of certain scenes and provide continuity between other scenes; it can establish dramatic-psychological links between one scene and another that may or may not be reflected in matters of image, character or language. And on the macro-structural level, quite independent of any function it might serve *vis-à-vis* details of character or plot, the score can organise filmic time.

But aside from the fact that it benefits from a culturally accepted semiotic code, how does the film score differ from the intelligently made soundtrack that features what Bellour calls 'arbitrary noise'?

In the typical film, the non-diegetic score only rarely rises to the foreground. The music is meant to be heard, of course, as the title credits roll, or when the main characters don their predictable mantles, or when certain dramatic ideas in the plot are introduced or recapitulated. Far more often, however, the music hovers comfortably in the distance. When well-crafted, the score fulfills its emotional-structural duties yet tends not to be noticed; as Claudia Gorbman reminds us in her so aptly titled book *Unheard Melodies*, 'film music is normally subordinated to more "directly" significant sounds on the soundtrack' (1987: 59). Whether subordinated or not, the score emanates from somewhere beyond the screen; by definition, the non-diegetic score exists apart from the filmic narrative.

'Arbitrary' noises that have nothing at all to do with the narrative tend to be heard as intrusive, and the more remote they are from the context of a scene the more boldly they stand out. Whether or not such noises escape 'translatability' depends on their contextualisation (the ticking sounds heard in Malick's *The Thin Red Line* (1998), for example, are diegetic only early in the film, when they seem to emerge from the clock during Witt's flashback memory of his mother's death; elsewhere they serve to recall that scene and perhaps symbolise the inexorable passage of time or the approach of fate). In any case, noises not directly related to the narrative call attention to themselves far more than does the non-diegetic music of the underscore.

But 'arbitrary' noises that maintain ties to the narrative – noises that violate expectations not because of their content but because of their treatment – tend to be subsumed into the mix of quasi-realistic noise. Even though their volume levels may be exaggerated in one direction or the other (the amplified sound of wind-blown grass in *Days of Heaven* and *The Thin Red Line*, for example, or the muted gunshot in *Badlands* (1973) as Holly's father kills her dog), these noises are nonetheless 'motivated'. Along with dialogue, they belong to the narrative's 'directly significant' sounds. To use a term developed by Christian Metz (1985), they are 'aural objects' contained within the filmic space; whether they are judged as synchronous or asynchronous with the action, as empathetic or anempathetic to the narrative's emotion (Chion 1985), the noises are components of the *mise-en-scène*, as functional as costumes, lighting and props.

There is resistance to using musical terminology for the description of filmic sounds. Citing the work by Bordwell and Thompson (1979) that for more than two decades has been a favoured text for introductory classes in film, Rick Altman (1992: 15) observes that 'current approaches to film sound systematically borrow a musical model'. But then he argues that such a model is inappropriate, for while film sounds indeed have the qualities of pitch, loudness and timbre, these terms suit only the notation for instructions contained within a musical score and have little to do with actual sonic phenomena. By 'stressing the formal concerns of music's internal, self-referential aspect', Altman argues, 'musical notation diverts attention from [filmic] sound's discursive dimensions, concealing the fact that sound is in reality multiple, complex, heterogeneous and three-dimensional' (1992: 16). I make no assumption that a sound, musical or otherwise, is unidimensional. And contrary to Altman, I maintain that musical terms – all of which can easily be translated into plain English – are appropriate for the description of not only individual filmic sounds but also the compositional ways in which those sounds are utilised.

Artfully arranged, filmic sounds can indeed serve as a score and perform functions similar to those normally assigned to non-diegetic music. But because its components are so closely linked with the narrative, the cinematic manifestation of *musique concrète* – that is, music made entirely of natural, concrete sounds, either unadulterated or somehow electronically manipulated – escapes attention even more elusively than does the traditional underscore. Thus when such a score is effective, it is all the more so for its subtlety.

Badlands is filled with instances during which noise – 'motivated' by the action yet sometimes skewed enough so that it qualifies as 'arbitrary' – impacts heavily on the filmic narrative. At certain moments, jarring bursts of diegetic sound serve as punctuation marks for dialogue; the blare of the passing train as Kit and Holly discuss their final round of plans has the effect of an exclamation point, for example, as does the intrusive rumble of another train as one of the arresting officers comments on Kit's resemblance to James Dean. At other moments, noise is severely suppressed; early in the film, the cattle yard's crashing gates are completely silent, and at the end of the film so is the departing airplane. And like *Days of Heaven* (and, for that matter, like *The Thin Red Line*), Malick's debut film features a raging fire whose voice is stifled.

Most of the sound in *Badlands*, however, is not nearly so notable as its counterpart in *Days of Heaven*. Malick's treatment of the off-screen speaking voice is certainly sophisticated here; indeed, Chion praises it for bringing 'new poetic power to the voice-over, breaking conventions of narration to destructure the spectator's point of view' (Chion 1999: 56). And there is much to ponder in the pre-existing music that Malick employs both as a title theme and as a recurring motto; the borrowed material (in this case, the 'Musica Poetica' segment from Carl Orff and Gunild Keetman's 1950–54 first volume of *Schulwerk*) is a piece created for young children, and it ironically reflects the naïveté of the protagonists as they romp on with their crime spree. But on the whole, *Badlands* seems a sonically tentative work, a film in which the director reveals only his potential for the highly creative use of sound.

The Thin Red Line, as so many reviews in the popular press have noted, is a sonically spectacular film. It teems with music, off-screen monologue and diegetic noises, and these are so tightly interwoven with the narrative that if one considers the film as a whole to be intelligently organised then one must apply the same judgement to the sound. One does not find in *The Thin Red Line*, however, discrete 'sound pieces' of the sort that characterise *Days of Heaven*.[3] A possible reason for this is the film's language content. Like *Days of Heaven*, Malick's treatment of the Guadalcanal story contains action-filled moments during which spoken or shouted words serve merely as ingredients in a mix of diegetic background sound. Although such moments abound in *Days of Heaven*, in *The Thin Red Line* they are greatly outnumbered by moments in which the dominant element is naturalistic dialogue or interior monologue. Because the narrative of *The Thin Red Line* is a complex web of subplots, some of them fragmentary and arguably nonlinear, the audience member's understanding of the language during these scenes is of crucial importance. The words are highly meaningful, and thus they must be highly intelligible if the spectator is to be at all successful in weaving the various plot strands into a comprehensible whole. With language so constantly in the film's foreground, there is little space for attention-grabbing episodes of *musique concrète*.

Another possible reason for the different sonic approaches evident in *Days of Heaven* and *The Thin Red Line* is the latter film's duration. A running time of almost three hours does not explain, of course, why an aurally sensitive director might chose to avoid embellishing his soundtrack with discrete 'sound pieces'. But such a length, in combination with such an eclectic narrative, might well explain why a director would opt to use sound primarily for a different purpose. Indeed, it seems that in Malick's long and circuitous *The Thin Red Line* the most potent use of sound is organisational.

There are certainly dramatic qualities expressed by the sonic imagery, and the shifts from one aural landscape to another serve not only as punctuations but also as emotional charges. The spectator is lulled by the maternal throbs of the ship's engines and then thrust violently into the chaos of hostile artillery fire, rubbed raw by the rustle of sharp-edged swamp grass and then mollified by utter silence. More impressive, though, are the associations of certain types of sound with certain characters or situations. The rustle of grass, whether in the swamp or on the hillside, becomes a symbol for action; the whistle of wind, whether on land or sea, suggests fear. The confused chatter of anonymous soldiers typically serves as the aural background for the fustian pronouncements of Lt Col Tall; the sound of water – dripping from canoe paddles, trickling over blood-stained stones, splashing wildly under the feet of members of a reconnaissance mission – seems always to be linked with the character of Private Witt.

To turn back to *Days of Heaven*, having made passing, anecdotal reference earlier to the first several scenes, let us now examine the opening in detail: in particular, the formal structures of 1) the roll of title credits that features Ennio Morricone's orchestration of music from Saint-Saëns' *The Aquarium*; 2) the scene at the steel mill – accompanied only by diegetic noise – during which Bill kills the foreman; and 3) the entire sequence that begins with the music-supported credits, includes the noise-supported mill scene as well as the brief streamside scene that precedes it, and then ends after the narration with the zoom-in on the character of Linda.

The Saint-Saëns music, which will recur throughout the film, begins with an oscillating melody that over the course of eight measures descends from the pitch E to the pitch B, and it is followed by a cascading figure whose formulation of pitches fairly obscures a sense of tonal centre. The melody and the cascade figure (which we might call the music's A section) together last 38 seconds, and then they are subjected to an exact repeat (the music's A' section). In obvious contrast, the music's B section features an ascending melody that clearly establishes the tonality of A minor. Repeated, this melody lasts a mere 12 seconds and is followed by a cadential figure, centred on the pitch E, whose two iterations (sections C and C') occupy a total of 20 seconds. With a resolution not in the 'dark' key of A minor but in the relatively 'bright' key of A major, the cadence settles into a coda that is extended for 14 seconds. For the purpose of this analysis, the important issue is the relationship – in terms of length – of the tonally ambiguous introductory material to the tonally clear material that constitutes the second part of the musical composition (see Fig. 1).

The scene at the mill features a similar proportional relationship of 'intro-ductory' material to 'conclusive' material. Considering the contrasting emotional content of the credit roll and the scene involving murder, it is not surprising that different tempos are at play here (whereas the Saint-Saëns music features a relaxed 80 pulses per minute, the mill scene – measured by the repetitive thumps of the machinery – features an energetic 120 pulses per minute). There is also a difference in sonic design (see Fig. 2). As does the introductory music, the mill scene begins with two statements of equal length, each of which begins with several 'measures' in steady tempo and then slows to a halt; these statements are brief, however, and they are separated from the 'conclusive' section by a relatively lengthy intermediary phrase that features not only steady pulses but also sustained screeches; after the climactic segment that features the killing, the scene quiets down with a coda marked by the opening lines of Linda's narration. Despite this difference in design, however, the sequence of shots that leads directly to the killing (that is, the sequence that begins with the close-up of the glaring foreman, identified as section D in the figure) begins at almost exactly the same spot – in terms of temporal proportion – as does the introductory music's settling into an unambiguous tonal centre.

If the similarity of proportion seems merely coincidental, consider the entirety of the film's opening sequence (see Fig. 3). The credit roll lasts 122 seconds and the mill

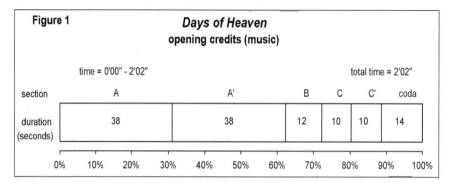

Figure 1

Days of Heaven
opening credits (music)

time = 0'00" - 2'02"   total time = 2'02"

section	A	A'	B	C	C'	coda
duration (seconds)	38	38	12	10	10	14

0% 10% 20% 30% 40% 50% 60% 70% 80% 90% 100%

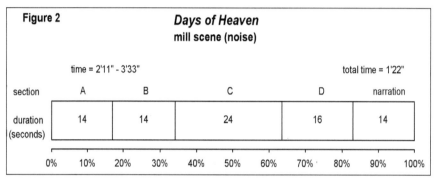

Figure 2

Days of Heaven
mill scene (noise)

time = 2'11" - 3'33"   total time = 1'22"

section	A	B	C	D	narration
duration (seconds)	14	14	24	16	14

0% 10% 20% 30% 40% 50% 60% 70% 80% 90% 100%

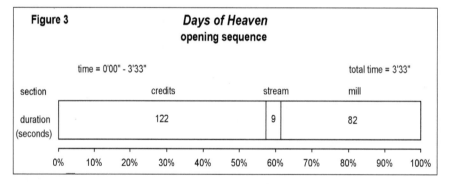

Figure 3

Days of Heaven
opening sequence

time = 0'00" - 3'33"   total time = 3'33"

section	credits	stream	mill
duration (seconds)	122	9	82

0% 10% 20% 30% 40% 50% 60% 70% 80% 90% 100%

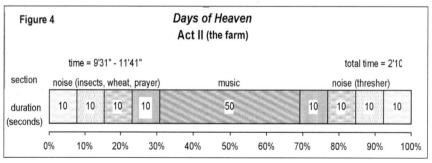

Figure 4

Days of Heaven
Act II (the farm)

time = 9'31" - 11'41"   total time = 2'10

section	noise (insects, wheat, prayer)				music	noise (thresher)			
duration (seconds)	10	10	10	10	50	10	10	10	10

0% 10% 20% 30% 40% 50% 60% 70% 80% 90% 100%

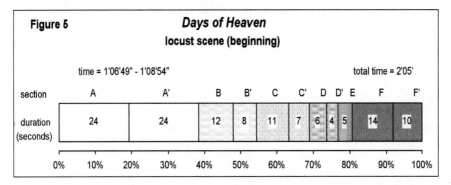

Figure 5 — Days of Heaven — locust scene (beginning)

time = 1'06'49" - 1'08'54"   total time = 2'05'

section	A	A'	B	B'	C	C'	D	D'	E	F	F'
duration (seconds)	24	24	12	8	11	7	6	4	5	14	10

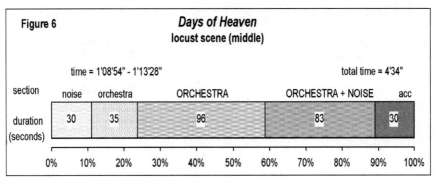

Figure 6 — Days of Heaven — locust scene (middle)

time = 1'08'54" - 1'13'28"   total time = 4'34"

section	noise	orchestra	ORCHESTRA	ORCHESTRA + NOISE	acc
duration (seconds)	30	35	96	83	30

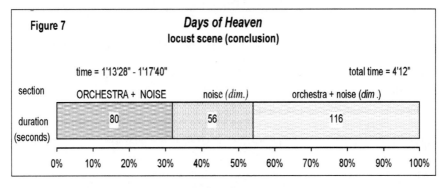

Figure 7 — Days of Heaven — locust scene (conclusion)

time = 1'13'28" - 1'17'40"   total time = 4'12"

section	ORCHESTRA + NOISE	noise *(dim.)*	orchestra + noise *(dim.)*
duration (seconds)	80	56	116

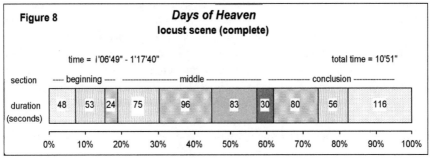

Figure 8 — Days of Heaven — locust scene (complete)

time = 1'06'49" - 1'17'40"   total time = 10'51"

section	---- beginning ----				-------------- middle --------------			-------------- conclusion --------------	
duration (seconds)	48	53	24	75	96	83	30	80	56	116

scene lasts 82 seconds, and these are separated by the streamside scene that lasts a mere nine seconds. Just as the transition from the close-up of the antiquated photograph of Linda to the long shot of the mill is a smooth one, so the gentle *musique concrète* of the streamside scene seems to 'flow' almost naturally out of the extended coda of the orchestral score. In contrast, the jump cut to the mill is articulated not just by a shift in imagery but also by the ear-jarring introduction of industrial noise. And this sudden change of audio-visual focus, which arguably serves to establish the tone of the film's ensuing narrative, occurs at precisely the same proportional moment as does the establishment of tonal centre during the opening credits and the establishment of Bill's murderous character during the mill scene.

In all three cases, the larger portion (the 'introductory' material) is related to the whole as the smaller portion (the 'conclusive' material) is related to the larger portion. The proportional relationships are exemplified in what is perhaps the best-known of the many numerical series described by the thirteenth-century Italian mathematician Leonardo Pisano Fibonacci, in which the last number at any given point is the sum of the previous two numbers (that is, 1, 2, 3, 5, 8, 13, 21...). The ratio of the penultimate number to the ultimate number is sometimes called the 'Divine Proportion' or the 'Golden Section'. It is often found in nature and has figured into works of visual art since the days of ancient Greece. In twentieth-century music, the ratio is found most strikingly in the compositions of Béla Bartók (Rothstein 1995: 156–71), and it is clearly evident in the three interfolded sequences that make up the opening of *Days of Heaven*.

Another fine example of tightly organised noise-as-music occurs 9½ minutes into the film, as the narrative settles into the actual work that must be done at the farm. At this point, the sonic ambience of the farm has already been established, most strikingly by the blur of insect chirps that segues into the rhythmic whirring of the wind gauge and the sudden near-silence that accompanies the shot of the bison. For a full minute, however, as Linda engages in conversation with her new friend and the playful banter of the three main characters is masked by a babble of foreign languages from their co-workers, the sounds are entirely 'motivated'.

This situation changes abruptly with the shot of the scarecrow's flapping clothes followed by the shot of the men waving signal flags (see Fig. 4). Despite the windy imagery, for the first ten seconds the sound – extremely quiet – is that of insects. In each of the three ten-second segments that follow, the volume level as well as the complexity of the sound markedly increases. After the hushed insect sounds, the close-up of the Farmer is paralleled by magnified sounds of wheat being crunched, rubbed and blown into the air; the insects' hum, louder than before, is penetrated by the priest's prayer; the underscore (a variation on the oscillating title theme) creeps into the mix and builds in intensity. After these four progressively louder and sonically more complex ten-second segments, a 50-second montage of apparently eager work – depicted mostly in long shots – is dominated by orchestral music that suggests that at the farm all is well.

Then, as the camera focuses on Abby, the soundtrack reverses its course. During the first ten-second segment, the orchestral music fades and eventually ends – doubtless with emotional significance – on an unresolved half-cadence. In the next ten-second segment there is a swell in the noise of the thresher, which was foregrounded in the mix at the very moment that Abby became the central figure in the imagery. For ten seconds more the noise of the thresher shares sonic space with distant shouts and the sound of the wings of birds as they flee the harvest. In the final ten-second segment, the thresher noise dissipates.

If we regard this perfectly symmetrical 130-second sequence as a 'sound piece', its conclusion is marked – as was its beginning – by an approximation of silence. Precisely at the moment at which the 'arch form' of the *musique concrète* composition balances itself, the Farmer makes his first longing gaze in the direction of Abby. For a moment, nothing happens. Then a quiet underscore of piano music, overlayed with Linda's naïve commentary on her perception of the relationship between the Farmer and Abby, shifts the narrative to an entirely different plane.

A third example of canny sonic organisation occurs just over an hour into the film, in the extended climactic scene during which the onset of the plague of locusts leads to Bill's killing of the Farmer. Like the scene just discussed, this 'sound piece' is prefaced by more or less realistic dialogue (in this case, between Bill and Abby) punctuated by the telling whirr of the farmhouse's wind gauge. Then, as in the previous example, the camera focuses on the farmyard and the 'sound piece' begins with a sudden drop in volume level (see Fig. 5).

For 24 seconds there is nothing but the quiet noise of animals and wind (section A); for another 24 seconds, as the scene shifts to Linda in the kitchen, there is nothing but quiet chopping sounds and a mere hint of insect noise (section A'). But then there is an acceleration of imagery augmented by an increase of both sound levels and emotional intensity. In the B section, Bill actually sees a few of the locusts, and in the B' section the peafowl begin to eat the locusts. In the sections marked C and C', respectively, Abby encounters a locust in the bathroom and Linda begins to swat at locusts she finds in the kitchen. Building toward a peak of tension, the sections marked D and D' feature close-up shots of ducks eating locusts and then locusts eating wheat. The brief section marked E introduces the sound of the siren; the sections marked F and F', whose total duration balances neatly with the durations of the scene's two opening sequences, feature a maximally loud array of noise as the narrative is swept with a feeling of panic.

In sharp contrast to this almost naturalistic prelude, the middle portion of the locust scene begins with a sudden move to a surreal sonic plane (see Fig. 6). After the Farmer's cry of 'Smoke 'em out!' and the roar of a tractor, the volume level drops precipitously, and for 30 seconds the soundtrack consists primarily of a sustained insectile hum embellished with tone clusters – analogously buzzy and high-pitched – from the violins of the non-diegetic orchestra. Toward the end of this 30-second section the volume level of the orchestral strings rises and for the next 35 seconds – after the imagery shifts from close-ups of the locusts to shots of the farm workers – the full orchestra continues the crescendo. A burst of 'white noise' from a rising cloud of locusts marks the start of the third section, during which the orchestra – now unambiguously foregrounded – plays a richly developed meditation that lasts 96 seconds.

In the fourth section, the diegetic noise that previously had been suppressed rises to balance with the sound level of the orchestra. During this segment, 83 seconds in length, the filmic narrative is especially rich, and the imagery echoes the beginning of the climax of the scene at the steel mill. As the workers dump baskets of locusts on the bonfire, the camera focuses on the Farmer and his hatred for Bill; Bill and the Farmer engage in dialogue, but their apparently heated words – like those exchanged between Bill and the foreman – are all but drowned out by the surrounding din. Appropriately, the underscore at this point is filled with harmonic tension, but then – as the flames accidentally spread to the wheat – the music suddenly withdraws in deference to raw noise. After it has been established that the blaze is out of control, the music re-enters and partakes in a ghastly counterpoint with the noise of shouts, alarm bells, flames and wind. At the end of this section the sound level subsides so that the audience can hear Abby say to Bill: 'He knows!' Immediately afterward, in an ear-catching gesture that parallels the camera's shift away from the Bill/Abby/Farmer triangle and back toward the disaster, a surge in the music's tempo as well as its volume level ushers in the last section of the locust scene's middle portion.

The concluding portion of the locust scene begins, aurally and visually, with the flutter of birds attempting to escape the flames (see Fig. 7). For 80 seconds the camera dwells on the blaze. The underscore here is appropriately forceful and dire, yet it remains relatively quiet; even quieter is the fire's noise, which ironically decreases as the flames gain in intensity. After the noise of the holocaust diminishes to barely a whisper, the image shifts to the interior of the farmhouse for the confrontation between Abby and the Farmer; there is no underscore at this point, and for 56 seconds the dominant sounds are sharply percussive (footsteps, objects roughly handled, the click of the pistol). Orchestral music is introduced as the image shifts again to the outdoors for the Farmer's confrontation with Bill, but the music quickly yields to the relatively soft percussive noise of mechanical tinkering and the horse's clopping hooves. This final section lasts 116 seconds, and much of it is played in near-silence; tellingly, after Bill runs away from the scene of the killing – as the camera recapitulates the equine imagery with which this extended sequence began – the shift of narrative time and space is marked with the return of the oscillating Saint-Saëns theme.

The entire locust scene – beginning with the image of a contented horse in the farmyard and ending with the image of a frightened horse in the still-burning field – lasts ten minutes and 51 seconds (see Fig. 8). The first two sections feature significant increases of sound level and sound complexity; indeed, the loudest, densest moments of the scene occur at the ends of these two sections, and the end of the second section is further intensified by a sudden acceleration of the music's tempo. Sound levels in the third section move in the opposite direction. Thus the transition from the second section to the third section represents the scene's dynamic peak, the point toward which all the preceding material builds and the point from which all the ensuing material recedes. Is it mere coincidence, one might wonder, that this peak sonic moment is also the moment at which Malick's camera begins its long gaze at the out-of-control yet perversely hushed blaze? Is it likewise just a coincidence that the temporal proportions of this long scene so closely resemble those of the nested segments that make up the film's opening sequence?

In a perspicacious talk on the possibilities of various noises as elements in composition, the American avant-garde composer John Cage suggested that 'if this word "music" is sacred and reserved for eighteenth- and nineteenth-century instruments, we can substitute a more meaningful term: organization of sound' (1961: 3). Schreger's claim that there is 'no more intelligent use of sound than in *Days of Heaven*' is perhaps hyperbole. But surely there are few films in which intelligent organisation of sound is more evident upon close analysis.

Days of Heaven is so obviously sonic a film that one suspects that the director – and his editor, Billy Weber, who worked on all three of the Malick films discussed here – wallowed in the opportunities afforded by the new Dolby technology. One hesitates to call this an aurally 'manneristic' work, yet the film's use of sound does tend toward the extreme. Collages of naturalistic noise – especially noise associated with the elemental forces of wind, earth, fire and water – rival the landscape cinematography for the audience member's attention. In terms of the film's narrative, the psychological environments conjured up by collages of noise are every bit as meaningful as the film's physical settings. And at least a few of these collages can be isolated from their filmic context and heard as enduringly memorable compositions in the *musique concrète* genre. If *Days of Heaven* is not manneristic in its use of sound, it is at the very least strikingly auteuristic.

Notes

1   Along with Malick, these are Michael Cimino, Francis Ford Coppola, Milos Forman, Philip Kaufman, Stanley Kubrick, George Lucas, Alan J. Pakula, Ken Russell, Martin Scorsese, Jerzy Skolimowski and Steven Spielberg.
2   Among the many books that deal with the film score's history and semiology are Tony Thomas' *Music for the Movies* (Cranbury, N.J.: A. S. Barnes, 1973), Mark Evans' *Soundtrack: The Music of the Movies* (New York: Hopkinson and Blake, 1975), Roy M. Prendergast's *Film Music: A Neglected Art* (New York: W. W. Norton & Company, 1977), Christopher Palmer's *The Composer in Hollywood* (London: Marion Boyars, 1990), George Burt's *The Art of Film Music* (Boston: Northeastern University Press, 1994) and Royal S. Brown's *Overtones and Undertones: Reading Film Music* (Berkeley: University of California Press, 1994).
3   Discrete 'sound pieces' certainly do not figure into Malick's *The New World* (2005) which in terms of both music and sound effects is quite conventional.

References

Altman, Rick (1992) 'The Material Hetereogeneity of Recorded Sound', in Rick Altman (ed.) *Sound Theory, Sound Practice*. New York: Routledge.
Bellour, Raymond (1975) 'The Unattainable Text', in *Screen* 16, 3, 23–4.
Bordwell, David & Kristin Thompson (1979) *Film Art: An Introduction*. New York: McGraw-Hill.
Cage, John (1961) 'The Future of Music: Credo', in *Silence*. Hanover, N.H.: Wesleyan University Press. [Originally a speech delivered to an arts group in Seattle in 1937, first printed in 1958 in the programme booklet for a Cage retrospective concert in

New York's Town Hall.]

Chion, Michel (1985) 'Le Son au cinéma', in *Cahiers du cinéma*, Paris, 122–6.

_____ (1994) *Audio-Vision: Sound on Screen*, trans. Claudia Gorbman. New York: Columbia University Press.

_____ (1999) *The Voice in Cinema*, trans. Claudia Gorbman. New York: Columbia University Press.

Gorbman, Claudia (1987) *Unheard Melodies: Narrative Film Music*. Bloomington: Indiana University Press.

Kerman, Joseph (1994) *Write All These Down: Essays on Music*. Berkeley: University of California Press.

Metz, Christian (1985) [1975] 'Aural Objects', trans. G. Gurrieri, in Elisabeth Weis and John Belton (eds) *Film Sound: Theory and Practice*. New York: Columbia University Press, 154–61.

Meyer, Leonard B. (1956) *Emotion and Meaning in Music*. Chicago: University of Chicago Press.

Rothstein, Edward (1995) *Emblems of Mind: The Inner Life of Music and Mathematics*. New York: Avon Books.

Schreger, Charles (1985) 'Altman, Dolby, and the Second Sound Revolution', in Elisabeth Weis and John Belton (eds) *Film Sound: Theory and Practice*. New York: Columbia University Press, 348–55. [Originally 'The Second Coming of Sound', *Film Comment*, 14, 5, 1978.]

CHAPTER TEN

'Everything a Lie': The Critical and Commercial Reception of Terrence Malick's The Thin Red Line

Martin Flanagan

Terrence Malick's return to filmmaking with *The Thin Red Line* (1998), after a much-publicised twenty-year hiatus since the release of *Days of Heaven* (1978), could lay claim to being one of the most keenly anticipated comebacks in modern cinema history. Although acclaimed as an esoteric visual poet rather than a crafter of popular entertainments, the coverage of Malick's return in the press, in specialist film magazines and in broadcast and online media testified to a substantial amount of public interest in the director whose reputation had been made by *Badlands* (1973). When *The Thin Red Line* achieved wide release in early 1999, much was made of the fact that Malick was one of a triumvirate of major directors whose work was set to return to cinemas during that year, the other two being George Lucas and Stanley Kubrick (see, for instance, Handy 1997). In the event, the three projects that those respected, if controversial, artists delivered to audiences in 1999 (*The Thin Red Line*; Kubrick's *Eyes Wide Shut*; Lucas' *Star Wars Episode I: The Phantom Menace*), as disparate as they were in style and form, all met with some cautionary critical responses, often centring on accusations of an autocratic approach to the creative process. That the three directors had all prospered in the 1970s, now critically enshrined as something of a 'golden age' in American film, was frequently invoked, with many commentators, especially in Malick's case, speculating that the autonomy of these works might presage a return to the non-conformist commercial and aesthetic spirit of that decade (Handy 1997; Taylor 1999).

The industrial and critical context around the release of *The Thin Red Line* bears scrutiny precisely because of the divergence between the economic conditions of the early 1970s, when Malick made his first two features, and the institutional structure of Hollywood at the time of his re-emergence. Malick made *Badlands* for an estimated $350,000, at a time when the major studios, in decline throughout the 1960s, were reconstructing themselves around the creative identities of filmmakers like Lucas, Francis Ford Coppola, William Friedkin and Peter Bogdanovich. As has been well documented, by Schatz (1993) amongst others, the net result for American cinema of this period of experimentation was an eventual return to classical formulae of narrative-driven commercial conformity when figures like Coppola, Lucas and Steven Spielberg began to translate personal expression into broad box-office appeal. During Malick's absence in the 1980s, Hollywood consolidated the gains of the post-*Star Wars* (George Lucas, 1977) era by concentrating resources on sequels and 'high-concept' spectacles. Multinational conglomerates like Sony acquired key studios, folding them into media empires, and a series of high-profile mergers and acquisitions registered a profound impact upon the Hollywood landscape. Such institutional changes had inevitable consequences for the artistic freedoms enjoyed by individual filmmakers. Despite a strong independent sector that still encouraged individual vision (albeit often in tandem with major studio distribution muscle), American cinema was a very different organism, both in terms of industrial organisation and prevailing stylistic climate, when Malick returned in the mid-1990s. Bearing in mind the fates of his peers from the 1970s (Bogdanovich, Friedkin, Michael Cimino), questions were asked about how Malick would fit into the new topography of American film, and of how his narratively slender aesthetic would sit with audiences. Malick would handle a budget of $52 million – 150 times the cost of *Badlands* – on *The Thin Red Line*. In the late 1970s, the commercial failure of *Days of Heaven* had threatened to bracket Malick with the likes of Cimino, director of the notorious *Heaven's Gate* (1980); even taken aside from its commercial performance and on the terms of its obvious aesthetic merits, *Days of Heaven* seemed to belong, in tone, temper and ambition, to another era completely. For his more supportive critics, Malick's comeback would crystallise a hoped-for return to the (heavily romanticised) 1970s ethos of artistic and commercial boldness; *The Thin Red Line* would mean something beyond its already culturally loaded subject matter. When Steven Spielberg, in some ways the anti-Malick (in terms of industriousness, public recognition and commercial achievement), released his own World War Two movie, *Saving Private Ryan* (1998), only months before *The Thin Red Line*, the stakes were raised even further.

This chapter will briefly consider the relationship between the Spielberg and Malick films in the service of establishing the proper industrial context for evaluating the achievement of *The Thin Red Line*. Diverging, to some extent, from the critical tendency to read Malick's films exclusively from within the auteurist paradigm, we will then explore the relationship of the text to pre-existing generic and narrative modes through a close reading of a key sequence in the film and extensive recourse to the critical and promotional discourses surrounding it.

Marketing War: The Challenge of Saving Private Ryan

If there was ever any real 'battle' for the favours of the film-going public between *Saving Private Ryan* and *The Thin Red Line* (separated as the films were by US release dates five months apart), it was won by Spielberg's movie on the territory of publicity and promotion. The seeds of this outcome can be found in the obvious difficulty experienced by backers Twentieth Century Fox in crafting a marketable identity for Malick's film. Fox's promotional campaign comprehensively failed to locate *The Thin Red Line* within public discourse surrounding World War Two, something that *Saving Private Ryan* had achieved with notable success. Despite widespread criticism of its historical verisimilitude, Spielberg's *Schindler's List* (1993) had cemented him in the popular consciousness as an active contributor to the public record of the war (an image compounded by Spielberg's later involvement in creating the Survivors of the Shoah Visual History Foundation). Publicity for *Saving Private Ryan* widely acknowledged the fact that Robert Rodat's screenplay was based upon the true story of Private Fritz Niland, a member of the 101st Airborne who had lost three brothers in combat and was returned home to his mother by military decree (Ambrose 2001: 102–3). Going beyond the film's modest link to a real-life case, the promotional discourse orchestrated by Paramount and Dreamworks played up Spielberg's new role as artistic chronicler of the Second World War, a figure through whose cinematic imagination people could rediscover the experience of a conflict gradually becoming lost to eyewitness testimony. Packaging for the UK video release of *Saving Private Ryan* bore the legend 'The Film that Inspired the World to Remember', before going on to detail the seemingly endless awards bestowed upon both Spielberg and the film, placing special emphasis on accolades that confirmed its approval by contemporary military bodies and the veteran community:

> In addition, Spielberg received his third Directors Guild of America Award, the American Legion 'The Spirit of Normandy' Award, a USO Merit Award from the USO of Metropolitan Washington, as well as the highest civilian public service award from the Department of the Army (excerpted from video packaging, *Saving Private Ryan*, CIC Video, UK, 1999)

Spielberg went on to produce *Shooting War* (Richard Schickel, 2000), a television documentary on World War Two combat photographers that further augmented the connection between the heavily fictionalised work *Saving Private Ryan* and the historical record of the war. More famously, Spielberg would collaborate with his *Saving Private Ryan* star Tom Hanks on the major HBO miniseries *Band of Brothers* (2001), blending *Saving Private Ryan*-style photographic techniques with a scenario based on the experiences of a real infantry unit.

Such promotional discourses and spin-offs deliberately presented *Saving Private Ryan* as an overdue jog of the collective memory by a director whose carefully cultivated image inferred a direct pipeline to the mass psyche ('The Film that Inspired the World to Remember'). Malick, on the other hand, was an enigmatic figure who had opted out of the public sphere two decades before, having little apparent influence

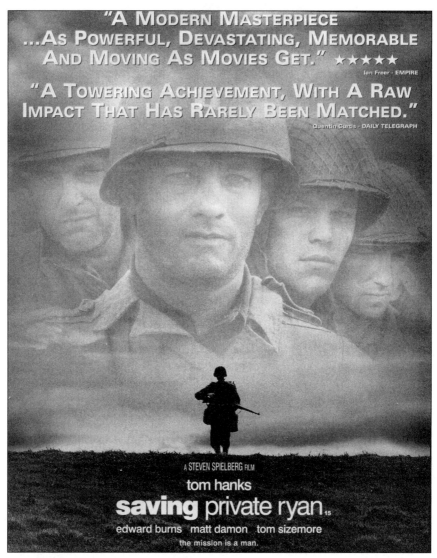

'The film that inspired the world to remember': promotional poster for *Saving Private Ryan*

on American cinema's development in the intervening period. Fox never chose to emphasise any potential that *The Thin Red Line* might have to contribute to or even change perceptions of World War Two, instead opting to separate the film from other artistic and public discourses concerning the war. Spielberg's movie had stoked perceptions of the conflict as an honourable one, focusing on the moral conundrum of placing one life above the greater human cost to preserve it, and finally concluding that the value of an entire way of life is maintained through such symbolic individual cases; the director even dubbed the film a 'morality play' (Gritten 1998). (John Streamas identifies Spielberg and Malick's contrasting ideologies with respect to the myth of World War Two as 'Good War' in his chapter in this collection.) By contrast, Malick's

NOMINATED FOR 7
ACADEMY AWARDS®
INCLUDING
BEST PICTURE
BEST DIRECTOR - TERRENCE MALICK • BEST SCREENPLAY - ADAPTATION

"Awesome...Astonishing...Amazing...
Every frame is a masterpiece...an eye-popping,
mind-blowing, soul-stirring epic...★★★★★"
UNCUT

"A lose-yourself-in epic that reaches beyond
mere entertainment...impossible to
ignore, impossible to forget. ★★★★★"
Ian Nathan - EMPIRE

"Extraordinary...Stunning work from one
of cinemas true visionaries."
Geoff Andrew - TIMEOUT

THE
THIN RED LINE 15
EVERY MAN FIGHTS HIS OWN WAR
PHOENIX   www.fox.co.uk
INSIDE FILM

A cineaste's dream: ambiguity and metaphysics in *The Thin Red Line*

film, outwardly at least, had little to say about such difficult moral choices, thereby sacrificing the good-for-the-soul didacticism that attracted conscientious middlebrow spectators to *Saving Private Ryan*. In *The Thin Red Line*, the audience would be given no guide (even to the extent of being denied a clearly identifiable protagonist to clarify themes on their behalf), in effect being left to venture through a moral swamp alone.

Fox's official website for the film quickly dispensed with any expectations that American intervention in the war would be presented in a manner that, like *Saving Private Ryan*, would progress from initial and perturbing ambiguity to ultimate legitimacy. The blurb on the website carefully detaches Malick's film from the global reach and historical exigencies of the war and relocates it to the realm of metaphysics, emotional stress and selfhood (uncommon territory for a war movie even in 1998):

> The story is more than a tale of men fighting a key battle, one which would ultimately stem the Japanese advance through the Pacific Islands. It explores the intense bonds that develop between men under terrible stress, even evil [...] The horrors of war helped them lose their idea of self and of the world around them. They were no longer fighting solely for patriotic reasons or the larger world and its issues which had brought them there; they were fighting for survival and for the men next to them. (Anon. 1998)

This description arguably does a measure of justice to the text, but as promotional literature is hardly guaranteed to establish any connections with the popular, romantic perceptions of World War Two furthered by movies like Spielberg's. The blurb goes on to feature assorted studio executives and star actors attesting to the power of Malick's vision, demonstrating that, from the outset, Fox's promotion of Malick's film tried to take an opposite tack to the *Saving Private Ryan* campaign. Where that film had been opportunistically promoted as an event of huge public significance, a chance to remember and pay tribute, *The Thin Red Line* was marketed as a cineaste's dream, an aesthetic event, its campaign stressing the wizardry of a genuine auteur surrounded by star acolytes. Such would be the attraction of Malick's return to major filmmaking, Fox gambled that it could afford to play down the film's generic profile amongst the canon of war films ('more than a tale of men fighting a key battle ...') while simultaneously resisting *Saving Private Ryan*'s dubious (but successful) marketing tactic of engaging public sentiment for the war. Malick's personal reputation was thus left to serve as the fulcrum of promotion for a film which needed to appeal to a broad audience to justify Fox's investment.

Critical and commercial responses

The perceptions of *The Thin Red Line* engendered by its promotional campaign generally compounded the view of Malick as a visionary auteur returning from the wilderness; this also represented the key angle of much of the press coverage attending the film, both evaluative (reviews) and journalistic (set reports, and so on). The artistic achievement of the film was open to debate – one commentator, Jonathan Romney (1999) in UK newspaper the Guardian, declared himself impressed but, to denote the film's critic-proof unreadability, awarded the film a rating measured in question marks instead of the usual stars. However, there was uniformity in the way that many reviewers slanted their approaches to *The Thin Red Line* towards the implications of Malick's personal return. This return was celebrated not only as the rediscovery of a singular talent, but as a heraldic moment for the eventual restoration of the kind of directorial autonomy and free expression last observed in the Hollywood of the 1970s. Bruce Handy, in an anticipatory *Time* magazine piece of late 1997, stated that the intrigue of the project derived from 'the chance it offers to watch the more indulgent filmmaking style of the 1970s collide with that of the 1990s' (1997: 99), attributing to the film at an early stage the anachronistic quality noted by many commentators. This strategy typically included a standard comparison to Coppola's legendarily indulgent but artistically vindicated Vietnam epic *Apocalypse Now* (1979) (see also MacCabe 1999; Nathan 1999; Rosenbaum 1999). *Los Angeles Times* critic Kenneth Turan compared Malick to the archetypal figure of the Japanese soldier, emerging from some South Pacific jungle, unaware of the cessation of the war: 'Time has stood still for him … and for better or worse, he has made something that has more in common with his own personal and delicate last film than anything out there today' (Turan 1998). Charles Taylor (1999), in a wholly negative online review, deflated cinephile hopes that a Malick success might spearhead a return to the arty ethos of the 1970s:

It's as if by creating a swelling chorus of praise for Terrence Malick, they believe they can bring back the glory days of American movies of the '70s when, at good movies and bad, the constant seemed to be that audiences were treated like adults, and it wasn't assumed they would reject the unfamiliar or unresolved. And there seems to be an unspoken fear that if *The Thin Red Line* fails without any support, the studios will use it as an excuse to quash other chancy projects and feed us more of the same pap.

Although Taylor's citation of a 'swelling chorus of praise' for Malick's film glosses over the degree of equivocation characterising many critical responses, his statement does communicate the weight of critical expectation that formed around *The Thin Red Line*. As with Kubrick's return, the dreams of an army of commentators, scholars and film buffs, for whom the auteur model was still an article of considerable faith, appeared to rest upon Malick's shoulders. Of course, Malick's inactivity since *Days of Heaven* was always likely to create such an unreasonable level of expectation; Scorsese and Coppola, prolific workers by comparison, had disappointed on enough occasions in the 1980s to reduce the 'event' status of their releases and allow a sense of pleasurable surprise when they did turn in a late work of stature. Both Malick and Kubrick had fed their own myths by withdrawing from the public eye and leaving no indicator by which to forecast their return, a scenario that could be exploited by studio publicists but which also precluded the possibility of objective evaluation of their films, raising expectations both aesthetically and commercially (a Malick film had never been an outright box-office hit before *The Thin Red Line*, but its $52 million budget – actually fairly moderate by contemporary standards – warranted a large return, a situation exacerbated by the success of Spielberg's film).

As far as popular and critical discourses of cinema were concerned, then, *The Thin Red Line* took on the added import of a make-or-break commercial gambit for an auteur whose name was emblematic of an extraordinarily fertile period in the history of Hollywood as artform. Indeed, when Fox executive Bill Mechanic, who had overseen production of Malick's film, lost his position in summer 2000, a slate of risky projects (including *The Thin Red Line* and David Fincher's acclaimed but unprofitable film *Fight Club* [1999]) was widely blamed. Certainly, when it came to audiences, *The Thin Red Line* proved a curious specimen; as Irwin (1999) points out, even after the Academy Award nominations of 1999 had been announced, with the movie receiving consideration in seven major categories, its box-office share continued to decline (flouting conventional wisdom which states that Academy recognition can revitalise the financial life of a flagging movie). The final US gross achieved by *The Thin Red Line* amounted to $36.4 million, as opposed to the $216 million earned domestically by *Saving Private Ryan*. Worldwide, Malick's film is estimated to have taken $81 million in receipts, while Spielberg's grossed a massive $479 million (against a budget of $70 million).

Such commercial underachievement accelerated the process by which *The Thin Red Line* came to be seen as a barometer for the ongoing struggle between art and commerce in Hollywood. The venerable British journal *Sight and Sound* would pronounce 1999 a year when cinema looked 'healthier than ever', citing *The Thin Red Line* alongside films like *Fight Club*, *Being John Malkovich* (Spike Jonze, 1999) and *The Limey* (Steven Soderbergh, 1999) as constituting 'a really inventive stream of US productions' (Anon. 1999: 3). However, the economic realities of late 1990s major studio production and accounting would confer the status of financial flop on *The Thin Red Line*; in the same climate, even Kubrick's *Eyes Wide Shut*, though achieving a worldwide gross of approximately $160 million, was adjudged a relative failure given the star power of leads Tom Cruise and Nicole Kidman. In *The Thin Red Line*, also, major stars were present, although the precise and slightly perverse manner in which they were used contributed to a range of unorthodox aesthetic strategies employed by Malick to create an experience that would defamiliarise the combat movie for audiences and attempt to reconfigure the terms on which narrative cinema could engage with the legacy of World War Two.

Territories of genre in the Battle for Hill 210

While not wishing to underestimate the internal diversity of a genre that continues to achieve mass resonance, it seems futile to argue that *The Thin Red Line* fits comfortably into the lineage of the war movie that has developed from works like *Objective, Burma!* (Raoul Walsh, 1944), *The Sands of Iwo Jima* (Allan Dwan, 1949) and *The Dirty Dozen* (Robert Aldrich, 1967) through to contemporary treatments of World War Two such as *Saving Private Ryan*, *U-571* (Jonathan Mostow, 2000) and *Pearl Harbor* (Michael Bay, 2001). If that group of texts can be said to share certain family resemblances, they are attributes that are either absent or drastically underplayed in Malick's film: tightly plotted narratives structured around a series of action sequences; star names in showcase roles as stoical platoon leaders or heroic pilots; scripts that seek to 'humanise' and focus the unwieldy experience of war through a sustained emphasis on the camaraderie and sense of brotherhood bred even in the least forgiving of environments. Of course, the World War Two film walks a historical tightrope as well as a formal one, and many of the harshest criticisms of *The Thin Red Line* centred on accusations of misrepresentation or trivialisation of the realities of warfare. Tom Whalen points to the film's controversial voiceover, and its airily metaphysical counterpoint to the brutality of some of the images, as the source of his misgiving:

'What keeps us from reaching out and touching the glory?' wonders Witt. Well, in the narrative context the answer might be that we'd get a finger shot off. (1999: 163)

More sympathetically, Colin MacCabe accuses Malick of having 'no interest in World War II ... C-Charlie company are engaged in a conflict which is as old as time, which is simply a modern version of the Trojan War' (1999: 13). Critical consensus suggested that Malick was more concerned to explore World War Two as a psycho-dramatic crucible comparable to the killing spree of *Badlands* or the fatal love triangle of *Days of Heaven*, than as a matter of historical record or public remembrance. Such observations frequently made simultaneous reference to Malick's rejection of generic and narrative formulae, as if the renunciation of formal convention was somehow inseparable from the lack of fidelity shown to historical fact (a situation complicated by the fact that Malick's source material, James Jones' novel, was itself a 'fictionalisation' of the author's real experiences). Even *Film Comment*'s Gavin Smith, one critic who embraced Malick's approach and seemed to approve of the application of such a transcendental aesthetic method to an apparently ignoble and utterly corporeal subject, noted that 'Witt isn't the protagonist of a war film ... but of an adventure in sensory and spiritual wonder' (1999: 11). Other than the much-maligned use of voice-over, the perceived absence of the generic tropes of the war film became one of the most the most contentious areas in critical discussion around *The Thin Red Line*. A central sequence of military strategy and execution in the film, depicting an attempt to 'reduce' a Japanese defence position obstructing the eventual capture of a crucial airfield, will now be analysed to provide a more detailed reading of Malick's aesthetic and how, rather than rejecting generic strategies wholesale, it strives to incorporate certain aspects of genre and then move beyond their limitations.

The sequence detailing the capture of Hill 210 represents perhaps the greatest concentration of combat action in the film; occurring as it does roughly halfway through the running time, it could be argued that this is the peak of the movie's appeal to formal and generic convention. Yet, the sequence does not make for comfortable or obvious viewing. Audience identification is complicated by the fact that the assault is led by John Cusack as Captain Gaff, a recognisable star but a character who seems to appear from nowhere to take us through the highlight of the movie. Malick, contrary as ever, seems to want to simultaneously disavow and celebrate the presence of star names throughout, a fact noted by many critics (Taylor 1999; Turan 1998). Furthermore, the withholding from us of a master shot of the objective means that the spatial relationships of the scene are never fully clarified for the audience, a strategy that mirrors Malick's more general refusal to map out the territory of his narrative according to the codes of the war movie. However, more traditional techniques like slow motion, point-of-view shots and rapid cutting do gradually come to feature in the scene, establishing a degree of formal affinity with the war film. The sequence thus encapsulates the more general way in which *The Thin Red Line* alternately embraces and denies formal convention.

As the approach begins, a typically prowling crane shot follows the soldiers from a position slightly above and to the left as they weave in and out of the tall

Battle for Hill 210: embracing and denying formal convention in *The Thin Red Line*

grass, frequently disappearing from view only to resurface seconds later (the angle reinforcing the fact that the unit's cautious approach is almost insect-like). The image cuts to track Gaff's progress as he makes his way up the incline of the hill. The next shot disturbs our expectation slightly with a spatial shift to a viewpoint apparently proximate to the Japanese mounted gun position, peering out over the edge of a jagged rock formation (the clue to the significance of the location being handfuls of spent bullet shells littering a ledge). Recalling the codes of the war film, we briefly expect to see the crawling soldiers come into sight, emphasising their vulnerability to a still unseen, omniscient foe. But before this can happen there is a further cut, causing us to question where the last image really originated from; the film is refusing to join the dots for us in spatial terms. We pick up the progress of the unit from a head-on position, several of the soldiers passing closely by the camera. Hans Zimmer's tentative score has, by this point, faded out completely, leaving only ambient sound. We then receive the closest thing to a master shot in the sequence, a long shot that encapsulates the military target and its daunting impenetrability. Our gaze is directed towards the pinnacle of the hill, apparently the site of the threat, where hidden opponents would enjoy a clear line of sight to any approach save for a few spots where the rock juts out of the hillside. As Gaff's unit falls in behind one of these privileged spots, we understand the precariousness of their situation and the need for a stealthy and decisive attack. Darkening clouds just visible at the top of the frame, it is an oppressive and daunting shot, depicting an inhospitable natural fortress at odds with some of the images of natural beauty seen at other stages of the film (Malick was frequently criticised for his propensity to overstate the beauty of nature in intended contrast to the unnatural horrors of war – see Taylor 1999; Turan 1998; Whalen 1999).

We move in close to the fatigued soldiers, and the handheld camera shakes uncertainly, capturing their tiredness and disorientation. Malick elects to jump cut between Doll (Dash Mihok) and Bell (Ben Chaplin), the men positioned at either extreme of the group, insinuating the cumulatively shattering effect of such physical exertion and mental vigilance. We are being given as little time to recover as the soldiers; Gaff lays out some strategy, and is soon inching along the rock to get a better look and fix some co-ordinates to relay to air support. A point-of-view shot conveys Gaff's limited vision as he peers around the edge of the protective rock, Malick fusing the image to Gaff's consciousness. Here, convention is used to lay stress on the importance of the moment: elsewhere in the film such unambiguous signifiers of subjective point of view are used sparingly. Bell relays the instructions via radio, but the resulting artillery blast from above is quickly snatched from our view (Malick minimising the sense of spectacle) as we cut away to a shot of Colonel Tall (Nick Nolte) watching from a safe distance, straining to see his orders carried out and the high-point of his military career secured. As Gaff adjusts the co-ordinates, Bell extorts the air support to 'fire for effect' – a line that could be read as ironically acknowledging the heavy dependence on spectacle of modern war films. However, rather than indulge in such spectacle, the next pair of shots attempts to convey the unpredictability of being on the ground amidst such mayhem, cutting from the worried face of Private Dale (Arie Verveen) to a rotating, dizzying view of a clear blue sky from which the shell that is about to be unleashed could emerge at any moment. The next cut gives us the spectacular blast that Malick has been withholding for so long (albeit held in distancing long shot), showing the Japanese bunker coming under repeated artillery fire, before cutting to Dale again, lying on the ground and covering his ears. Through the resulting smoke, the unit progresses up the hill, the rate of cutting steadily increasing and the attack now launched. We cut to a view from inside the bunker, looking out of a slot from which a Japanese machine gun protrudes, the shot embodying the deliberately limited, distanced view of events that we have been given throughout the sequence.

As if to compensate for such alienating effects, the film now slips into the closest it will get to conventional generic mode, relying on swift cutting and the thunderous rhythm of discharging weaponry to move the sequence along, although Malick still refrains from giving us any overhead shots that might clarify the still obscure spatial relationships between the opposing forces. As the Americans move from one sheltering rock outcrop to the next, we are still tied to their limited view. The uncertainty puts us in their position, with the terrain ahead as unpredictably threatening as Dale's blue sky; a similar strategy is used later in the raid on the Japanese bivouac, when jungle mists make it impossible for the American patrol to anticipate the emergence of their opponents, and Zimmer's metronomic percussion and the sound effects of whistling bullets become the only means of orientation for both soldier and spectator.

Back on Hill 210, an infantryman is wounded and Witt (Jim Caviezel), nominally the lead character of the narrative but marginal in this sequence, peers down at him, seemingly fascinated by the sight. Japanese soldiers begin to emerge from the hilltop, but, ensuring that we still share the viewpoint of Gaff and his comrades, they are kept in the distance (and are not seen in any detail or individual focus until their position has been fatally breached, perhaps the most generically typical aspect of Malick's war narrative). A swirling sound effect renders the confusion felt by Private Doll, who, either conquering his panic or perhaps stretched by it beyond reason, launches himself (in slow motion) towards the summit of the hill, throwing a grenade and then desperately firing his revolver at the source of enemy aggression. As the soldiers regroup behind yet another rock, the camera lurches around disturbingly, as if it has lost its own composure. Characteristic Malickian grace notes occur in the midst of the confusion, with shafts of light piercing through the long grass (such moments are usually relayed to a reverse shot of Witt, establishing the different register with which he seems to perceive events; although a peripheral figure in the action of the attack, Witt's viewpoint is frequently adopted). The American soldiers become more individualised, each fighting their own battle, their styles ranging from Gaff's calm leadership to Doll's crazed and improvisatory approach (reflecting the absence of self-possession suggested by his surname). As the Japanese forces, glimpsed in detail for the first time, leave their foxholes, the Americans (apparently smaller in number) seem to be able to wander around fairly unthreatened, perhaps indicating that Tall has made good on his promise to push supporting forces up the hill once the vital inroad has been made. Gaff blows on a whistle, signalling the capture, and we see the stunned faces of Bell and Doll as the action suspends and time slows down again, and they can consider what has just happened. While the brutalising effect of combat is clearly shown in the actions of Corporal Queen (David Harrod), who shoots a surrendered opponent in his rage and has to be restrained by Gaff, Doll and Bell share the sheer unreality of their survival with a tender embrace. That the battle continues to reverberate in the minds of the combatants long after the end of hostilities is shown in the shot of a trembling Japanese officer who flinches at the smallest sound.

The sequence combines sound and image in a way that is arguably more visceral than poetic; although elsewhere in the film Malick's visual symbolism can be found at its most expressive, the concern in the Hill 210 sequence is to anchor the narrative in a combat episode that aims not to provide consequence-free thrills but to give a sense of the unknowability, the openendedness of battle. At the end, we feel that Gaff's men were fortunate to find the right conditions for cover on the approach, and that the outcome was far from inevitable. That single cutaway shot of Nick Nolte's Colonel Tall, watching the artillery drop from half a mile away through binoculars (as far from the direct physical consequences of the action as a film director ordering some poor stuntman into a burning set), brings out an implicit critique of hierarchical military structure, suggesting that Malick is interested in more than constructing pretty pictures of 'paradisiacal' nature (Whalen 1999: 163).

Conclusion: Mythologising Malick

Ultimately, *The Thin Red Line* failed to attain the commercial success and public resonance of the inferior *Saving Private Ryan*. In style, narrative approach and genre, Spielberg's film addressed a global audience and styled itself through various extra-textual discourses as a version of the war that would be at once shockingly frank (in the powerful opening battle scenes) and dependably familiar. *The Thin Red Line* instead sought, perhaps, to remove the war from such a comfortable zone of audience contact, to dismantle the protective barriers of generic expectation and to recover some of the living contradictions of that traumatic experience. In many ways, Malick's film pulls off the considerable effect of making us feel that we are in the moment of war to a far greater degree than does Spielberg's; for all *Saving Private Ryan*'s searing shrapnel, we still feel safe in the cinema seat, a detached observer, whereas the (frequently mundane) flashbacks of *The Thin Red Line* remind us that a soldier's most intense moments might be concentrated on dreams of home, on finding a way of traversing the massive distances between South Pacific jungle and middle America in an instant. Perhaps this reminds us of the spatial paradox inherent in our own position as spectator: static, surrounded by protecting signs of familiarity, yet simultaneously transported to the landscape depicted on screen. The tremendous but ambiguous power of the film is predicated on such a juxtaposition of the familiar (stars, genre, historical subject matter) with the unknown.

The unknown elements seemed to be the problem in selling the film. Considered as the third part of a Malickian trilogy, *The Thin Red Line* shares with *Badlands* and *Days of Heaven* an interest in isolating a mythic quality in overdetermined historical markers such as the two world wars or 1950s suburbia, in turning away from common modes of representing American cultural history. However, the film also has a more material and contemporary orientation, positioned, as it is, at an intersection of discourses: social and aesthetic, historical and cinematic, institutional and personal. Terrence Malick's enigmatic reputation, and his indelible association with American cinema's 1970s resurgence, undoubtedly brought a touch of magic to the film's release, but perhaps also unbalanced expectation; there is no way of returning to the *laissez-faire* ethos of 1970s Hollywood, itself something of a myth, unless it is on the terms of the studios and their parent corporations.

The project depended on a conjunction of directorial vision and industrial muscle that was rare in 1990s Hollywood. One could ask how exactly Fox was supposed to communicate the quality of this film to the public if not through the burnishing of Malick's legend. Undoubtedly, the film suggestively calls to be situated in an ongoing body of work that draws a line through *Badlands* and *Days of Heaven*, but so rich (and, in places, so unique) is the cinematic experience of *The Thin Red Line* that viewing it as a golden age throwback, marooning Malick in an era associated with noble failure – where film art is intrinsically associated with excess – seems like a reductive move.

Popular notions of American movie authorship continue to lean heavily on the 1970s, but are constantly being reformulated as cinema's landscape changes. In the years since Malick's 1999 comeback, as I have observed elsewhere, discourses around mainstream Hollywood cinema (critical, popular and promotional/industrial) have tended to reinforce the 'cachet, 'cult' value or just plain star name of the auteur director' (Flanagan 2004: 32). Encouraged by the wealth of information about directorial intentions that can be provided via DVD commentaries and other 'special features', along with the capacity of the Internet to facilitate fan communities, the romantic model of the auteur appears to be in rude health. Yet at the same time as a director's cult flourishes, filmmakers also come under greater public scrutiny: tools have emerged that make it simple to instantly gauge a film's reception with major US critics (rottentomatoes.com, metacritic.com), or to check the average box-office takings for an established director, writer, producer or actor (boxofficemojo.com). Amongst developments like these, Terrence Malick's association with projects with agonisingly long gestations, and predilection for modes of narrative that may be intimidating to mass audiences, is out-of-step with the accessibility and rate of productivity of a younger, 'Sundance'-era generation of filmmakers making adult-oriented features that mix strategies of art cinema with populist forms and genres (say, Steven Soderbergh or Ang Lee); yet his myth remains intact. This is curious at a time when the impulse to conformity within the most notable of his 'movie brat' peers (George Lucas, and recently Martin Scorsese) is marked.

If anything, the legacy of Malick's return with *The Thin Red Line* has been to fix sheer singularity as his abiding identity within the ranks of American filmmakers, as demonstrated by the gushing, but frequently perceptive, tributes paid to him by actors and technical collaborators in the documentary *Rosy-Fingered Dawn* (Barcaroli *et al* 2002). Malick might be the one director of his generation who has not adapted his style either to the safe studio movie or the standard subject matter and budgets of the American independent mode; since *Days of Heaven* he has insisted upon working in an epic art film register (although of course with only three features since 1978, he has not had the opportunity to burn through as much financial goodwill on the part of the major studios as contemporaries like Cimino, Friedkin or Brian De Palma). With figures such as Scorsese and Spielberg ensconced firmly in making prestige studio fare (which is not to deny their own authorial coherence), very few candidates present themselves to be described as '[the] last Mohican of the personal epic mode', as Malick is by David Sterritt (2006). As evocative and witty as Sterritt's comment is, the tendency to characterise Malick as a lost warrior from the film battles of the 1970s – atavistically associated with a pined-for, apparently defeated filmmaking culture of artistic risk – endures.

Of course, no director is impervious to the vicissitudes of the marketplace and how it circumscribes audience expectations. Sterritt's comment related to *The New World*, Malick's most recent feature, which opened in a limited US release on Christmas Day 2005 (timed to qualify for the 2006 Academy Awards; the film ultimately earned a nomination for cinematographer Emmanuel Lubezki). *The New World* consolidates many of the stylistic and narrative developments of *The Thin Red Line* (especially around the use of internal monologue and the idiosyncratic approach to identification through stars, with the recurrence of 'principal' characters even more loosely applied than in the previous film). Released and part-financed by the 'mini-major' company New Line Cinema, the film was not a theatrical success, returning around $30 million world takings against a production budget of a similar figure. In the US, however, the movie has been discovered by a much larger audience on DVD, earning more than $26 million in rental revenue by the end of July 2006 (all figures from boxofficemojo. com). Producer Sarah Green insisted that Malick retained final cut, despite the widely reported withdrawal of the film after its initial coastal US engagements to be recut, with 17 minutes being removed in the process (Wildman 2006). The slow evolution of a 'cult' around those critics and audiences who passionately loved the film was palpable enough to be the subject of a *Village Voice* article wherein J. Hoberman attempts to pinpoint the peculiar feelings of transience and intangibility that accrue around both

Malick's work and his public profile. Citing some of the laments of fans of *The New World* that the film would soon vanish from theatres (indeed, the longer version had only lasted a matter of days), Hoberman sees such anxious devotion as reflective of how the film builds its very own 'Golden Age', glorious but unrepeatable, into its construction (Hoberman 2006). Critics in general continue to approach Malick as a mercurial and undefinable talent. Mimicking the reception of *The Thin Red Line*, responses to *The New World* could only critically process the film's style by applying the core aesthetic issues relating to his whole body of work, thus validating Malick in terms of an auteurist totality. Many accounts of the film familiarly dwell upon Malick's philosophical bent (Sterritt 2006), the divergence of his style from mainstream narrative formulas and film language (Foundas 2005; Hoberman 2005; Burns 2006), the centrality of nature to his overall thematic (Howell 2006), and so on. One of the fresher angles taken by reviewers instead considered the representation of Pocahontas (Q'Orianka Kilcher) within Malick's general sexual politics (Taubin 2006).

Directors with provably coherent styles and non-studio backgrounds are as likely to be employed in directing a medium-to-big budget film as at any time in modern Hollywood (Flanagan 2004: 20–22), but few of that host of auteurs are like Malick. There is clearly still something at stake when a Terrence Malick movie emerges; rather perversely, we could conclude, the more films Malick makes, the more his commentators insist upon the historical unfeasibility and incongruity of his position. Put another way, the less the structure of Hollywood cinema seems to have room for his particular working methods and talent, the more he is needed by American culture.

References

Ambrose, Stephen E. (2001) *Band of Brothers*. London: Pocket Books.
Anon (1998) '*The Thin Red Line*: Movie Info'. Available at: http://www.foxmovies. com/thinredline/htmls/movie_info.html [Accessed: 5 January 2002]
_____ (1999) 'Alive and Kicking', *Sight and Sound*, 9, 12, 3.
Burns, Sean (2006) '*The New World*'. Available at: http://www.philadelphiaweekly. com/view.php?id=11418 [Accessed: 4 November 2006]
Flanagan, Martin (2004) '*The Hulk*, An Ang Lee Film: Notes on the Blockbuster Auteur', *New Review of Film and Television Studies*, 2:1, 19–35.
Foundas, Scott (2005) 'Back to the Garden'. Available at: http://www.laweekly.com/ film+tv/film/back-to-the-garden/26/ [Accessed: 5 November 2006]
Gritten, J. (1998) 'When the Going Got Tough'. Available at: http://www.scruf-fles.net/spielberg/movies/saving-private-ryan/saving_private_ryan_article_1.html [Accessed: 6 January 2002]
Handy, Bruce (1997) 'His own sweet time', *Time*, 150, 15, 92–99
Hoberman, J. (2005) 'Mr. and Mrs. Smith'. Available at: http://www.villagevoice. com/film/0551,hoberman,71140,20.html [Accessed: 5 November 2006]
_____ (2006) 'Paradise Now'. Available at: http://www.villagevoice.com/film/ 0610,hoberman,72427,20.html [Accessed: 10 November 2006]
Howell, Peter (2006) '*The New World*'. Available at: http://www.thestar.com/NASApp/ cs/ContentServer?pagename=thestar/Layout/Article_Type1&c=Article&cid=113

7754956176&call_pageid=1022183557980&col=1022183560753 [Accessed: 4 November 2006]

Irwin, Lew (ed.) (1999) 'Studio Briefing: Despite Oscar nods, *Thin*'s biz thins out'. Available at: http://www.imdb.com/SB?19990224#4 [Accessed 13 January 2002]

MacCabe, Colin (1999) 'Bayonets in Paradise', *Sight and Sound*, 9, 2, 10–14.

Macnab, Geoffrey (1999) 'Review: *The Thin Red Line*', *Sight and Sound*, 9, 3, 53–54.

Nathan, Ian (1999) 'Review: *The Thin Red Line*', *Empire*, 117, 16.

Romney, Jonathan (1999) 'Treading the *Line*'. Available at: http://www.guardian. co.uk/Archive/Article/0,4273,3834076,00.html [Accessed: 5 January 2002]

Rosenbaum, Jonathan (1999) 'Malick's Progress'. Available at: http://www.chireader. com/movies/archives/1999/0199/01159.html [Accessed: 5 January 2002]

Schatz, Thomas (1993) 'The New Hollywood', in Jim Collins, Hilary Radner & Ava Preacher Collins (eds) *Film Theory Goes to the Movies*. London: Routledge, 8–36.

Smith, Gavin (1999) 'Let There Be Light: *The Thin Red Line*', *Film Comment*, 35, 1, 8–11.

Sterritt, David (2006) 'Film, Philosophy and Terrence Malick', Undercurrent 2, July 2006. Available at: http://www.fipresci.org/undercurrent/issue_0206/sterritt_ malick.htm [Accessed: 5 November 2006]

Taubin, Amy (2006) 'Birth of a Nation', *Sight and Sound*, 16, 2, 44–5.

Taylor, Charles (1999) 'The Big Dead One'. Available at: http://www.salon.com/ent/ movies/reviews/1999/01/cov.08reviewa.html [Accessed: 13 January 2002]

Turan, Kenneth (1998) '*Red Line*: A Distant Epic'. Available at: www.calendarlive. com/top/1,1419,L-LATimes-Movies-X!ArticleDetail-5039,00.html [Accessed: 5 January 2002]

Whalen, Tom (1999) '"Maybe all men got one big soul": The Hoax Within the Metaphysics of Terrence Malick's *The Thin Red Line*', *Literature Film Quarterly*, 27, 3, 162–165.

Wildman, David (2006) '*The New World*: An Interview with Producer Sarah Green'. Available at: http://www.weeklydig.com/movies/articles/the_new_worldan_interview_with_producer_sarah_green [Accessed 9 November 2006]

CHAPTER ELEVEN

The Greatest Generation Steps Over
The Thin Red Line

John Streamas

On a tropical battlefield on Guadalcanal an American soldier holds gold teeth he has extracted from the mouths of dead Japanese soldiers. Our glimpse of this, in Terrence Malick's film *The Thin Red Line* (1998), is significant not because it adheres to its literary source – in James Jones's novel a sadistic Charlie Dale uses his new pliers toward 'one whole quart mason jar full of gold teeth as the beginning of his collection' (1998: 491) – but because it adheres to history. Memoirs and histories of the war recall scenes of a sadism that is peculiar to its Pacific combatants. Reporter Ernie Pyle, who covered the war in both Europe and Asia, wrote that Pacific battle was, on both sides, more savage: 'In Europe we felt that our enemies, horrible and deadly as they were, were still people ... But out here I soon gathered that the Japanese were looked upon as something subhuman and repulsive' (in Dower 1986: 78). Combat veteran and literary critic Paul Fussell titled an essay 'Thank God for the Atom Bomb' to declare his relief over the bomb's foreclosing his transfer from the European front to the Pacific, where he believed he would participate in an invasion of Japan and experience 'the unspeakable savagery of the Pacific war' (1988: 24). He cites examples of American soldiers' brutality – of their owning Japanese skulls, treating 'surrendering Japanese as handy rifle targets', extracting gold teeth from *living* Japanese – and, with the example of Americans carrying the 'charm' of a severed Japanese hand, concedes that these men 'would probably not have dealt that way with a German or Italian – that is, a "white person's" – hand' (1988: 25–6). Historian John W. Dower writes that in both the United States and Britain 'the Japanese were more hated than the Germans before as well as after Pearl Harbor', and he attributes this hatred to racism (1986: 8).

Our glimpse of the soldier's brutal desecration in Malick's film is, therefore, less brutal than the historical realities cited by Fussell. Yet the consensus among reviewers and critics seems to be that myth – not history – is Malick's dominant mode. Reviewers such as Roger Ebert (1999) and Susan Stark (1999) praise his moments of historical particularity such as the soldier's desecration, but they describe the film as a myth, noting its lyrical and contemplative qualities. Many admirers passively tolerate its atmospheric multiplicity of voices and its lush landscapes, or else they admire these as audiences admire fascinating but not compelling artistic experiments. But, like detractors, they often prefer the passages that adhere most closely to linear narrative and that look most like history. This tension between myth and history is important because the myth described by these critics and reviewers seems to be the very myth that, in the 1970s, informed anti-war films of Vietnam such as Francis Ford Coppola's *Apocalypse Now* (1979), and because *The Thin Red Line* is Malick's first film since the 1970s. To the extent that reviewers rightly notice Malick's lyricism and lushness, and to the extent that he succeeds in narrating human nature's ruination playing on the face of non-human nature, then *The Thin Red Line* is a myth that rejects historical analysis. Yet, because Malick also shrewdly uses particularities of the Pacific War to anchor some of his story in history, the problem posed by the film is a struggle between narrative modes: is myth or history better able to expose and resist the most brutal aspects of human nature? I argue that Malick prefers the mythic but that he is most persuasive when he invokes history. Moreover, his myth, deriving from the anti-war culture of the 1970s, is inadequate against the revived myth of the global war as the Good War.

If myth-making is the construction of grand narratives in the service of social agendas, then obviously, at various historical junctures, competing agendas will construct competing myths. Malick's myth was born in the 1970s, when mainstream American culture fused anti-Vietnam War politics with new racial or environmental narratives and produced movies such as *Apocalypse Now* and *The Deer Hunter* (1978). Thomas Doherty characterises these films as 'explorations of what was being called "the dark underside of the American soul"' and says they 'caught the cultural dislocation in the loss of a faith forged in 1941–45' (1999: 285). He argues that *The Thin Red Line* develops the position of those films: 'In ideology no less than topography, *The Thin Red Line* evokes the Vietnam combat genre … The taciturn Sergeant Welsh expresses the generic allegiance when he utters a line that is commonsensical in the Vietnam jungle but heretical in World War Two territory: "If you die, it's gonna be for nothing"' (1999: 314). Welsh says this to the film's central character, Private Witt, who subsequently looks up – characters in this film often look skyward, into the clouds or the moon or the distant tops of palm trees – and sees the full moon in the evening sky. Malick then shows the strange image of wild dogs pulling and chewing what appear, in the twilight, to be corpses of soldiers. Reviewers who complain about the indistinguishability of Malick's characters – charging that they 'are not well-developed as individual characters', that 'they look much alike' (Ebert 1999), and that 'they all speak the same generic, prettified ersatz poetry in the same generic, prettified ersatz Southern accent' (Hunter 1999) – understand the obvious point here of nature's obliviousness to the identities of the individual dead; but they neglect the larger and more important point – expressed not by Welsh but by Witt, and then mostly in voice-overs – of nature's indifference even to the individual living. A narrator says, 'War don't ennoble men. It turns them into dogs, poisons the soul'; and so, in this sense, war reinscribes nature's effacement of individual men, individual voices. That such opposites as the unchangeable paradise that is nature and the interchangeable hells that are war could effect the same effacements produces a tension at the heart of Malick's myth. In a scathing review essay, Tom Whalen observes that, as the men wage war, 'nature stays implacable, mysterious, grand. It's as if Malick wants us to reconsider or approach ingenuously the questions behind the Judeo-Christian myth of the Fall' (1999: 163). Whalen believes that Witt's question, 'Why does nature vie with itself?', represents Malick's own argument for seeking 'the source of ruin in nature rather than man' (ibid.). More likely, Malick fails to distance the film sufficiently from Witt's consciousness, to show that humans, having fallen, seek the source of their misery in the paradise from which they fell – except that they still inhabit, and even kill each other in, this paradise. In *The Thin Red Line*, as in *Apocalypse Now*, the jungle is both paradise and hell. Malick's myth is, then, as Whalen suggests, a reinvented myth of the Fall, filtered through a Vietnam-era political consciousness. Such a project contains internal contradictions, which will be discussed shortly.

While Malick was away, a competing myth arose – or, rather, was revived – and seized the American consciousness. This is the myth of the Good War, a narrative of World War Two in which the Allied nations achieved an unchallenged unity and patriotic pride in their fight against the pure evil of fascism. The curious timing of the release of Malick's film positions it therefore as either a shrewd corrective to the surging revival of America's Good War myth or else a luckless victim of the revival. Early admirers who likened it to anti-war films of the 1970s unwittingly diminished its prospects for commercial success. For by late 1998, when *The Thin Red Line* was released, Americans were forgetting the Bad War that was Vietnam, and their impetus was provided partly by the ageing of the generation that had fought the Good War. Also in 1998, Steven Spielberg's film *Saving Private Ryan* and Tom Brokaw's book *The Greatest Generation*, reaping more profits and awards than Malick's film, lifted the Good War to moral and political greatness and unassailability. For Spielberg, such greatness inhered in American individuals, for Brokaw in an American generation.

Idealised, the Good War resists historical analysis. *The Thin Red Line*, however, rejects idealisation even in its first lines. At the beginning of the film, Witt in voice-over asks, 'What's this war at the heart of nature?' None of the men and women profiled in Brokaw's book asks any such question – not in their old age, at least, when Brokaw celebrates them. If those who fought in combat asked these questions during the war, in such places as the Guadalcanal jungle, they probably asked silently, internally, which Malick realises by placing the questions in voice-overs. But these are questions that, when the war is over and the victory is celebrated, are swept into the farthest recesses of memory, not to be dredged up when celebrants such as Tom Brokaw come calling for stories of heroism and glory.

The Greatest Generation is the most problematic of several recent best-selling Good War revivalist books because it is the most nostalgic and reverential. Brokaw announces at the beginning his goal of extending his own 'small gesture of personal appreciation' to the World War Two generation (1998: vii). He privileges the local knowledge of individual experience and then deduces from that knowledge a grand generalisation that seems bold but is too vague to be subjected to historical analysis. For example, he recalls saying to a group of American veterans gathered for the fiftieth anniversary of D-Day that 'this is the greatest generation any society has ever produced'; he adds that, when challenged on this claim, he says, 'I have the facts on my side' (1998). What facts – and *whose* facts – prove greatness? Should it matter that, though Brokaw celebrates only Americans, only the continental US among all major combatants 'never experienced battle or destruction' (Jeffries 1996: 170)? Or that, among 'the more than 50 million humans who were killed by the war, fewer than 1 percent were Americans' (O'Brien & Parsons 1995: 3)?

Brokaw profiles 51 members of the greatest generation, persons who during the war 'all seemed to have a sense of purpose', of 'something greater connecting all of us' (1998: 11). That he really means 'all of us' is indicated by his earnest effort to tell the stories of wartime persons of colour, women and 'ordinary' Americans – though, significantly, a disproportionate number of his profiles celebrate famous politicians and media stars, almost all of them white and male. He fumbles Dorothy Haener's story, clumsily praising her as a 'seminal figure in the postwar women's movement' (1998: 99) even as he charges that her labour activism succeeded 'when she didn't single out women as an issue' (1998: 98). It is not enough to say that the war provided temporary work and wages for women. According to Brokaw, it also helped women even more than their best-known national organisation. And its benefits were permanent – as if the truly temporary phenomenon was the postwar retreat to male-governed domesticity and familialism. Brokaw would have us believe that women's empowerment owes more to a Good War created and waged by men than to women's own later activism. And he fares no better with racialised narratives: 'The war started the country on the road to long-overdue changes that finally came in the 1960s for women and blacks,' he writes, adding that 'the World War Two experience accelerated the solution in ways large and small' (1998: 386). Asians and Europeans whose homes were battlefields may be excused for laughing derisively at such a naïve and chauvinistic claim, in which Brokaw virtually thanks a global war for spawning national social movements. We need not situate Dorothy Haener against Korean 'comfort women' to compare degrees of pain, but Brokaw the journalist should know that a global war's effects on women must be regarded in all involved nations, not just his own.

The Greatest Generation aims so much praise at wartime unity and purpose that it becomes a bloodless, obsequious book. Whereas Paul Fussell in his memoir narrates in vivid detail the routine horrors of combat, Tom Brokaw in his celebration narrates abstract courage and honour with shallow awe. This is most telling when, near the end of his book, he creates a visual image that could almost come from Malick's film *Badlands* (1973). None of the historic events he has witnessed in Washington, DC, he says, 'moved me more than the sight of my uncle and his friend, a local farmer, walking among the headstones [of a South Dakota cemetery], framed by the wide steel-gray sky and the great curve of a prairie horizon, decorating the graves of the hometown veterans on … Memorial Day' (1998: 389).

In his acknowledgments, Brokaw says he was 'encouraged' by reading the memoirs of Fussell and William Manchester. But much of Fussell's book-length memoir *Wartime* is devoted to ridiculing both military incompetence and the idealisation of war, and Brokaw refuses to spoil his celebration with such unpleasant topics. He also turns away from the ugliness of the war, refusing even to consider its sanitising for public consumption. Fussell recalls that, even in the dispatches of John Steinbeck and Ernie Pyle, 'people at home were kept in innocence of malaria, dysentery, terror, bad attitude, and "psychoneurosis"' (1989: 286). Such innocence was still enforced long after the war, even after the Vietnam War, as in the popular 1977 photographic collection *Life Goes to War*, which shows no dismembered American bodies; and, of the three decapitated heads shown, 'all, significantly, are Asian' (Fussell 1989: 269). Recalling that during the American Civil War, poet Walt Whitman predicted that the 'real war will never get into the books', Fussell charges that during World War Two soldiers were driven to 'verbal subversion and contempt', as 'optimistic publicity and euphemism had rendered their experiences so falsely that it would never be readily communicable' (1989: 267–8).

In the novel of *The Thin Red Line*, Welsh surveys a platoon of soldiers pressed tight to the earth, fearing enemy fire and dreading their commander's orders to rise and charge again into the mortars:

> 2nd Platoon would make a great photograph to send back home, Welsh's eyes told him – without in the least disturbing his thinking – except that of course when the newspapers, government, army, and *Life* got ahold of it, it would be subtly changed to fit the needs of the moment and probably captioned: TIRED INFANTRYMEN REST IN SAFETY AFTER HEROIC CAPTURE OF POSITION. THE FIRST TEAM AT HALFTIME. BUY BONDS TILL IT HURTS YOUR ASSHOLE. (Jones 1998: 209)

Later, after a soldier named Train discovers a valuable Japanese sword – its hilt adorned with gold, ivory, rubies, 'emeralds, some small diamonds' – a Press Officer urges upon him the spectacle of a presentation of the sword as a trophy to a general: 'And think what a newsreel shot it will make … You'll have *your* face, and *your* voice, in every movie theatre across the nation' (Jones 1998: 346, 347, 348).

Crafting the Good War myth involved, then, more than euphemism and other verbal sleights. The 'real war' got into neither books nor visual imagery. Critic George H. Roeder, Jr. says, 'During the war the U.S. government, with extensive support from other public and private organisations, made the most systematic and far-reaching effort in its history to shape the visual experience of the citizenry' (1993: 2). That the film industry complied in this effort is the subject of the study *Hollywood Goes to War*, in which authors Clayton R. Koppes and Gregory D. Black, regarding together the government's propaganda bureau the Office of War Information (OWI) and the film industry, write: 'In the OWI/Hollywood vision, the war produced unity. Labour and capital buried their differences for a greater cause; class, ethnic and racial divisions evaporated in the foxholes and on the assembly line; even estranged family members were reconciled through the agency of war' (1990: 325). But compliance extended beyond the propaganda and image-making industries. Like Jones's fictional creations Welsh and Train, real-life soldiers such as Paul Fussell knew about the censorship and euphemism, and surely many Americans on the home front understood that a myth was being constructed about the war. Roeder writes that 'Americans were wary of attempts to control what they saw and what they thought', but he adds that the myth – during the war and since, and especially since the early 1990s, with the fiftieth anniversaries of its events and the ageing of its participants – 'fills a need', that it serves as a moral reference point: 'Most Americans believe that it affirmed that the United States can serve the cause of protecting human dignity, that it can get a job done, and that it is possible at least sometimes to see clearly the difference between good and evil in the amoral domain of international relations' (1993: 2–3). No such myth emerged during the 1960s and 1970s, and so, when war erupted in the Persian Gulf just as the Good War approached its golden anniversary, American leaders could promise 'no more Vietnams', meaning of course that verbal and visual reports from the new front would be sanitised again, and a new unity and moral purpose could be born of a revived myth.

It was in this time of revival that Tom Brokaw named the greatest generation. And it was also in this time that Terrence Malick created *The Thin Red Line*, a film more suited, as already suggested, to the culture of demythologising that characterised the 1970s. And yet the charge against Brokaw and other revivalists that they embrace a chauvinistic and childish acceptance of managed truths is also a charge that they reject historical analysis – a charge that might also be properly leveled against Malick. A myth's strength is inversely proportional to its capacity or even willingness to pass a test of historical scrutiny. This is not to privilege officially sanctioned history, which often enough conforms to such national myths as the Good War, as Jones's Captain Stein realises when he equates lies with 'the great conspiracy of history' (1998: 381). But the history of the peoples of a given place and time, massing together all their particularities, stands opposed to myth. If Malick's version of *The Thin Red Line* retells the myth of the Fall, and if it filters this myth through the political and demythologising vision of the 1970s, then it must resolve the internal struggle between the narrative modes of myth and history.

Stephen Hunter, who hates the film, regarding it as a jumble of bad philosophising and 'artsy photography', concedes that 'a small, good movie' is buried in the middle:

> This involves C-for-Charlie's adventures taking a grassy knoll called Hill 210 … Cleverly Malick does not show us the enemy for the longest time: instead, they are represented merely by their effects – streaks of tracer spurting off the ridge line, the random squall of mortar rounds incoming, the relentless body-piercings of the machine guns. (1999)

Detroit News reviewer Susan Stark, who likes the film, praises most its way of balancing its visual and philosophical aspects with 'a counterpoint of horrifying carnage' (1999). For film scholar Thomas Doherty, the film suffers for being 'more a meditation on nature than an evocation of war' (1999: 312). Yet Doherty, unlike the newspaper reviewers, addresses the issue of race in the Pacific War. Whereas wartime Hollywood constructed the Japanese in racialised stereotypes, as Koppes and Black amply demonstrate with such examples as *Little Tokyo, USA* (Otto Brower, 1942) and *Objective Burma* (Raoul Walsh, 1944), postwar Hollywood set few combat films in the Pacific, for, as Doherty writes, movies about 'Japanese villainy during World War Two make dubious exports into an increasingly lucrative Japanese market, where box-office rentals sweeten the dividends from North American theatres' (ibid.). It is with this in mind that Doherty suggests that either commercialism or revisionism dictates Malick's showing 'Japanese soldiers mainly as shadows in the grass or defeated victims of American war crimes' (ibid.). Either motive – or the likelier one recognised by Hunter, that Malick delays showing Japanese as a clever construction of dramatic tension – demonstrates the film's engagement with racial realities. Moreover, Doherty fails to note that, though the American's collecting of Japanese gold teeth is a revisionist racial reality, the film's first depiction of brutality is the image, no less a part of racial reality, of two mutilated American corpses. Also true to the realities of tragic errors that Paul Fussell recalls in sardonic anger, Sergeant Keck's mistake of throwing a grenade's pin rather than the grenade occasions no bleak satire or moral outrage. It is a regrettable episode in a seemingly unending procession of regrettable episodes. Reviewers prefer the particularities of these scenes, perhaps reasoning that, as a real battle was fought on the real island of Guadalcanal, Malick's dramatic particularities establish at least a relationship, however true or deviant, to history.

Malick suggests, however, that all violence is equally regrettable and that combat scenes need not accumulate in order to make their point. Similarly, men whose survival depends on their exclusive attention to a violent objective lose their particularities. In this way, *The Thin Red Line* raises a question that confronted anti-war protestors of the 1970s: is the protest pacifist, aimed at all wars, or is it aimed at this particular war? After the Vietnam War ends, *Apocalypse Now* answers with a probe into the darkest parts of human nature, those parts that make wars; but, by situating the southeast Asian jungle as the geographical embodiment of those parts, it retains some particularities of the anti-Vietnam War protests. *The Thin Red Line* attempts the same for World War Two, and both its leveling of all violent particularities as well as its brief engagement with racial realities suggest that it could sustain the effort, except that Malick must reckon with an opposing myth of a sort that Coppola, making *Apocalypse Now*, never faces. For no national myth arose from the Vietnam War. The brutal particularities of war might have been no worse in Vietnam than they had been in Guadalcanal, but no Good War narrative sanctioned their sanitising so that they might advance national unity and morality. Drawing upon Joseph Conrad's fiction and the history of Western imperialism in Asia, Coppola constructs a myth where no myth has existed before, and onto it he applies particularities of battle. Myth and history still clash within the world of the film, but at least Coppola's myth faces no Good War narrative. Malick's myth, meanwhile, though its reinventing of the Fall of human nature seems to draw from foundational narratives of Western culture, is doomed in any attempt to subvert the competing Good War myth. It forgets that Americans have been conditioned to *want* to believe in the Good War. Defeated even before it can engage the particularities of the film's sense of history, Malick's myth seems weak and ineffectual against the elderly heroes of Brokaw's greatest generation. Yet Malick, because he regards all wartime violence as equally deplorable, seems to prefer myth as a narrative mode better equipped than history to expose and resist the most brutal aspects of human nature. The owl, the crocodile, the bats, the snakes, the dogs and all the other wild beasts in the film are indifferent to the races and nationalities of the island's human combatants; but the film forgets that this war is the Good War, which reduces all the beasts' indifference to a mark of insignificance; and so the internal attempts of a soldier such as Witt to embrace their pre-lapsarian indifference, or what he often calls 'the light', seem too naïve and unrealistic. Malick may prefer myth, but in *The Thin Red Line* history prevails. Scenes of desecration and other particularities are his most persuasive claim against the dehistoricising myths of good wars and greatest generations.

I wish to examine last an aspect of Malick's film that, partaking of both of the narrative modes of myth and history, indicates the film's shortcomings and achievement. Though the story is set on Guadalcanal in the Solomon Islands, and though the battles there were crucial episodes in the Pacific War, few narratives of Pacific combat acknowledge the existence of its indigenous people. Lamont Lindstrom necessarily reminds us that the Pacific islands were invaded by both Japanese and Allied forces: 'These Islanders only occasionally appear and move across the narrative screen ... They were to enjoy coprosperity; they were victims to be saved from either European colonialism or evil Japanese empire; they were exotic and primitive jungle dwellers; and they were loyal allies in a good war' (2001: 108). Yet Tom Whalen, listing the differences between Jones's novel and Malick's film in a way that favours the novel, implies that Jones is wiser for having no native people in his story (1999: 163). His implied reason is voiced by Roger Ebert, who recalls that the film opens upon two AWOL soldiers living 'blissfully with tribal people who exist in a pre-lapsarian state' (1999). Surely the opening blend of lush images – of trees and beach and ocean with native children swimming and playing with stones, native women gathering plants for their baskets, native villagers singing and clapping – strongly suggests that Malick situates the islanders outside of history, in the realm of nature and myth. Wartime photographers of islanders, argues Lindstrom, construct them in one of six roles, the first of which is Exotic Savage: 'the savage in plumes and shells stands juxtaposed to uniformed servicemen ... The native is also like a child, and island children were favorite subjects for military photographers' (2001: 111). This role of Exotic Savage seems fitted to Malick's images of islanders. Even Thomas Doherty believes that 'the beauty of the lush foliage and the innocence of the noble Melanesian savages belie any intimation of a heart of darkness in the heart of nature' (1999: 312).

Yet I would argue that Malick tries to complicate his images of indigenous peoples, an effort that in his subsequent film, *The New World* (2005), even drives the central narrative. When Witt wonders why the islanders' children never fight, a native mother explains that in fact sometimes they do fight even as they seem to be playing. Late in the film, Witt returns to a village transformed – skulls sit on open shelves and people move in a violent agitation. The islanders are not outside history, after all, and Malick tries commendably to raise them above the plane of exoticised objects. The effort

History or myth?: complicating the role of the native in Guadalcanal

mostly fails. The lasting images, as reflected in critics' comments, are those that show the native people as Lindstrom's Exotic Savages. Still, Malick's willingness to show the islanders in both myth and history is a historically necessary response to the best-selling obfuscations of *The Greatest Generation*, in which Americans are the war's only participants worth noting.

In *The New World*, the colonising Englishmen call the indigenous people the 'Naturals', which has the effect not only of exoticising the natives but also of rendering the colonisers themselves as somehow unnatural. Glimpses of native children at play recall glimpses of islander children in *The Thin Red Line*, and John Smith's brief stay with the Indians recalls Witt's AWOL stay with the islanders. Perhaps a higher narrative consciousness is at work in *The New World*, conceding that Smith's image of pre-lapsarian natives is naïve and limited, and that both Captain Newport's sense of foreboding and John Rolfe's tentative romancing of Pocahontas are truer and more realistic. And yet again Malick makes his setting, even the Virginia swamp, into an Eden made sinful only with the encroachment of the colonisers, and Wagner's music swells as the film closes first on Rolfe's telling the story of Pocahontas's death and then on an image, looking upward, into the trees of the Virginia forest that, Smith claims, alone holds the only truth. Even at its noblest and most omnipotent, Malick's narrative consciousness remains the coloniser's, in which the Naturals cannot rise above their exoticisation. Malick struggles again, as in *The Thin Red Line*, to create an indigenous history out of the coloniser's mythmaking. But at least he engages the struggle.

A half-year before the release of *The Thin Red Line*, and just before the release of his own film *Saving Private Ryan*, Steven Spielberg wrote for a special issue of *Newsweek* an article on his childhood fascination with war movies, a fascination that sobered during the Vietnam War. He opens his last paragraph by saying, 'Of course every war movie, good or bad, is an anti-war movie' (1998: 68). Considering that he has just observed that, after Vietnam, realism 'was all that mattered' in war films, and that during World War Two Hollywood complied with the government's demand for one-sided visions of triumph, this closing claim seems naïve and even disingenuous. To do no more than show realistic images of brutality and violence, of dead and dying soldiers, is not enough to be anti-war, for it removes these images from history and therefore from the political and social causes of particular wars. In James Jones's novel, Sergeant Welsh, having just figured that the image of fearful soldiers clinging to the earth would be wilfully construed by *Life* as an image of soldiers at rest after a heroic capture of their enemy, realises with satisfaction that he has deceived the government by falsifying his first name and middle initial, so that, if he is killed, 'the government wouldn't have anybody to send a Regrets card to for him' (1998: 209). Jones writes a curious sentence to move from Welsh's first observation – of the soldiers on the ground – to his second: 'But all of this visual thinking had nothing to do with what Welsh was thinking on another, deeper level' (ibid.). Malick's film of Jones's book is about 'visual thinking' and this other, deeper thinking. He places history and myth on the visual level, but only myth abides on the deeper level, where it must stand alone, unfortified by history, against the dominant Good War myth. Steven Spielberg, regardless of whether he would judge *The Thin Red Line* a 'good or bad' war movie, would surely have to concede that it is more anti-war than his own film, for, unlike *Saving Private Ryan*, it opposes war by burrowing into those deeper levels – in history and, futilely, in myth – where all wars start.

References

Brokaw, Tom (1998) *The Greatest Generation*. New York: Random House.

Doherty, Thomas (1999) *Projections of War: Hollywood, American Culture, and World War II*, revised edition. New York: Columbia University Press.

Dower, John W. (1986) *War Without Mercy: Race and Power in the Pacific War*. New York: Pantheon.

Ebert, Roger (1999) Review of *The Thin Red Line*. *Chicago Sun-Times*, January. Available at: <http://www.suntimes.com/ebert/ebert_reviews/1999/01/ 010802.html> [Accessed: 22 June 2001]

Fussell, Paul (1988) '*Thank God for the Atom Bomb*' and Other Essays. New York, Summit.

_____ (1989) *Wartime: Understanding and Behavior in the Second World War*. New York: Oxford University Press.

Hunter, Stephen (1999) 'The thin long movie', *Washington Post*, 8 January 1999. Available at: <http://www.washingtonpost.com/wp-srv/style/movies/reviews/thin-redlinehunter.htm> [Accessed: 22 June 2001]

Jeffries, John W. (1996) *Wartime America: The World War II Home Front*. Chicago: Ivan R. Dees.

Jones, James (1998) [1962] *The Thin Red Line*. New York: Delta.

Koppes, Clayton R. & Gregory D. Black (1990) *Hollywood Goes to War: How Politics, Profits and Propaganda Shaped World War II Movies*. Reprint. Berkeley: University of California Press.

Lindstrom, Lamont (2001) 'Images of islanders in Pacific War photographs', in T. Fujitani, Geoffrey M. White & Lisa Yoneyama (eds) *Perilous Memories: The Asia-Pacific War(s)*. Durham, NC: Duke University Press, 107–128.

O'Brien, Kenneth P. & Lynn Hudson Parsons (eds) (1995) *The Home-front War: World War II and American Society*. Westport, CT: Greenwood.

Roeder Jr, George H. (1993) *The Censored War: American Visual Experience During World War Two*. New Haven, CT: Yale University Press.

Spielberg, Steven (1998) 'Of guts and glory', *Newsweek*, Special issue, Summer, 66–8.

Stark, Susan (1999) '"Thin Red Line" takes war to a stirring level'. *Detroit News*, 15 January. Available at: <http://detnews.com/1999/entertainment/0115/redline/redline.htm> [Accessed: 22 June 2001]

Whalen, Tom (1999) '"Maybe all men got one big soul": The hoax within the meta-physics of Terrence Malick's *The Thin Red Line*', *Literature/Film Quarterly* 27, 3, 162–6.

CHAPTER TWELVE

The Other World of War: Terrence Malick's Adaptation of The Thin Red Line

Stacy Peebles

When Terrence Malick's *The Thin Red Line* was released in the USA on 23 December 1998, it had already been foreshadowed by Stephen Spielberg's *Saving Private Ryan*, which came out almost five months earlier on 24 July 1998. Malick's film never acheived *Saving Private Ryan*'s popularity; at the 1999 Academy Awards, Oscars for Best Director, Best Cinematography, Best Film Editing and Best Sound all went to the earlier film. Both are World War Two films, but other than their shared subject matter and their coincidentally similar release dates, the stories that Spielberg and Malick chose to tell are very different. After *Saving Private Ryan*'s graphic opening sequence of the Normandy invasion, it assumes a familiar narrative, hearkening back to the type of war films that we have seen before: a ragtag group of soldiers from ethnically and geographically diverse backgrounds set out on a seemingly impossible mission, along the way overcoming obstacles both external and internal to that group, and ultimately complete the mission that they have grown to believe in. *The Thin Red Line* contains many of the same elements, and yet audiences failed to recognise them, and critics such as Janet Maslin of *The New York Times* claimed that the movie was too long and too confusing to be a good war movie or even a good movie, period (1998: E1).

This dismissive reaction may stem from the fact that in the making of his war film Malick drastically changes the boundaries of that familiar genre, expanding and elaborating upon the classic genre elements until the end result becomes almost unrecognisable as such. This chapter will explore the ways that *The Thin Red Line* transcends the war film genre, in doing so examining Malick's adaptation of James Jones' 1962

novel and the effect of his dramatic excision of the book's bodily and sexual themat-
ics to emphasise instead the transcendental soul; it will also consider director Andrew
Marton's 1964 adaptation of the novel which is both a bridge between Jones and
Malick as well as a classic example of a war genre piece.

Jones' novel centres around the campaign for Guadalcanal, and the soldiers in
C-Company who are ordered to overtake a complex of hills nicknamed The Dancing
Elephant and later push through to a beach village that the soldiers call Boola Boola.
In the last section of the novel, C-Company's replacement commander makes a stupid
error that results in the death of a great number of the company, although most of the
main characters survive. Marton and Malick both alter characters' names, actions and
the final events of the novel, and beyond that each of the three storytellers choose different aspects of the war experience to highlight. For Jones, this experience is undeniably corporeal: he explores in great detail both the graphic violence of combat as well
as the soldier's sexual or ecstatic response to that violence. The body is overwhelmingly
present in the novel and somewhat of a focus in the first adaptation. Malick, however,
effectively subtracts the body from this war story, and an examination of a few representative moments reveals what a substantial subtraction this proves to be.

It is clear from the first pages of *The Thin Red Line* that Jones' novel will not be
a romantic or sentimental story, and further that any beautiful or elegant image will
be subverted by some form of obscenity. After a description of the lovely view of the
island, two soldiers reflect: '"So this is Guadalcanal," a man at the rail said, and spat
tobacco juice over the side. "What the fuck you think it was? Fucking Tahiti?" another
said' (1998: 2). The later scenes of combat make this figurative violence literal, and
often graphically so. Two scenes stand out as particularly visceral, and they occur in
quick succession in the novel. During the push for The Dancing Elephant, C-Company sends out small platoons of men to overtake the Japanese-held bunkers. In one
platoon, Sergeant Keck in the excitement pulls out a grenade from his pack, but mis-
takenly by its pin. Realising that it will explode, he leaps back and sits against a dirt
hummock to shield the others from the blast. It is a heroic move, but the results are
neither heroic nor dignified: 'His entire right buttock and part of his back had been
blown away. Some of his internal organs were visible, pulsing busily away, apparently
going about their business as if nothing had happened. Steadily, blood welled in the
cavity' (1998: 240). Keck's final, self-effacing words are 'What a fucking recruit trick
to pull.' He dies, and the men quickly turn to other concerns. Just a few pages later,
Private Tella is gut-shot while in exposed territory, and starts to scream horrifically.
Jones describes his wounds in detail:

> He had been hit squarely in the groin with a burst of heavy MG fire which
> had torn his whole belly open. Lying on his back, his head uphill, both hands
> pressed to his belly to hold his intestines in, he was inching his way back up
> the slope with his legs. Through the glasses Stein could see blue-veined loops of
> intestine bulging between the bloodstained fingers. (1998: 242)

One medic is shot and killed trying to quiet his screaming, and finally Welsh manages
to dart out to him and administer a lethal dose of morphine.

A classic example of the war genre: Andrew Marton's *The Thin Red Line* (1964)

In this campaign for Guadalcanal, and in combat generally, the body becomes almost hyperreal, its extreme vulnerability painfully apparent as its internal surfaces are suddenly on display for the uninjured to observe and contemplate. It can be literally turned inside out, as these scenes attest, and Jones dwells in this liminal space between survival and oblivion, the internal and the external. Mikhail Bakhtin discusses these qualities in his discussion of the carnivalesque,[1] and elements of the grotesque, the carnal and the carnival appear throughout Jones' novel. When a small group of men enter the jungle to explore after the company's first bivouac, they come upon a mass grave of Japanese soldiers, and Jones includes an explicitly Bakhtinian reference: '[a] curious Rabelaisian mood swept over them leaving them immoderately ribald and laughing extravagantly' (1998: 73). They proceed to desecrate the bodies and search for souvenirs, and Corporal Queen decides to pull one of them out by the leg. The task proves much more difficult than he anticipated, and as he strains to extract it Jones calls the scene 'some mad, comically impure travesty of the Resurrection,' just as Bakhtin refers to carnival as the obscene, base reversal of religious ceremony (1998: 76).

In this sphere where existence is focused so completely on the physical self, the soldiers' responses to their situations are often sexual. Obviously in this kind of all-male environment it is natural that thoughts or conversation turn to women back home, whether those references are reverent or obscene. But Jones writes more frankly about this incredible sexual energy and its different outlets. One such outlet is circumstantial homosexuality, and characters such as Fife, Bead and Doll all pursue homosexual union. More often, however, these sexual energies find expression in other, more potentially troubling ways, and this other expression is one of the most striking and memorable aspects of Jones' novel. Jones writes of characters' sexual arousal from observing or experiencing combat, or in some cases from killing other men. This excitement can stem from viewing a dead body, from successfully averting enemy fire, or from murdering an enemy soldier, and it suffuses the novel from beginning to end. When the group of men encounters the mass grave in the jungle, they also find a bloody shirt, which for many of them is the first physical evidence of the killing that they will soon be part of. As they look at the piece of fabric, 'there was a peculiar tone of sexual excitement, sexual morbidity, in all of the voices – almost as if they were voyeurs behind a mirror watching a man in the act of coitus; as though in looking openly at the evidence of this unknown man's pain and fear they were unwillingly perhaps but nonetheless uncontrollably seducing him' (1998: 66). Later, they feel a corresponding guilt, as if they had been 'caught masturbating together' (1998: 69). Similarly, Bead associates his guilt for killing a Japanese soldier with memories of his mother beating him up for masturbating (1998: 179); and when Doll kills his first Japanese, he reflects that it is an experience that 'required extra tasting. Like getting screwed the first time' (1998: 204). Sex and violence, then, are not simply two different graphic elements of this novel, but two sides of the same coin. It is perhaps Bell that best articulates this idea, as his longing, sexual thoughts of his wife gradually turn to a broader consideration of sex in general. 'Could it be that *all* war was basically sexual?' he wonders. 'Not just in psych theory, but in fact, actually and emotionally? A sort of sexual perversion? Or a complex of sexual perversions? That would make a funny thesis and God help the race' (1998: 286).

A dark carnival of the sexual and the grotesque, Jones' novel takes these soldiers' monistically inseparable minds and bodies through what Captain Stein sarcastically refers to as 'the long-awaited, soul-illuminating experience of combat' (1998: 338). They may become much more familiar with the disturbing workings of their minds and bodies, but hardly their souls, which lie tamped down somewhere below the incapacitating fear and sexual ecstasy of combat. Though Marton's 1964 adaptation is not as detailed, it admirably attempts to convey something of the novel's tone. While the violence is relatively standard for a film of this time, with few truly graphic images, the sexual element is interestingly translated. Fife and Doll have a very close relationship in the film, and Fife is figured as effeminate; he fusses over Doll like a mother hen, and when the company successfully takes Boola Boola, they celebrate by dressing Fife up in women's clothing from a trunk they find. He dons a kimono, turban, bra, stockings and even makeup, willingly at first and then with increasing discomfort at the other men's enthusiastic reactions. The men chant, 'Take it off! Take it off!' and treat Fife uncannily as they would a showgirl, grabbing at him and trying for kisses. Soon after this, they are attacked by Japanese and Fife is killed, still wearing his come-hither costume.

Even more interesting are several scenes that draw obvious connections between sex and war or murder. When Doll kills his first Japanese, we see a close-up of his face as he chokes the soldier, and he screams in high-pitched, almost orgasmic gasps; Welsh happens upon the encounter, and voyeuristically smiles as though catching Doll in the sexual act. Doll will later dream of this moment in concert with images of his wife, and we see the same shot of his screaming face superimposed upon images of the couple in bed. Later, when Welsh kneels to administer the morphine to Tella, the soldier screams out 'More! More!' in a parody of sexual union, and then slumps in seeming bliss as the drug kicks in. And in the final minutes of the film, Doll shoots a Japanese soldier while in a close, intimate embrace, after which the man slumps post-coitally on top of him.

Again, the sexual material is not as prevalent or as graphic as Jones describes, but this carnal connection of combat and sexuality is still undeniably present, effectively translating part of this essential element of Jones' novel and his description of the experience of war. Malick's decision to completely excise the body from this war story, then, is a drastic one that alters both the content and thematics of the narrative. Action similar to that in the novel takes on a completely different tone; Keck sits on the grenade, but we see no damage, as the camera keeps it just out of the frame. We also see little of Tella's wounds, only enough to know that they are serious and mortal, and Malick relies more on the characters' expressions to tell the story. Similarly, his cries for 'more' are plaintive and sad, punctuated by a soft 'goodbye' when Welsh rises to leave. Bell's sunlit memories of his wife are sensual without being overtly sexual, as the images consistently fade or change just before any real sexual details or nudity would be shown. Bell's fear of cuckoldry is absent here, and instead he thinks of her solely in lyrical terms: 'One being. Flow together like water. Till I can't tell you from me. I drink you. Now. Now.' The body is simply not as much of a concern for Malick, and although Jones may be rather unique in giving the body such a powerful and disturbing starring role, its near-total absence in a film about war – which, after all, is by definition the maiming and killing of men – is very surprising, at times jarring. So, if Malick shifts the body from centre stage, where Jones very deliberately placed it, then what takes its place?

Essentially, the soul that is so nearly obliterated in Jones' narrative comes to the fore, although it is by no means a strictly Christian one. While much of the story's plot and dialogue is drawn from the novel, all of the extensive voice-over is Malick's own addition, and it is here that the focus on the 'soul' becomes apparent. Most of the voice-over is Witt's, the character who undergoes the greatest changes from novel to adaptation. In the book he is a small, thin Kentuckian who joins and abandons the company five different times. He is not educated, and though he is dedicated in some way to the men in C-Company, he is not a particularly appealing character; Fife reflects at one point that 'there was something oddly snakelike about Witt at certain times such as this – like a coiled rattler ready to strike and certain it is right and … completely satisfied in its own tiny mind' (1998: 107). At one happy moment he nearly hugs Stein, but restrains himself because 'it might have looked faggoty' (1998: 324). He 'hated niggers because they all wanted to vote' and Jones describes him as having a 'peanut head' and 'the eyes of some ferretlike animal' (1998: 442).

Wholly absent in Marton's film, in Malick's version Witt emerges as the protagonist. The spontaneous and rather petty company-hopping he undertakes in the book is presented in the film as the wanderings of a free spirit; his musings are poetic, hardly the thoughts of a prejudiced, small-minded flake. He is played by Jim Caviezel, who is far from ferretlike, and his character is given to beatific half-smiles whether looking at water dripping off a leaf or at a comrade dying from a painful wound. Malick uses Witt's character to make the most significant thematic changes in his adaptation, and his ideas as well as those of the film as a whole echo Ralph Waldo Emerson's *Nature*, his first major work and the manifesto of transcendentalism. 'Philosophically considered,' Emerson states, 'the universe is composed of Nature and the Soul,' (1836: 3) and he sermonises that through isolated communion with nature, one can achieve a communal spirituality:

> Standing on the bare ground – my head bathed by the blithe air and uplifted into infinite space – all mean egotism vanishes. I become a transparent eyeball; I am nothing; I see all; the currents of the Universal Being circulate through me; I am part or parcel of God. (1836: 6)

For Emerson as well as for Witt, and also Malick, nature and spirituality are inextricably intertwined. Witt is capable of pausing even in the midst of chaos and contemplating the shape of a leaf or the trajectory of a drop of water; in fact, if there were no voice-over, we would hardly hear him speak during the course of the film. He exists comfortably and serenely in nature, and strives to actualise the spiritual connection he feels with his fellow soldiers as well as the native children of the area and captured Japanese men: 'Maybe all men got one big soul,' he muses, 'where everybody's a part of it. All faces of the same man, one big self. Everyone looking for salvation by themself. He's like the coal drawn from the fire.' Welsh, Witt's ideological opposite, tells Witt that 'in this world, a man himself is nothing. And there ain't no world but this one,' but Witt will counter him on both points. On the latter, he responds, 'You're wrong there, Top. I seen another world,' and indeed through his eyes the Guadalcanal campaign does look dramatically different; though Malick enters the consciousness of other characters in the film, he always returns to Witt, and the film's images are invariably framed the way that Witt would see them – quiet, calm and untainted. The transcendentalists believed that the world of nature was the spiritual realm, and that no additional heavenly plane existed, but Emerson also writes that 'few adult persons can see nature … The lover of nature is he whose inward and outward senses are truly adjusted to each other; who has retained the spirit of infancy even into the era of manhood' (1836: 5–6). Thus Witt's 'other world' is not the Christian's idea of a distant heaven, but instead the world around him, the world that Welsh, aged beyond his years, cannot see.

In a striking departure from Jones' novel, the film ends as Witt voluntarily distracts a group of Japanese soldiers so that his own company will be saved. Emerson and Thoreau would be proud; Witt takes a nonconformist action that both asserts his own individuality and affirms his connection to humanity. Immediately after he is shot, we see scenes of light filtering through trees and of Witt swimming, his character again associated with this profound affiliation with nature. We hear his voice-over a few minutes later, and he has become the transparent eyeball: 'Oh my soul, let me be in you now. Look out through my eyes. Look out at the things you made. All things shining.' This almost exactly restates Emerson's own words in another essay titled 'The Over-Soul': 'We see the world piece by piece, as the sun, the moon, the animal, the tree; but the whole, of which these are the shining parts, is the soul' (1841: 237). Coupled with his ubiquitous voice-over and narrative prominence, this heroic and redemptive action makes Witt the clear protagonist, and thus makes his transcendent soul – which, after all, is also all humanity's – the centre of the film. 'Nature is made to conspire with the spirit to emancipate us' (1836: 26) Emerson writes, and here nature and the spirit are embodied in Witt, who emancipates his fellow soldiers from some of the chaos of war, and, through his perspective, perhaps the viewer as well.[2]

If Malick's film emancipates us in some way from the vulnerable confines of the body and the madness of war – and war films – then what kind of movie is this that blends the battle for the Pacific theatre with Emersonian meditations? Contrasting Malick's version with Marton's is again helpful here, since in many ways the earlier film is a much more typical World War Two movie. Here, Welsh the cynical veteran is set against Doll, the green soldier who vows to think for himself during the war in order to get back to his wife in one piece. After Doll kills his first Japanese, Welsh offers advice that might be fatherly if it were not so cold and nihilistic: 'So now you know there aren't any heroes. Just guys who get so scared they go crazy and kill ... Look kid, that Jap was just a hunk of meat. A hunk of meat. Now, you remember that.' As the film progresses, the two forge a grudging partnership, even as Welsh grows increasingly concerned with Doll's willingness to take reckless chances and embrace the dangers of combat. In the assault on The Dancing Elephant, which here is a cliff perforated with caves, Welsh tries to hold Doll back from a seemingly suicidal charge. 'You're crazy, Doll! Crazy!' he shouts. 'Yeah, if that was a word', Doll dully responds. In the caves, Doll goes on a killing spree, mowing down enemy soldiers, but fails to see one of them who tries to shoot him. Welsh throws himself in front of Doll and takes the bullet. 'Welsh! Why? Why did you do it?' Doll asks, cradling the older man in his arms. Welsh responds tiredly, 'Because I'm stupid. What's the matter, kid? It's only meat.' He then dies.

Here we see many of the classic war story elements: the reluctant partnership, the successful mission, the heroic sacrifice. These kinds of characteristics have been discussed in detail by genre critics, who work to group narratives into recognisable categories. Genre itself of course is a slippery term, and as a grouping mechanism can refer to anything from the setting to the occupation of the main character to the creator of the story. Stanley Solomon has defined genre in film as 'the recognisable ordering of narrative patterns to produce related experiences from film to film' (1976: v), and Stuart Kaminsky also notes that these narrative patterns may have deeper roots in folk tales, myth and archetypes, which may account for their popularity (1985: 2–3). Finally, Thomas Doherty gives the best working definition of genre, while also noting the similarity to archetype and myth: 'Peering into the animal memory of mankind, Carl Jung saw myth as "the history we already know". Genre is the movie we've already seen' (1993: 86).

The war film genre is an extremely broad one and thus Solomon calls it 'the most difficult of all genres to define ... the subject incorporates attitudes towards war, responses, preparations, results, aftermaths, and so on' (1976: 243). The most common and obvious subgenre of the war film is the combat film, which takes as its subject the actual theatre of war, but as Solomon notes offshoots include the prisoner-of-war film, the special-mission film and the war-in-the-air film. There are also anti-war films, which are distinguished because they 'operate mainly in a realistic mode that serves to deglamorise the romantic elements associated with fighting for a cause, for freedom, or for the attainment of noble or heroic ends' (1976: 252); the classic of this subgenre is *All Quiet on the Western Front* (Lewis Milestone, 1930). And finally, there are the great number of movies which take war not as their focal point, but as a backdrop; these include classics like *Gone With the Wind* (Victor Fleming, 1939), *Casablanca* (Michael Curtiz, 1942) and *The African Queen* (John Huston, 1952). Kaminsky and Solomon each identify the characteristics or narrative patterns that make up the classic combat genre film, which include a sense of the mission at hand and a need for committed response, the depiction of a successful strategy, a stark and open landscape, and the development of a unity within the combat group that can withstand the chaos of war (Kaminsky 1974: 229; Solomon 1976: 245–7). If we consider these the basic building-blocks of the typical combat narrative, then we can start to classify these three war stories.

The 1964 version of *The Thin Red Line* perfectly fits the bill. Doll and Welsh overcome their dislike of one another to join together and almost single-handedly take The Dancing Elephant, which is described by Colonel Tall as the crucial objective for Guadalcanal and therefore could be 'the turning point of the war'. Here the Elephant looks remarkably like the desert Southwest, rather than the tropics, and the two men even practice a little impromptu rock climbing during their final push. When Welsh makes his sacrifice for Doll, the soldier that he has, in his own way, nurtured and then saved, he refers to himself as a stupid hunk of meat; the film obviously intends that we think the opposite, however, in the same way that we accept Witt's sacrifice in Malick's film as right and proper. In this final scene, any cynicism about the futility of war is undercut by Welsh's final humanistic and ultimately nationalistic action.

In Jones' novel, however, that cynicism is ubiquitous and unrelenting, and makes for a very different story. While Kaminsky and Solomon speak specifically about film, the generic criteria are also easily applicable to literature. The original *The Thin Red Line* does not meet them – it is a different kind of narrative, one that like the anti-war film strives to deglamorise combat. The jungle is hot, wet and impossible, and when the men happen upon a beautiful view or image, it is described as being cruelly so; the men watch a 'diabolically' lovely sunset and later have to 'endure' a brilliantly clear night (1998: 158, 291). Welsh's cynical view of life is one that many of the men will come to accept: 'Politics amused him, religion amused him, particularly ideals and integrity amused him; but most of all, human virtue amused him. His did not believe in it, and he did not believe in any of those other words' (1998: 24). The overt antagonism within the company only seems to increase as the novel unfolds, and no one manages to see any kind of 'greater good' in the chaos and mess that they have to endure. 'It was not heroic', Jones asserts. 'It was merely undignified' (1998: 90).

Jones takes this subgenre a step further, however, and creates a narrative that is not just anti-war, but also anti-war-*film*, writing specifically against the kinds of war movies that might meet Kaminsky's requirements. Repeatedly throughout the novel characters compare their own experiences with fictional ones. When Welsh dashes out to give Tella the lethal dose of morphine, he denies the gruesome reality of it by fitting it mentally into an already-written script – specifically, the classic World War Two film *The Sands of Iwo Jima*:

> It had no reality to Welsh. Tella was dying, maybe it was real to Tella, but to Welsh it wasn't real, the blueveined intestines, and the flies, the bloody hands, the blood running slowly from the other, newer wound in his chest whenever he breathed, it had no more reality to Welsh than a movie. He was John Wayne and Tella was John Agar. (1998: 250)

Though they may be able to reference these fictions for psychological distance in times of crisis, the complete disjunct between onscreen war and real war is also cause for deep anger. The characters are acutely aware of this genre, and the status of their own narratives outside of that sphere. Bell perfectly articulates this anger, and reflects on what he finally thinks of art:

> If this were a movie, this would be the end of the show and something would be decided. In a movie or novel they would dramatise and build to the climax of the attack. When the attack came in the film or novel, it would be satisfying. It would decide something. It would have a semblance of meaning and a semblance of an emotion … Even if the hero got killed, it would still make sense. Art, Bell decided, creative art – was shit. (1998: 237)

Through Bell, Jones aligns himself not just against gung-ho war fictions, but essentially against war fictions as a whole, whether their ultimate message is pro- or anti-war. He even criticises his own effort in the last sentence of the novel: 'One day one of their number would write a book about all this, but none of them would believe it, because none of them would remember it that way' (1998: 510). Jones chooses to tell his war story much in the same way that Tim O'Brien (1990) writes about Vietnam, questioning the validity of memory and moral truth.

If Marton and Jones respectively create a genre and an anti-genre narrative, then Malick's adaptation occupies an entirely different position on the spectrum. All of the elements of a classic combat genre narrative are unquestionably present in Malick's film, but that presence is not represented or realised as one may expect. Malick takes these elements and intensely elaborates upon them, thus creating something profoundly different. He 'fulfills all the requirements' of a combat film, so to speak, but does so in such a baroque manner that the end result becomes more than the sum of its parts.

To begin with the most immediately striking characteristic of the film, Malick uses landscape as much more than a blank canvas upon which to place his showdown between good and evil. Instead of a bombed-out, ravaged plain that distantly reflects the soldier's haunted thoughts, here the lush setting leaps immediately to the foreground. Malick pauses repeatedly to show us perfectly-framed still lifes of flora and fauna, and even the grassy fields of battle shimmer serenely. Different characters are associated with the natural elements: Witt is associated primarily with the water he often contemplates and happily swims in; Staros prays to a candle flame or fire, and his name also suggests a kind of heavenly blaze; and Welsh makes himself out 'like a rock' and insists that there is no other world, 'just this rock'. Images of animals or vegetation provide pauses between scenes of combat or struggle, and the last shot of the film interestingly resembles the calm lines of a Japanese brush painting. The landscapes are anything but stark, and their beauty seems capable at times of consuming all the ugliness of battle.

The combat film's typical presentation of grudging but productive comradeship is also translated here into a more spiritual concern with universal unity. In the 1964 *The Thin Red Line*, Welsh and Doll's partnership leads to mutual respect and the successful invasion of a key enemy stronghold; it will help win the war. Through Witt's eyes, however, we see a brotherly love and desire for unity that transcends the rules of combat. He treats captured Japanese soldiers with humanity, and insists that he still 'sees a spark' in Welsh despite Welsh's denial of what he calls the 'beautiful light'. This human connection, far from being simply a pragmatic necessity for survival and success, is instead universal, transcendent and not bound by the corporeal self.

Early in the film, Witt remembers his mother on her deathbed, and in considering the possibility of his own death, thinks, 'I just hope I can meet it the same way she did, with the same kind of calm. Cause that's where it's hidden. The immortality I hadn't seen.'[3] Later, when we find out what happens to Witt, this moment stands out as something of a mission statement. The military mission of the novel, to overtake the Elephant and Boola Boola, is something the men strive for because they have no choice; no one, not even Tall, wants to complete the mission because of a burning patriotic fervor, but out of fear. In Malick's film, Witt's desire for calm and immortality are the real quest, because he seeks them for himself and also for the group; as he says, a man seeking salvation alone is like a 'coal drawn from the fire'. Welsh strongly counters him and asks, 'what difference do you think you can make, one single man, in the middle of all this madness? If you die, it's going to be for nothing.' In the end, however, Witt proves him wrong.

When the company is in a vulnerable position and their lines of communication have been cut, 1st Lieutenant Band orders Fife and Coombs to scout and see how close the enemy are. Witt steps up and offers to go along, saying that he wants to be there 'in case something bad happens'. The three scouts move upriver and sight a large number of Japanese who shoot Coombs. Witt sends Fife back to the company to warn them, sets Coombs up to float downstream to safety, and then leads the Japanese away from the company's position. 'They're coming. Let it go. I don't want you to be afraid', he tells Coombs quietly before leaving him. His mission is successful, both physically and metaphysically. His decoy plan works and he is killed, saving the company. On one level, Witt's action is simply a successful ploy for ensuring the safety of his company and perhaps aiding the campaign for Guadalcanal. In Malick's hands, however, it is much more than a political or nationalistic action; instead, it is a philosophical exertion of his will, and an attainment of the immortality he wondered about earlier. The final image of the seed plant is perfectly balanced, and emphasises the harmony that Witt has achieved for himself and for the other men.

Jones' novel tells a story about the dirty realities and physicalities of war that rather furiously resists the 'terrible lies' of film fictions, while Marton's adaptation presents exactly that kind of fiction, in perfect adherence to the Hollywood aplomb of combat genre films. Malick, however, takes a different direction. He preserves the basic plot of Jones' novel, but upon that foundation builds an entirely unique story; he recreates the genre characteristics with such elaboration and emphasis that they are no longer characteristics of that genre. It is a war film that, ultimately, is no longer about war; appropriately, it *transcends* the genre. In fact, we might better classify Malick's *The Thin Red Line* with his other films, *Badlands* (1973), *Days of Heaven* (1978) and *The New World* (2005), in a genre defined by the auteur rather than by related subject matter. What the definitive pieces of the Malick puzzle might be and what narrative patterns draw his own films together are questions that this volume as a whole may begin to answer.

Notes

1   See Bakhtin's *Rabelais and His World* (1968) for the full explanation of this theory.
2   Malick's philosophical interests are also reflected in his choice of soundtrack. Charles Ives' *The Unanswered Question* is used heavily in the film, and Ives had a strong interest in transcendentalism. His piano sonata *Concord, Mass., 1845* is intended to convey impressionistic portraits of Emerson and Thoreau, and Ives also wrote 'Essays Before a Sonata' to explain his transcendentalist references in detail.
3   This quote is again not drawn from Jones' novel, but is an altered version of a passage from the second novel in Jones' World War Two trilogy, *From Here to Eternity*: 'He only hoped that he would meet it [death] with the same magnificent indifference with which she who had been his mother met it. Because it was there, he felt, that the immortality he had not seen was hidden' (1951: 19).

References

Bahktin, Mikhail (1984) [1968] *Rabelais and His World*. Bloomington: Indiana University Press.
Doherty, Thomas (1993) *Projections of War: Hollywood, American Culture, and World War II*. New York: Columbia University Press.
Emerson, Ralph Waldo (1836) *Nature*, in *The Selected Writings of Ralph Waldo Emerson* (1992) New York: Modern Library, 264–377.
_____ (1841) 'The Over-Soul', in *The Selected Writings of Ralph Waldo Emerson*. (1992) New York: Modern Library, 236–251.
Ives, Charles (1920) 'Essays Before a Sonata', in *Essays Before a Sonata: The Majority and Other Writings*. (1999) New York: W. W. Norton and Co., 3–104.
Jones, James (1998) [1951] *From Here to Eternity*. New York: Delta Publishing.
_____ (1991) [1962] *The Thin Red Line*. New York: Delta Publishing.
Kaminsky, Stuart M. (1985) *American Film Genres: Approaches to a Critical Theory of Popular Film*, second edition. Chicago, Nelson Hall.
Maslin, Janet (1998) 'Beauty and Destruction in Pacific Battle', *The New York Times*,

23rd January, E1.

O'Brien, Tim (1990) *The Things They Carried.* Boston: Houghton Mifflin.

Solomon, Stanley J. (1976) *Beyond Formula: American Film Genres.* New York: Harcourt Brace Jovanovich.

CHAPTER THIRTEEN

Terrence Malick, Landscape and 'What is this war in the heart of nature?'

Robert Silberman

The appearance of Terrence Malick's *The Thin Red Line* in 1998 after a hiatus of more than two decades left no doubt about one aspect of the director's achievement and personal style in the cinema: the central importance of landscape and the natural world.

The film begins with a shot of a crocodile and a voice asking, 'What is this war in the heart of nature?' That war obviously extends to human society as well. For Malick, humanity balances on the edge between reason and irrationality, comedy and tragedy, fairytale adventure and deadly conflict, faith in moral values and nihilism. Landscape is important in Malick's films not only because of the possibilities for visual splendor, but because the director's ideas are expressed through his representation of nature.

In *Badlands* (1973) the youthful duo, Kit and Holly, proceed in classic road-movie fashion, fleeing across the Great Plains after Kit shoots Holly's father, a former co-worker and perhaps a couple whose fate is not shown. Among the possessions removed from the house Holly shared with her father and installed in the makeshift Swiss Family Robinson-style abode where Kit and Holly set up housekeeping by a river is a Maxfield Parrish print. A typical Parrish image of the Golden Age, it was an appropriate bit of décor for Holly and her father's home, an old-fashioned gingerbread confection. In the riverside hideout, in spite of its unusual status as a pastoral image brought to a pastoral setting, it suggests the overall framework that governs Malick's treatment of landscape and cinematic narrative. All four of Malick's films feature landscapes that provide appropriate backdrops for a movement from innocence to experience haunted by a dream of Paradise.

That could be overlooked in *Badlands*, where the action is low-key when not punctuated by violence, and the narrative becomes romantic only in rare moments, as when the couple dance in the car headlights to Nat King Cole's 'A Blossom Fell'. The flatness of the landscape matches the flatness of Kit and Holly's delivery and the generally deadpan tone; the film is an offbeat ode to a particular kind of American emptiness and moral emptiness. The magic of the world appears in escapist fantasies identified with the mountains of Montana that lurk on the horizon like a mirage, or the Parrish print with its glowing, Arcadian imagery. Such visions are repeatedly undercut, as in Holly's disarming realisation: 'Suddenly I was thrown into a state of shock. Kit was the most trigger-happy person I had ever met.' Yet the sense of romance lingers, like the reverberating lyricism of the musical score.

Days of Heaven (1978) opens with a montage sequence that includes two H. H. Bennett photographs from the Wisconsin Dells. One shows a pair of men paddling into a cavern by the river; the other, the photographer's young son leaping across a gap to a pillar of rock. These images are characteristic of Bennett's enterprise, which John Szarkowski has described as making 'essentially the same picture … a fairy-story landscape, rugged and wild in half-scale, with enchanted miniature mountains and cool dark grottos. Almost invariably he included in his picture a human figure: a picnicker, in but not quite of the landscape, and yet with friendly feeling toward it. It was a portrait of the American discovering the poetic uses of the wilderness' (1973: 44).

Malick's use of the Bennetts, like his use of the Parrish, indicates his preoccupation with the pastoral. Yet the action of *Days of Heaven* begins with an anti-pastoral: the urban industrial nightmare of the early twentieth century. The flight from city to country after Bill attacks a steel mill foreman is an attempted escape, but ends badly. Once again, the movement toward an idyllic isolation is presented as a move into a timeless realm, but history re-enters in the symbolic form of President Woodrow Wilson's passage by train through the emptiness of the Texas Panhandle, and the appearance of a flying circus as a parodic reminder of World War One. The West may promise infinite space and freedom, yet even the amber waves of grain reveal the landscape as a site of exploitation, for there are labour issues in the country as in the city. The farm foreman is country cousin to the mill foreman: both patriarchal authorities collide with Bill's rebellious masculinity. The conflict introduced by the Jamesian love triangle makes the West a scene of encroachment by the problems of society – sexual rivalry, greed, deception – so that the heavenly days end in an apocalyptic, hellish night. When Bill is hunted down and shot, the bystanders watching from the river bank have a stillness reminiscent of a Bennett photograph as the violence intrudes upon their leisurely enjoyment of nature. The fairytale is over, for as in *Badlands* there can be no escape from civilisation and the law. Preceding the final scene of the girl narrator and her friend walking away on the railroad tracks there is the departure of the troops, off to World War One. The political isolationism of the United States and the charmed personal isolation of the figures in the Western landscape are both at an end.

The Thin Red Line continues Malick's exploration of nature and human nature. The introductory sequence with Privates Witt and Hoke absent without leave in a village of Pacific islanders is not in the James Jones novel. In fact, this episode is only hinted at as late as the second draft of the screenplay (Malick 1996: 1), where it is described under the heading 'Credit Sequence': 'Waves lapping at the shore. Breadfruit and coconut trees. The peace of a green island paradise.' As Jonathan Rosenbaum (1999) noted, the influence of F. W. Murnau's *Tabu* (1931) may be visible here. But so is the entire weight of an American (and European) obsession with tropical exoticism, from Winslow Homer to James Michener and Rodgers and Hammerstein. The subject of the movie may be soldiers at war, rather than a couple or trio attempting to 'light out for the territory' (to borrow from Huck Finn), but Malick once again establishes an opposition between the world of nature as paradise and the world of modern human society as paradise lost. In *The Thin Red Line*, the intruders bring modern civilisation to the 'primitive' world in the form of modern warfare – a major concern of Jones who has one character describe war as 'the reality ... of the modern State in action' and another hold that 'American warfare had changed from individualist warfare to collectivist warfare', making the idea that individuals were free 'a fucking myth' (1962: 223, 238). Yet the crocodile suggests that a deadly aggressiveness is already there, in nature, as much as in the human nature shown, if not by the islanders, whose village is a sanctuary complete with communal hymn-singing to suggest its state of grace, then by the armies that despoil the island, apparently regarded by Malick as the 'poison' that destroyed Eden (Biskind 1998: 210).

Malick's image of the crocodile and initial questions about the war in nature are not consistently developed. That may be attributable to the way different characters represent different points of view, or to the possibility that Malick created the monologues as a post-production fix, like the voice-over in *Days of Heaven*: the voice-overs are not in the second draft of the screenplay, except when Bell addresses his wife (1996: 161). There may be an unavoidable tension in Malick's use of voice-over as an expression of the inner world of spirit and thought over against the external world of physical nature and action. In any event, a movie is not a philosophical treatise. The initial 'What is this war in the heart of nature?' is followed immediately by 'Is there an avenging power to nature?' – a query that suggests *Moby Dick* more than the movie, since the only other threatening animal shown is a snake slithering through the grass, and the idea of vengeance is not applied to the human conflicts. A (or perhaps the same) crocodile appears again only briefly, bound, in the back of a military truck as a mascot, nature (and brute aggression) controlled by 'unnatural' human domination.

The search for the origins of disharmony and death in the interior monologues Malick uses for his metaphysical investigation – 'This great evil, where did it come from? How did it steal into the world?' – can seem both grandiose and naïve.

As antidote, one might recall the question asked by the character Maria at the beginning of Joan Didion's *Play It As It Lays* (1970): "'What makes Iago evil?' some people ask. I never ask.' Malick's language, Rosenbaum (1999) observed, 'periodically turns all his soldiers into soul-searching poets who share the same literary style, for better and for worse.' As the film's mixed critical reception demonstrated, one person's philosophy is another's (mere) philosophising.

Thomas Doherty argues that Malick looks at the landscape 'like a natural scientist' rather than a military tactician and that '*The Thin Red Line* luxuriates in a sense of place, not history or politics' (1999: 83). He criticises Malick for 'pantheistic sightseeing' and remarks that the warship that disrupts the idyll for the AWOL soldiers should have 'et in arcadia ego' stencilled on its bow.[1] Such criticisms, however witty, ignore the combat narrative and the philosophical debate that informs the entire action. As Malick said of Heidegger's critics, 'If we cannot educate ourselves to his purposes, then clearly his work will look like nonsense' (Heidegger 1969: xvii). Doherty's statement that 'Malick's Guadalcanal diary is more a meditation on nature than an evocation of war' (1999: 83), and Tom Whalen's that *The Thin Red Line* is 'not a war film, but a meditation on the relationship of man to nature' (1999: 163), are inaccurate because, as the opening line of the film indicates, for Malick nature and war are inseparable, so that to meditate on one is to meditate on the other. Colin MacCabe goes so far as to say that Malick 'has no interest in World War Two', and the film seeks 'to replace history by nature, to transform World War Two into War itself' (1999: 13). Malick would not be the first filmmaker or writer making of a specific war a vehicle for consideration of 'War itself' – consider Abel Gance's *J'Accuse* (1937) or William Faulkner's *A Fable* – and such attendant themes as violence, suffering and death. But to say that Malick 'has no interest in World War Two' goes too far, even if he is not concerned with the kind of history or treatment of war that interests MacCabe.

Landscape in *The Thin Red Line*, as background and battleground, does more than provide scenic picturesqueness, display zoological and botanical exotica, or serve as an allegorical diagram like something out of *Pilgrim's Progress*. It is also territory and 'terrain', the word Jones uses in a 'Special Note' where he states that the specific locations and landmarks are imaginary (1962: ix). Territory and terrain are essential elements in war, where the landscape is both the site and the object of the struggle. The presentation of Guadalcanal from the water and then of its topography once the action moves onshore in part reflects a surveying, reconnoitering, territorial gaze, since physical possession is the goal of the military action. The central section of the film, the attack on the Japanese positions atop the hill, is developed in terms of landscape in both senses of the term, as an actual piece of land, and as a view of the land, presented through the points of view of the individual characters and the overall perspective created by the film. Before turning to the battle within the landscape, however, it is worth considering how Malick shows his interests are not removed from history and society. From the beginning of the film, in the scenes onboard ship, we are shown how the war in human nature is not only an abstract, metaphysical struggle but a worldly one

Nick Nolte plays high status as the ambitious Lt Colonel Tall in *The Thin Red Line*

as well. The politics of the Army, with its hierarchy of ranks and the kind of careerism that drives Colonel Tall, is a major concern for Malick, as for Jones.

Malick's adaptation, unlike the first film version, is in colour, which helps him to show the beauty of the dawn in the early view of the island from the ship – a sharp contrast with the dark, claustrophobic ship interiors – and later provide an appropriate illustration for Tall's recitation from Homer in Greek about 'rosy-fingered dawn'.[2] That sequence is at once a statement about the epic poetry of war, a display of the beauty of the landscape as ironic counterpoint to the horrors soon to appear in the combat, *and* an indication of Tall's background and status. Staros is a Greek-American (not the Jewish Stein of the novel, target of anti-semitism), but he is not a career officer, did not attend West Point and does not know classical Greek. When Tall relieves Staros of his command, he says, 'Look at this jungle. Look at those vines, the way they twine around the trees, swallowing everything. Nature is cruel.' This returns us to the opening with the crocodile and a shot of twining vines, yet it is an obvious piece of rhetoric, a rationalisation for Tall's action. Staros' compassion is shown in his initial refusal to obey Tall's order for a frontal attack, and nobly voiced in an interior monologue at the end – 'You are my sons. I'll carry you wherever you go.' It is clear that Tall is threatened by Staros, whose resistance impedes Tall's determination to gain the hill and professional recognition, revealed in an uncontrolled outburst: 'I've waited all my life for this … You don't know what it feels like to be passed over [for promotion].' When Tall moves up to rally the men, he performs the role of fearless leader;

like Robert Duvall's Kilgore in *Apocalypse Now* (Francis Ford Coppola, 1979), he stands unflinching under bombardment. That bravado is absent when he is alone in the overrun Japanese camp, facing a sprawled Japanese corpse and several covered American bodies. There he appears on the verge of breaking down. This private scene hints at the stress of the public performance, indicated in an interior monologue presented earlier as he moved to the front: 'Shut up in a tomb. Can't lift the lid. Played a role I never conceived.' Tall's philosophy of nature, then, may be a rhetorical argument for Staros's consumption, and no more credible than the blustery pep talk and praise he addresses to Captain Gaff.

The conflict between Staros and Tall over the proper conduct of war is one expression of Malick's central theme, the mysterious nature of nature – is it cruel or kind, ugly or beautiful? – and the corresponding problem of human action, of how one should act, given a set of assumptions about the world. The other major debate appears in the conversations between Witt and Sergeant Welsh, representatives of different philosophical positions that define attitudes toward nature and human nature. Witt, an idealist, upholds the existence of another world. Welsh, a materialist, insists, 'Property, the whole fucking thing is about property.' The battle-shattered Sergeant McCron exclaims, 'We're just dirt.' It is at once a statement of plain disgust and a reaction against any spiritual gloss. McCron later reinforces Welsh's scepticism by saying, 'Who is going to live, who's going to die? This is futile.' Malick builds here on a similar comment in Jones, when Bell asks, 'What power was it which decided one man should be hit, be killed, instead of another man?' But in Jones, Bell's thoughts lead him to the idea that in a movie a death would have meaning and decide something, whereas 'Here there was no semblance of meaning', and therefore 'Art … creative art – was shit' (1998: 237).

Malick leaves that out. He provides death with a 'semblance of meaning', primarily through Witt, whose behaviour answers Welsh's existential question about the significance of individual action: 'What difference do you think you can make, one single man in all this madness? If you die it's gonna be for nothing.' In the screenplay, Malick says of Witt, 'The idea of service to humanity, of comradeship, of the solidarity of men, is slowly perishing from the world, but in Witt it still runs strong' (1996: 134). Jones does not put Witt's idea of service into an historical framework, and does not describe it, as Malick does, as a 'mysterious summons of fraternal devotion' (1996: 178). The emphasis on Witt's service as a merciful angel comforting the frightened, wounded and dying, and therefore providing a counter to historical devolution, is part of Malick's Edenic mythologising. When Witt tends the wounded by the river, the voice-over speculates about a transcendental humanity: 'Maybe all men got one big soul who everybody's a part of, all faces of the same man.' This recalls Tom Joad in John Steinbeck's *The Grapes of Wrath*, who tells Ma Joad how Preacher Casy 'went out in the wilderness to find his own soul, an' foun' he jus' got a little piece of a great big soul' (1975: 570). Witt, in Jones's novel, is a stubborn hillbilly who loves his fellows passionately with 'an almost sexual ecstasy of comradeship' (1998: 276) and secretly believes he can save them. But he likes to describe himself as 'free, white and twenty-one' (1998:

322) and is described by Storm as 'Witt the Kentuckian', a 'peanut head' who 'hated niggers because they all wanted to vote' (1998: 442). In the film, Malick transforms Witt into a figure full of 'understanding and tenderness' (1996: 72), a figure Gavin Smith refers to as 'enigmatic and charismatic ... a serene Emersonian idealist' (1999: 8).

The battle, and the landscape at its centre, are therefore especially important because the attack on the hill makes possible the familiar war movie exercise of seizing machine gun nests and pillboxes, a dramatisation of the politics of command under fire and a test of the ideas set forth in the dialogue and interior monologues. The landscape is contested terrain and a site of death; it is also a philosophical proving ground. Filmmaking is not like war only because it involves logistics and hierarchical organisation. As Paul Virilio reminds us, movies and war both depend upon pictures: visually as well as ideologically, perspective and point of view are central to both (see Virilio 1989: 68–89). The characteristic shot through the opening passage of the attack is a gliding camera move through the tall grass at eye level, at once lyrical and frightening. Lyrical, because of the mesmerising tranquility of the setting, where figures can rise up out of the waving, windblown grass, then disappear as if swallowed up. Frightening, because of the unseen Japanese, whose threat is indicated by the discovery of mutilated remains of American soldiers. The pivotal event in the film occurs when two scouts are sent forward up the hillside, into the sea of grass, and then shot dead: just like that. It is a masterful, stunning moment, with John Toll's cinematography capturing the muzzle flashes that appear up the slope, beyond the scouts, from what Jones describes as 'the quiet, masked face of the deserted little ridge' (1998: 191). (In the final engagement, when Witt is surrounded, the Japanese emerge from the jungle with foliage stuck in their helmets. The armies are always outsiders, never at one with nature on the island, but their deadly game of hide-and-seek makes them employ concealment and camouflage.)

As Malick depicts the attackers moving up toward the Japanese emplacements, he introduces shots from the Japanese point of view, but at first withholds shots of the Japanese, only gradually showing them. Stanley Kauffmann calls these shots 'superfluous' and says they 'spoil the unitary point of view – our participation in the American advance' (1999: 24). They do, but that is the point. In war, as Bill Schaffer (2000) has observed, 'POV is everything'. And in war films, too. Kauffmann misses the unified strategy behind Malick's dialectical tactics. To conceal the Japanese keeps the enemy largely unseen. Yet at the same time the partial shots remind us that they are there, and the attackers are being viewed and targeted from above, increasing the tension by building suspense, and establishing a complex point of view that goes beyond simple identification with the Americans.

'The logistics of perception,' Virilio has noted, 'was from the start the geographic logistics of domination from an elevated site ... the "field of battle" ... is also a "field of perception" – a theatre of operation' (Der Derian 1998: 17). In *The Thin Red Line*, the American conquest of the hilltop gains the high ground and the dominant point of view. Elevated, panoramic shots are nevertheless rare, although Malick introduces a few as punctuation marks to open or close sections of the narrative, and provide a more encompassing view of the field of battle. Malick, like Jones, keeps his focus on one company with the larger engagement only occasionally glimpsed. But as the battle progresses to its savage finale with the Americans overrunning the enemy positions, the Japanese are shown, as is the 'denatured' and devastated area surrounding their encampment. The Japanese become the focus of the film's moral concern, since Malick displays an almost *Lear*-like interest in suffering as he shows the skinny, terrified prisoners shuddering in the dirt, killed mercilessly by the rampaging Americans or, if captured, pathetic.

The moral climax comes with the shot of a face emerging from the dirt and ash. The face 'speaks' to Witt, whose point of view we share in looking at it, of suffering and goodness, as an oracular voice of wisdom: 'Are you righteous ... loved by all? Know that I was, too. Do you imagine your sufferings will be less because you loved goodness, truth?' As the prisoners are shown in their pitiable condition, the voice provides the most extreme case of Malick's use of philosophical conversation, in a form of address that offers questions from the living and an admonition from the dead: 'Who's doing this? Who's killing us, robbing us of life and light, mocking us in the sight of what we might have known? Does our ruin benefit the earth? Is this darkness in you, too? Have you passed through the night?' In the film's central sequence, therefore, Malick leads the audience from a military version of landscape as terrain, as fortification and as property, to a spiritual version of landscape as a site of devastation, death and possible transfiguration.

A figure of speech that appears in the ongoing dialogue between Witt and Welsh is 'spark'. One of the most striking of all Toll's images captures the silhouette of a Buddha statue in the conquered Japanese camp, against a background of flames and smoke flying upward, the result of fires set by the Americans. That shot, moving up to the dark sky, concludes the entire attack section, and may allude to Asian aesthetics and spirituality of the kind Malick is drawn to, on the evidence of his theatrical adaptation of *Sansho the Bailiff*, the Mizoguchi masterpiece on suffering, sacrifice, goodness and forgiveness, directed in a workshop production by Andrzej Wajda in 1993 (see Shteir 1994; Biskind 1998; Andrew and Cavanaugh, 2000). As a kind of visual fire sermon, it offers another view of transcendence to go with the idyllic images of light and water Malick introduces at the start and the recurring shots of birds and of the moon that indicate a realm of peace beyond the landscape of war. The seeming exception occurs when Dale taunts a dying Japanese by saying, 'See those birds up there? They gonna eat you raw.' But Dale, who moves among the Japanese corpses with pliers, pulling their gold teeth, is eventually transformed from the monstrous epitome of cruelty to a poor soul sobbing in the rain – a conversion not present in the novel.

Malick's widescreen treatment of the South Pacific landscape in *The Thin Red Line*, like Kevin Costner's of the Great Plains in *Dances With Wolves* (1990) (which won Toll an Academy Award), is tinged with nostalgic longing for the epic sweep of untouched vistas. Malick's treatment of the sexual side of his sensual approach to the world, though it might seem far removed from the issue of landscape, presents images of home and domesticity also coloured with nostalgia and a poeticising style, as in a dissolve that opens an interior up to the sky. In the novel Bell tries to evoke 'that translucent, so realistic image of his wife' (1998: 505). Dreamy translucence, rather than earthy realism, is the hallmark of the film's flashbacks and imaginings. In an interior monologue, Bell, staring out at an islander in a dugout canoe, asks over a matching shot of his wife gazing at the shore in Hawaii, 'How do we get to those other shores?' Here the landscape – seascape – enters as a figure of speech, and as visual imagery revealing Malick's mystical, poetic strain and his powerful sense of romantic longing. An interior monologue near the end proclaims, 'Walked into the golden age. Stood on the shores of the new world.' This is the pure voice of pastoral, both an elegiac lament and a reminder of the optimism of the archetypal figure R. W. B. Lewis has called the American Adam. Hope and loss are balanced, as the vision of the new world is set against the observation that 'the good that was given us' was slipping away, 'scattered careless', which leads to a question that links religious language, personal complaint and existential questioning: 'What's keeping us from reaching out, touching the glory?'

Rosenbaum may be right that *The Thin Red Line* is a product of cinematic nostalgia, displaying a love for silent cinema, especially that of Murnau. It may also recall *Rashomon* (1951), Kurosawa's deliberate attempt to return to the visual style of the silent era, in its shots of the forest primeval pierced by shafts of light in a visual figure Malick uses, following a Jones description, to trace the gaze of a dying soldier. The larger issue is how the cinematic nostalgia, or more simply, the cinema, plays a part within *The Thin Red Line*. In *Badlands*, Holly looks through a stereopticon and sees a magical world of illusionary realism: the viewing device metaphorically suggests the movies. *Days of Heaven* offers its own version of reflexivity when the barnstormers screen Charlie Chaplin's *The Immigrant* (1915) for their hosts. These images of the cinema-like and the cinema have no equivalent in *The Thin Red Line*, except in distanced viewing through binoculars to scan an objective or, during fighting, to observe the progress of an attack. Yet it is still possible to invoke Stanley Cavell and his brief, suggestive remarks on beauty in *Days of Heaven*. Cavell argues that Malick's achievement is to explore, through the visual and specifically photographic aspect of cinematic representation, the play of absence and presence, the relationship between being and Being (1979: xiv–xvi). The use of 'glory', 'spark' and 'radiance' in the verbal language of *The Thin Red Line* is matched by equivalent visual language, such as the shots of light streaming down past the trees at Bead's death, or the use of the 'magic hour' at dusk as a glowing backdrop, notably for Welsh's conversation with Witt about the existence of another world. The edenic myth is in effect incorporated within the system of cinematic representation.

Heidegger, discussing Rilke in 'What Are Poets For?', warns against confusing nature and natural science (1971: 101). For Malick, nature leads to natural philosophy, not natural science. In *Days of Heaven*, a time-lapse shot of a seed sprouting underground is at once scientific and poetic punctuation, and indicates Malick's deeply-rooted fascination with the creative, not avenging, force of nature. His interpolated shots of bats, owls, parrots, lizards, a war-wounded young bird and other creatures in *The Thin Red Line*, like his play with exotic animals in *Badlands* and *Days of Heaven*, introduces a strange otherness to the landscape, that is, a world beyond the human, and a plenitude pointing toward an inclusive sense of Being. One of the interior monologues suggests pantheism by asking, 'Who are you to live in all these many forms?' But the next statements – 'Your death that captures all. You, too, are the source of all that's gonna be born. Your glory, mercy, peace, truth...' – suggest a Christian perspective. It is both ironic and fitting that *Days of Heaven* uses *The Carnival of Animals* by Saint-Saëns to complement the main score by Ennio Morricone, and that *The Thin Red Line* features Faure's 'Requiem-in Paradisium'. Music and sound – and silence – play an important role in shaping the sense of the landscape in *The Thin Red Line*.

Malick's fascination with the exotic in nature can be a sly joke, such as the llama and stuffed animals that appear in *Badlands*, as well as a sign of Being living 'in all these many forms'. Nature's extravagant richness poses a challenge to the powers of the imagination. The opposition in *The Thin Red Line* between Witt and Welsh is a metaphysical debate over existence and transcendence, but it is also a debate over art. Welsh says, 'In this world a man himself is nothin'. And there ain't no other one.' Witt replies, 'You're wrong there ... I seen another world. Sometimes I think it was just my imagination.' The 'other world' can be construed as a spiritual realm, with Witt as its prophet; it is also the realm of the artistic imagination, with Malick as its poet. The screenplay has Witt in effect paraphrase the gardener's lament for England from *Richard II*. He tells Storm, 'You ever had a garden? They're pulling up the young plants and watering the weeds.' The poet/filmmaker cultivates the renewal of paradise through the power of art, with landscape as the master metaphor. Military perception, where as Virilio observes, the function of the eye is always coordinated with the function of the weapon – see, aim, kill – is incorporated within cinematic representation and leads to spiritual or philosophical perception, the vision that can see another world (Virilio 1989: 2–3).

Near the start of the film, when Witt is in the brig for going AWOL, there is a brief flashback of him as a young boy with his father, playing in the hay in a farm field. The screenplay version is more complete, and more helpful as a guide to Malick's idealisation of Witt and of the pastoral myth. While C-Company is camped by an abandoned plantation, on what is to be his last night Witt has a vision of 'the farms and valleys of Kentucky – people are going about their work, raking hay and putting it up in barns – a land of peace and truth, bright with an unearthly light' (1996: 173). This passage helps explain the overall shape of the film because following this description, 'a woman appears. Gracious, noble, she looks out on those scenes, a smile on her lips. She might be some individual whom Witt has known; his sister or mother. She is all that is not strife or war or senseless death. She is peace, she is hope' (1996: 174). Peace, home, harmonious nature and a woman not identified with sexuality (and therefore incapable of betrayal, unlike Bell's wife) are all presented as one, the antithesis to the masculine wartime world where nature has conflict at its heart and the landscape is beautiful and alluring but deadly, as the shots on the hillside proved. This passage also explains the force of Witt's return to the native village, a joyless experience. The original communal harmony has been lost because of the intrusion of the war, and replaced by contention, suspicion and listlessness. As Witt leaves, the voice-over asks, 'How did we lose the good that was given us, let it slip away, scattered, careless?' Maybe the closest earthly approximation to paradise, 'another world' beyond the Hobbesian world of war, was just a product of his imagination. But at the moment of his death he is shown once again enjoying the pure pleasure of swimming with the village children, and we share that experience through the power of cinema.

Welsh's insistence to Witt that there is no other world is subtly challenged in the course of *The Thin Red Line*, as Malick tilts the balance toward Witt's saintly quietude. In the screenplay, Welsh exclaims 'Fool!' as he looks in Witt's direction, while C-Company retreats under the cover of his rearguard action, in which he moves 'like a jungle animal' (1996: 179). Also in the screenplay Welsh asks at Witt's grave, 'Where's your pride now?' before turning to a medic and saying 'Bury that soldier' (1996: 181). (Jones makes clear that Witt takes pride in his odyssey to return to the company.) In the film, the wording is changed, but the taunt hurled by Welsh – 'Where's your spark now?' – is belied by his emotion as he squeezes back tears. He had earlier said to Witt, with a hint of sarcasm, 'You still believing in the beautiful light, are you ?' To which Witt replies earnestly, 'I still see a spark in you.' At Witt's grave a spirit of peace, even sanctity, reigns; the setting is a kind of natural chapel, and Malick adds a shot of birds wheeling on high. Yet the whole sequence of Witt's heroic action and death is Malick's creation. For Jones, the jungle is initially described as 'alien, supremely confident … ominous to the human ego' (1998: 55) and near the end as 'eerie' and 'mad': 'Dripping trees, disturbed birds squawking … mud, perpetual wet, gloom, green air, stink and slithering animal life' (1998: 398–99, 446). In Malick, for all the mud and danger, after the initial glimpse of the crocodile and one brief early shot showing the men slogging up a stream bed, the jungle is not, as it is in Jones, nature at its most frightening.

Malick's narrative of C-Company's experience preaches a sermon of the triumph of the spirit. The final monologue, delivered on the departing ship with Doll at the rail watching the churning wake and the receding Guadalcanal, is a prayer for the indwelling spirit that begins with one more religious-spiritual question – 'The darkness and the light, are they workings of the same face?' – and ends with a kind of redemptive benediction that affirms Witt's position: 'All things shining.' The luminous visuals accompanying this speech, like the images of landscape throughout the film, provide an unmediated, nonverbal argument for the radiant splendour of the world and the victory of a faith in spirit, although that does not necessarily answer the fundamental questions that haunt the film. Near the end, in response to a smug speech to the men by their new commanding officer, Captain Bosche, Welsh says in an interior monologue, 'Only one thing a man can do. Find something that's his. Make an island for himself.' Welsh's isolationist faith in an island self is contradicted by his own conduct, as when he goes out to Tella and gives him morphine to alleviate his suffering. And it is no match for the behavior of Witt, who follows his own moral compass but acts for others. The final series of shots reveals islanders peacefully paddling canoes up the river, some brightly colored parrots, and then a coconut floating just offshore, sprouting new growth, an emblem of renewal and rebirth, like the shot of the young colt frisking up the river bank that closes John Ford's *Wagonmaster* (1950) as the Mormons cross over into their promised land. In spite of the opening image, the questioning about the war in nature, and the tragic action, Malick concludes on an uplifting note.

Norman Mailer wrote in *Cannibals and Christians* that the Jones novel was strong in its psychological understanding and 'workmanlike' (1966: 112) as a war narrative. He criticised Jones for being 'too technical' (ibid.), overburdened with technological information on the machinery of war. For Mailer, Jones had put the mystical side of his talents (1966: 113) 'on bread and water' – and therefore had created a book that would prove less memorable than *The Red Badge of Courage* (1951). Mailer argued that 'the mystery is what separates the great war novels from the good ones' (ibid.). Malick has answered Mailer in adapting Jones, for it is precisely the mystical side that Malick stresses, retaining some of the psychological concerns yet emphasising the philosophical issues. The ideas may be most explicitly presented in the spoken debates and in the interior monologues, but the foundation of their expression remains the visuals. And it is in the visuals of the landscape, notwithstanding all the complications and contradictions, that Malick is able to most clearly express his vision of the world as paradise and paradise lost, caught up in darkness and death but open to redemption through the radiance of unselfish individual action.

The New World offers few surprises in its treatment of landscape. In general, it offers a reprise of the approaches used to represent nature – and civilisation – in Malick's earlier films. At its centre is the opposition between the idyllic, as in the initial experience of the American West in *Days of Heaven* and the opening AWOL sequence with the Melanesian islanders in *The Thin Red Line*, and more desolate, despoiled states, such as the post-fire devastation in *Days of Heaven* and the overrun Japanese encampment in *The Thin Red Line*. *The New World* establishes a sharp division in representational terms right at the start, in the opening contrast between the pristine view of the New World as a dreamy reflection in the mirror-like surface of the water, and the view provided by a map, a form associated with exploration and adventure, but an instrument of rationality, order, territoriality and conquest.

The fundamental dichotomy is then extended as the film sets the majestic, unspoiled beauty of the landscape and the life in and around the native village against the conflict-ridden wreckage, human and structural, at the Jamestown settlement. The devolution that occurs until the boats return provides a nasty disproof of Captain Newport's assertion: 'Eden lies about us still. We have escaped the old world, and its bondage.'

The sustained opposition between the New World and the Old is capped in the concluding English sequence with the presentation of the court and civilised life as finery, as décor, and as poetry full of pastoral conceits: 'Let rolling streams their gladness show/With gentle murmurs as they flow/And their wild meanders flow rejoining … The new world's princess new life brings'. Above all, there is the architecture and landscape architecture. Instead of the great central structure of the natives, with its mystery and dramatic lighting, there is the grand hall where the first encounter between Pocahontas and the British court takes place. Instead of the forests and fields primeval or the cultivated patches of corn and tobacco of the New World, there are the topiary hedges and artfully shaped trees of the formal gardens that bewilder the native emissary, Opechancanough. The difference is clear between nature as a spiritual realm and a bounteous source of sustenance and nature as a garden for display and leisure. An especially neat touch is the bouquet of flowers that punctuates the panelled salon in John Rolfe's house, nature domesticated, like the large dog lounging on the floor, more at home than the caged exotic New World species present when Pocahontas meets the king and queen. Although Pocahontas frolics with her child amid the trimmed hedges surrounding their home in England, and even in her dress behaves in a free-spirited manner as she did in her original home, that is a throwback to her initial childlike enthusiasm and immediate relationship to the world, a glimmer of personal innocence not lost. More telling is the gloomy shot of her (supposed) final resting place in Gravesend, a grave end indeed for her journey from New World to Old.

If the basic perspective on landscape is familiar, so are many of the accompanying narrative elements: the interior monologues, the treatment of romance (unfortunately too often reminiscent of D.W. Griffith at his most cloying), and the concern with trust, bad faith and betrayal. One other landscape, briefly glimpsed, rounds out the opposition between Paradise and Paradise Lost: the desolate northern shore, far from Virginia, England and his beloved, where John Smith is shown pursuing his dutiful, futile quest for the Northwest Passage.

Malick has developed a complex cinematic style, but I am not sure he has overcome the tension between the historical and the modern, as in the play between a handheld camera technique and a more conservative approach, or in the echoes of Viet Nam hut burning when the settlers torch the native village. Nor do I believe, given his treatment of matters of the heart, tinged with melancholy and perhaps male self-pity, that *The New World*'s version of the Smith-Pocahontas relationship can bear the burden of serving as the centrepiece in addressing the overall social and political encounter between the two cultures. A romantic anecdote out of old-fashioned storybook history is one thing, a convincing extended narrative for today is another. Malick's Pocahontas goes far beyond being just an allegorical figure in a map cartouche, an emblematic image of America and the promise of 'new life'. Yet his representation of the natives combines idealisation and infantilisation, not without a bit of New Age spirituality, and at times comes too close to Karl May and Longfellow in spite of the dedication to authenticity in language, customs and setting.

Whatever the failings of *The New World*, there is no denying the magnificence of the representation of the landscape as first experienced by those who crossed the seas. Malick's images of nature once again could be regarded as a late chapter in American Transcendentalism, or a Heidegger-inspired meditation on Being and the world. But his achievement also suggests a compelling cinematic equivalent to the famous passage at the end of *The Great Gatsby* (1925) where Nick Carraway imagines the first glimpse by the Dutch sailors of 'a fresh, green breast of the new world', man brought 'face to face for the last time in history with something commensurate to his capacity for wonder'.

Notes

1 As Erwin Panofsky showed in a famous essay on two paintings by Poussin ('*Et in Arcadia Ego*: Poussin and the Elegiac Tradition', chapter seven in *Meaning in the Visual Arts*, 295–320), '*Et in Arcadia ego*' can mean both 'I also was in Arcady' [as a shepherd enjoying pastoral pleasures] and 'I, too, am in Arcady' where the speaker is Death.

2 Jones is not a particularly descriptive writer when it comes to the landscape and visual scene-setting, except at the beginning, where he describes the view from the deck as a beautiful one, in the 'early morning tropic sunshine', and notes the 'open distances and limitless sea vistas' (2). These are nicely rendered by Malick and Toll. A brief mention well into the book of 'a lovely striated tropic sunset to look at in the western sky' that 'was a time to think of peacefulness and women' (1998: 158) does anticipate Malick's elaborate development of the interior monologues and flashbacks and the frame story. Jones does, as Norman Mailer says, give enough descriptions for ten topographic maps (1966: 112), but at other times he offers brief, effective sketches that provide a basis for Malick and Toll's grand vision.

References

Andrew, Dudley & Carole Cavanaugh (2000) *Sanshô Dayû*. London: British Film Institute.

Biskind, Peter (1998) 'The Runaway Genius', *Vanity Fair*, December, 460, 202–20.

Cavell, Stanley (1979) *The World Viewed*, enlarged edition. Cambridge, MA and London: Harvard University Press.

Der Derian, James (ed.) (1998) *The Virilio Reader*. Oxford: Blackwell.

Didion, Joan (1970) *Play It As It Lays*. New York: Farrar, Straus & Giroux.

Doherty, Thomas (1999) '*The Thin Red Line*', *Cineaste*, 24, 2–3, 83.

Ebert, Roger (1999) '*The Thin Red Line*', *Chicago Sun Times*, 1 January. Available at: http://www.suntimes.com/ebert/ebert_reviews/1999/01/010802.html. [Accessed: 23 January 2002]

Heidegger, Martin (1969) *The Essence of Reasons*, trans. Terrence Malick. Evanston: Northwestern University Press.

_____ (1971) *Poetry, Language, Thought*, trans. Albert Hofstadter. New York: Harper & Row.

Jones, James (1998) [1962] *The Thin Red Line*. New York: Delta.

Kauffmann, Stanley (1999) 'On Films After Twenty Years', *The New Republic*,

January 25, 24.

Lewis, R. W. B. (1955) *The American Adam*. Chicago and London: University of Chicago Press.

MacCabe, Colin (1999) 'Bayonets in Paradise', *Sight and Sound*, 9, 2, 10–14.

Mailer, Norman (1966) 'Some Children of the Goddess', in *Cannibals and Christians*. New York: Delta, 104–30.

Malick, Terrence (1996) *The Thin Red Line*, second draft screenplay.

Panofsky, Erwin (1955) *Meaning in the Visual Arts*. Garden City, N.Y: Doubleday.

Rosenbaum, Jonathan (1999) 'Malick's Progress'. *Chicago Reader*, 1 January. Available at: http://www.chireader.com/movies/archives/1999/0199/01159.html. [Accessed: 23 January 2002]

Schaffer, Bill (2000) 'The Shape of Fear: Thoughts after *The Thin Red Line*'. *Senses of Cinema*, July–August, 8. [Accessed: 23 January 2002]

Shteir, Rachel (1994) 'The Elusive Playwright', *Village Voice*, 11 January, 84, 86.

Smith, Gavin (1999) '*The Thin Red Line*', *Film Comment*, 31, 1, 8.

Steinbeck, John (1975) [1939] *The Grapes of Wrath*. Viking Press, New York.

Szarkowski, John (1973) *Looking at Photographs*. New York: Museum of Modern Art.

Virilio, Paul (1989) *War and Cinema: The Logistics of Perception*, trans. Patrick Camiller. London & New York: Verso.

Whalen, Tom (1999) '"Maybe all men got one big soul": The Hoax Within the Metaphysics of Terrence Malick's *The Thin Red Line*', *Literature-Film Quarterly*, 27, 3, 162–66.

CHAPTER FOURTEEN

Terrence Malick's Heideggerian Cinema: War and the Question of Being in The Thin Red Line

Marc Furstenau and Leslie MacAvoy

In 1998, almost twenty years after the appearance of Terrence Malick's *Days of Heaven*, *The Thin Red Line* was released. During that time his reputation as a mysterious and enigmatic figure, the reclusive and inscrutable artist, grew to almost mythical proportions. While he had long maintained a distance, both geographically and professionally, from Hollywood, when it was announced that he would direct a new film, an adaptation of James Jones's 1961 war novel, he was able to acquire major studio financing and attract the interest of some of the most powerful and popular actors. Such influence, based on a relatively limited output, seems to derive instead from the general sense that the man is a genius, and Hollywood has long sought to associate itself with genius, eager to burnish its often tarnished image with the periodic production of 'works of art'. Malick can be placed in a long line of serious filmmakers with whom Hollywood has associated itself and from whom it has garnered some reflected prestige, beginning with F. W. Murnau, Fritz Lang, and even Alfred Hitchcock, and including such contemporary directors as Francis Ford Coppola, Martin Scorsese and Jane Campion. Such a list must also contain another filmmaker with whom Malick has in fact often been compared, and to whom Hollywood has also offered its vast resources in the hopes of being associated with an artist, namely Stanley Kubrick. Yet, as Carole Zucker has noted in an article on *Days of Heaven*, while Malick has achieved a reputation comparable to Kubrick's, which has provided him with considerable negotiating power and some currency as a serious, artistic filmmaker, nevertheless, 'unlike Kubrick, there has been little critical discourse surrounding Malick's films' (2001: 2). While Kubrick's significance has received considerable scholarly attention, Malick's reputation has for the most part merely been taken for granted, insisted upon in popular and journalistic discourse but not seriously pursued by scholars and critics.

Notoriously shy of publicity and determined to stay out of the limelight, Malick has, despite or perhaps because of this, long been an object of interest and speculation, primarily among journalists, film buffs and Hollywood insiders, and this only increased with the publicity around the production and release of *The Thin Red Line*. While Malick has, as we will argue, resumed what we see as his philosophical project with *The Thin Red Line*, a film that aspires to the status of philosophy and that manifests key themes and issues specifically from the work of Martin Heidegger, much of the discourse around his return to filmmaking has dealt instead with the more trifling issues of his long absence, his legendary aloofness, and the more complex aspects of the film have been characterised as examples of his infamous 'difficulty'. In so far as Hollywood requires him to be viewed romantically as an 'artist' or as a 'genius', journalists and publicists are content to describe him as reclusive, complex, enigmatic and ultimately inscrutable.[1] Malick's films are often judged to be perversely obscure, a positive quality from Hollywood's point of view, which values obscurity as an indicator of artistic seriousness. Yet, given that his first career was as a philosopher, the clues to Malick's films are readily available, and the supposed obscurities of his films may be illuminated by placing them within a specific philosophical tradition. Those who have engaged critically with his work, however, tend to go no further than the more popular accounts, and frequently express frustration and often disappointment at Malick's pretensions. A recent example is Tom Whalen's account of what he describes as the failures of *The Thin Red Line*, which he identifies mainly through a comparison of the film with James Jones's original novel. Whalen accuses Malick of perpetrating a 'metaphysical hoax', enumerating a variety of discrepancies between the film and its literary source, towards which, he argues, Malick does not display the appropriate fidelity. Both Jones's novel and the war itself have, he insists, merely 'become for Malick a place to play with his philosophical conundrums about nature and our relationship to it' (1999: 166). While for Whalen this is the source of Malick's failure, for us it is precisely Malick's use of such material – the popular formats of the war novel and the combat film – for philosophical purposes that makes his film unique and worthy of careful consideration. The question for us is just how Malick puts identifiable philosophical themes in play in the film, how he raises fundamental questions about the cinema, images and representation through the liberties he in fact takes with the source material.

Malick's films, especially *The Thin Red Line*, are instances of what may be called a Heideggerian cinema. Malick's approach to filmmaking is strongly influenced by the philosophy of Martin Heidegger, of which he has a thorough and intimate understanding. It is well known that after his return from Oxford, Malick briefly taught philosophy at MIT. He seemed to be headed towards the life of a traditional philosopher, building upon his earlier achievements, and settling into a career of teaching and writing. After having travelled to Germany in the mid-1960s to meet Heidegger, Malick translated *Vom Wesen des Grundes* as *The Essence of Reasons* (Heidegger 1969), and seemed well-positioned within the world of academic philosophy. Yet Malick chose instead to pursue the study of the cinema, and transformed his knowledge of Heidegger into cinematic terms. In 1969 he entered the American Film Institute's Center for Advanced Film Studies, where he made his first film, the short *Lanton Mills*. But the character of Malick's philosophical investigation into the cinema became clear only with the release in 1973 of *Badlands*, and then, five years later, with *Days of Heaven*, his stunning and evocative portrait of the beauty and fragility of earthly existence.

Malick himself is notoriously silent about his films, which he hopes are capable of functioning without any subsequent comment on his part. Yet this is not to say that the films simply speak for themselves. They invite and provoke the participation of those who view them, and insist upon a critical response. In this they perform their first and perhaps most traditional philosophical function, as they propose an argument which solicits and requires an answer, as they initiate a dialogue between film and audience. Stanley Cavell, the American philosopher and author of several significant books on cinema, was among the first, and remains one of the few, to answer the call of Malick's philosophical cinema, quickly recognising the affinities between his and Malick's projects as well as the films' explicit Heideggerian concerns. In the forward to the second edition of his ontological analysis of the cinema, *The World Viewed*, Cavell offers some brief comments on *Days of Heaven*, with which, he argues, Malick has found a way to make visible certain key Heideggerian themes, particularly the theme of the Being of beings and the presence of beings (1979: xv). Cavell argues that Malick has 'found a way to transpose such thoughts for our meditation', and has transformed them into cinematic terms 'by having discovered, or discovered how to acknowledge, a fundamental fact of film's photographic basis: that objects participate in the photographic presence of themselves; they participate in the re-creation of themselves on film; they are essential in the making of their appearances' (ibid.).

This characteristic is common to virtually all film, which makes objects and individuals present for the viewer despite their actual absence, and thereby foregrounds the more general human capacity to make present things that are absent, to produce representations of otherwise intangible concepts and ideas through conceptualisation. The paradox of present absence is reproduced in virtually every cinematic representation; the images on the screen force the viewer to acknowledge the fact of the object's or individual's independent existence, as well as the necessity of its existence for the production of the image, while nevertheless recognising its actual absence. The cinema as such, argues Cavell, produces reflexive images. 'Objects projected on a screen', he insists, 'are inherently reflexive, they occur as self-referential, reflecting upon their physical origins. Their presence refers to their absence, their location in another place' (ibid.). Beyond such inherent reflexivity, however, in order for a film to achieve the status of art, to put the film image's reflexive character to some purpose, the filmmaker must endeavour to explore the significance of the distance between the thing seen and the thing itself, between the object and its realisation as idea or image. The structures of presence and absence, which have long provided the contours of metaphysical thinking, and which are recreated or reenacted through the technology of the cinema, have also functioned to distance human beings from a world which is rendered conceptually as an idea or as an image.

The core of Cavell's view is that there is a connection between metaphysical and cinematic representation. Metaphysical views are representations of the world which, according to Heidegger, become so sedimented that we forget that they are representations or interpretations. The presenting of what is absent through those representations becomes occluded. The cinema also provides us with representations of the world, and in this it importantly resembles metaphysics. But the cinema also contains the often unrealised possibility of presenting its representation, of drawing attention to the fact of its representing. The task of a philosophically engaged cinema is to address both the inherent reflexivity of the film image, as well as the potential consequences of the transformation of the world into an image, the consequences of a metaphysical thinking in which the world is understood to have been grasped through its representation. For Cavell, Malick has accomplished these objectives in *Days of Heaven*, and has provided images that refer to their status as images while simultaneously registering the necessity as well as the danger and poignancy of living in a world of images. For both Cavell and Malick, the cinema can serve as a medium for addressing the philosophical problem of (the representation of) presence or Being, which is of central importance to Heidegger, and modern, self-reflexive philosophy generally.

Following a long hiatus, Malick has offered another meditation on the relationship between cinematic and metaphysical representation. *The Thin Red Line* at once offers a vision of the world and a profound reflection upon the process of producing visions of the world. Describing *Days of Heaven*, Cavell wrote that 'the film does indeed contain a metaphysical vision of the world; but I think one feels that one has never quite seen the scene of human existence – call it the arena between earth (or days) and heaven – quite realised this way on film before' (ibid.). In our analysis of *The Thin Red Line*, we find a similar realisation, a visual investigation of the human situation, of our living in a world which is at once beyond our capacity to fully conceive, but for which we have devised a complex arsenal of techniques for conception – even further, given that this is also a war picture, a complex arsenal with which to literally dominate the world. In this regard, Malick is performing the function of the artist, of the poet during what Heidegger called 'destitute times', in which the world is voided of mystery and depth, as language, thought and representation themselves are put to merely instrumental ends. Heidegger accorded to poetry and to art an important and specifically restorative function. The poet's task, as Heidegger insists in 'What Are Poets For?', is to reveal through the use of evocative, poetic language what metaphysics has obscured: the presencing of Being through language. Philosophy, thus, must become poetry, and poetry must become philosophical. We argue that Malick has assumed the role of poet-philosopher, putting the cinema to poetic and philosophical ends, revealing the relation between Being and the medium of film, revealing through the use of poetic, evocative imagery the cinema's unique presencing of Being. Neither obscure nor oblique, Malick's cinema must be understood to be performing a valuable gesture of clarification, and its primary value derives from its concern with traditional, cinematic representation of modern war.

•••

To a certain extent, a disenchantment with technology and modernity is a feature of the destitute times to which Heidegger refers. Like many of the generation who lived through World War One, he was very aware of the challenge to humanity posed by the technological capacity of modernity. The barbarism of that war, in which the fruits of Western scientific progress were mobilised to develop weapons with an unprecedented capacity to destroy life, called this progress into question. But what is definitive in Heidegger's notion outstrips this sense of disenchantment. To understand the role of the poet in destitute times, we must grasp what Heidegger thinks is missing in these times such that they are destitute, and how this has occurred. There are four elements to the discussion which must be clarified: Heidegger's understanding of the nature of human existence and the relation to Being that it involves; the deficiency of this relation in modern technological society; the loss that this entails; and, finally, the role of the poet in light of this situation.

Heidegger's philosophical thinking is guided by the question of Being, which is formulated in many different ways throughout his work. The basic problem is this: what is the relation between Being (*Sein*) and beings (*Seiendes*)?[2] That is, if beings or entities are all things that are – that is, they all are because they participate in Being – then what is Being, and what is this participation or involvement in Being that we refer to when we say that all beings are? Being is the ground of beings, and so Heidegger often formulates the question of the relation between Being and beings as a question of ground or origin. The claim that there is a relation between Being and beings is predicated on the view that there is a difference between Being and beings – that Being is not just the sum of all beings. Heidegger calls this difference the ontological difference. But if Being is not the totality of all beings, it is also not some prime substance out of which all beings emerge and are differentiated. Being must be understood in the dynamic sense signified by the verb 'to be'. All beings are, and each being is different, in its own mode of Being: not all beings are in the same way. The way a being is is the way it is present. An entity's mode of Being is its mode of presencing, its way of being present. Thus, Heidegger will often speak of Being as presence or presencing. Being is like an activity in which entities are all involved and through which they become present, and this is the sense in which beings participate in Being. Being is the ground of beings because beings come to presence through Being.

These central elements of Heidegger's thought are at play in 'What Are Poets For'. Using the poetry of Hölderlin and Rilke as a basis for his reflections, Heidegger holds that living things have been flung or thrown into Being from an undisclosed source or centre (1971a: 101–2). Different kinds of entities (for example plants, animals, human beings) are flung into different modes of Being and thus have different natures. As it happens, the mode of Being for human beings entails a greater degree of consciousness than that of other living things, and this consciousness is such that the world is set up for the human being as an object from which it is separate and distinct (1971a: 108). This form of consciousness also allows human beings to take their own existence as an object, thereby permitting them to embrace or appropriate as their own the path upon which nature has thrown them (1971a: 109–10). In other words, human beings can will their natures because they can make their existence (their Being) an object of their consciousness. This consciousness of their own existence makes it possible for human beings to ask the question of Being or ground with which all philosophy begins, according to Heidegger. This possibility is distinctively human and we express our Being most fully in pursuing it.

However, this form of consciousness is not without its dangers. That we can make our own nature the object of our will also means that we can assert ourselves as the foundation of our own nature and thus deny that human existence is grounded in anything other than itself (1971a: 111). Furthermore, that consciousness is able to distinguish itself from the world ultimately enables the objectification of the world. This phenomenon lies at the heart of the subject-object distinction, the theoretical attitude, and the subject's understanding of itself as independent of the world and the entities in it. These elements of human consciousness contribute to a particular way of thinking, a technological rationality, in which things in the world (including people) are viewed purely instrumentally. In texts such as 'The Question Concerning Technology' (1977) Heidegger argues that the objectification of the world performed in the detachment of the theoretical attitude transforms the relation of the thinker to the thing such that the thing is stripped of its independent reality, and is instead conceived as something that only has value and only is in relation to some instrumental end. Everything in nature – including people – comes to be seen as a resource to be exploited.

This technological thinking is deeply implicated in the destitution of modern times according to Heidegger. We become forgetful of the fact that we are not really the ground of our own Being, and we obscure from ourselves our relation to Being, to the rest of nature, and to one another. In modern technological society, where our self-understanding as self-founding producers who exercise mastery over the rest of nature becomes most fully manifest, this forgetfulness becomes acute (1971a: 112f). Since we understand ourselves as the ground of our own Being, we understand ourselves as possessing unlimited power, not only over the rest of nature, but over nature in ourselves. Specifically, we think we can cheat death: 'the self-assertion of technological objectification is the constant negation of death' (1971a: 125). In short, in highly developed technological society, we think of ourselves as immortal, as free of the constraints that are placed upon other living things. But if we are immortal, then we have become the gods. Since previously human beings defined themselves as mortal in relation to the immortality of the gods, this shift indicates that 'the gods have fled', and that we have lost a sense of our place in relation to other beings and to Being. Since this place defined our humanity, its loss signifies that we have become in-human. As Heidegger writes, 'the time remains destitute not only because God is dead, but because mortals are hardly aware and capable even of their own mortality. Mortals have not yet come into ownership of their own nature' (1971a: 96).

At stake here for Heidegger is not just that human beings are arrogant or that they run the risk of destroying the earth. What is most critical is that we become forgetful of what it means to be human, which means understanding oneself as standing in a particular relation to Being, a relation that actually connects us with all other beings. Thus, the forgetfulness of our humanity goes hand in hand with a forgetfulness of Being, and this is to be overcome through a reawakening of the question of Being, which involves bringing human beings back to themselves as human through reminding them of their mortality, their finitude, their existence. In various texts, Heidegger refers to human existence as a dwelling. To dwell is to be humanly through preserving what Heidegger in his essay 'Building, Dwelling, Thinking' calls the four-fold: 'In saving the earth, in receiving the sky, in awaiting the divinities, in initiating mortals, dwelling occurs as the fourfold preservation of the fourfold' (1971b: 151). Here Heidegger emphasises that human existence is finite: it entails living on and of the earth and under the sky, being situated between earth and sky. It also entails the temporal finitude of an entity that is aware of its death and thus of its life as possibility, and it involves the transcendence of an entity that can ask about what is beyond the horizons of its finitude. To dwell, for Heidegger, is for an entity to exist in a manner that draws these aspects of finitude together and preserves them in its way of Being.

This dwelling is lost in destitute times, and in such circumstances, the task of the poet is to reawaken in human beings a sense of their Being as human and mortal. The poet is to draw us back to ourselves, to remind us of the 'fugitive gods' and of our place in relation to Being and other beings (1971a: 94, 137–8; 1971b: 151), and since this leads to a reopening of the question of Being, this task becomes a very philosophical one. It is to be accomplished through language because our access to Being is in language because things are in language: 'all beings … are qua beings in the precinct of language' (1971a: 132). But since even language is increasingly instrumentalised, the disclosing of our relation to Being can only happen through poetic, evocative language (1971a: 133). Such language draws attention to the manner in which the entity is made manifest in language and thus presents itself as mediating our relation to Being as it allows the entity to become present. Thus, the use of poetic language permits the philosophical point to be made that things are through language and that instrumental language or the language associated with different metaphysical views allows entities to be seen – to be – in some ways but not in others. Discourse realises certain possibilities of Being for entities and forecloses others, but in destitute times we have lost a sense of language's function in this regard, and the use of poetic language becomes necessary. Philosophy and poetry become intertwined. Heidegger construes poetry rather broadly to include all art, for poetry is poiesis, a bringing-forth or creation. Poetry or art draws attention to its poiesis – its creative bringing-forth – in a way that technological production does not (1977: 10–11). Poetry makes present what the instrumentality of this technological bringing-forth conceals.

The Thin Red Line is Heideggerian cinema, and Malick has assumed the role of a poet in destitute times. Yet Malick has chosen the cinema for his poiesis, and one might question whether it can be used for such a poetic presentation. The cinema is obviously a visual medium, and Heidegger complained that traditional epistemological models were based upon visual perception, and that this tendency contributed to the interpretation of beings as things present-at-hand. Such an interpretation is bound up with the theoretical stance of the subject in relation to the object that underlies the technological thinking that Heidegger criticises. Against the tradition, Heidegger argues that beings come to presence through language, through speaking and hearing. Surely, then, the cinema seems a strange choice for poiesis.

While this objection suggests that language has priority over the visual image, it is important to recall that for Heidegger language is subject to instrumentalisation as well. Language, too, can perform a representational function by objectifying through propositions in which what the thing is is reduced to its representation, and language can operate to obscure that it functions in this way (1971a: 126–7). This is why Heidegger stresses the necessity of poetic presentation that breaks through this barrier of representations with intuitive images brought forth from the thing itself by poetry:

> The nature of the image is to let something be seen. By contrast, copies and imitations are already mere variations on the genuine image which, as a sight or spectacle, lets the invisible be seen and so imagines the invisible in something alien to it ... poetic images are ... not mere fancies or illusions but imaginings that are visible inclusions of the alien in the sight of the familiar. (1971a: 126–7)

Since the goal of poetising is to allow the intuition of images, the cinema perhaps is a very apt medium. This is not to say that the choice of cinema is without risk, however. The cinema is a product of specific technological advances, and often serves a strictly instrumental function. This is particularly true of the war film – the genre within which *The Thin Red Line* falls. In choosing to elaborate an alternative vision of the cinema's task through this genre, Malick defies many of our expectations of a war film, and the significance of this choice becomes more apparent when considered in view of the thought that *The Thin Red Line* is Heideggerian cinema. First, this choice of genre is apt for conveying the decidedly Heideggerian content of the film, which illustrates technological thinking and the alienation from Being that it produces and shows how, when this alienation is at its most acute – namely in war – the question of Being may be reawakened. Second, the film does not simply represent this content; it enacts it poetically and disturbs the viewer's forgetfulness of Being. The choice of genre draws attention to the film as a mode of presentation or presence.

Malick is able to use the setting of war in *The Thin Red Line* to thematise the central concerns raised in 'What Are Poets For?' War is a context in which technological rationality and instrumentalisation reach an extreme, where the specific instrumental tasks of warfare trump all other human ends, even humanity itself. Technological rationality alienates us from Being or ground, from nature, from one another, and from our very humanity. This alienation is manifest in the destruction of war in which not only are people killed but the earth is scarred, the animals it shelters are killed or displaced, and the humanity of the combatants themselves is jeopardised as they commit acts, the atrocity of which they only fully come to understand later. Malick's film presents all of this, and demonstrates the tension between the goals of instrumental thinking and the ends of humanity most clearly in the conflict between Lt Colonel Tall and Captain Staros. While Staros clearly understands that in war men will die, he nevertheless acutely feels the loss of each of his men and heavily bears his responsibility for them. Tall, on the other hand, has waited fifteen years for the opportunities that the war provides, and he will accomplish his military objective whatever the cost. He has slight regard for the welfare of the men under his command, seeing little difference whether they die from enemy fire or from lack of water. Although Tall calls the loss of men a 'sacrifice', he clearly does not understand it to be a sacrifice, for he has instrumentalised his troops.

But if war involves the calculation of technological rationality at its extreme, it also functions as the limit situation which, because of its extremity, raises our consciousness of this kind of rationality and its dehumanising effects. If technology is the negation of death, modern warfare – the use of technology to destroy life – is the negation of that negation. Since war is consciously willed, it is essentially the will to death, an affirmation of death. In this, war is a distinctively human phenomenon, despite its inhumanity. All living things are 'thrown' towards death by nature. But, as Heidegger puts it, only human beings can will the path onto which nature has thrust them, only human beings can take over their nature and affirm it as their own end (1971a: 109–11). If existing involves understanding human finitude, then existing means understanding oneself as limited, as existing in relation to what one is not, to what is beyond. Life in advanced technological society is a mode of existence in which one tries to deny existence (that is, the possibility of death). But where there is no awareness of death, can there be any true awareness of life? The will to death suppressed in technological life erupts to the surface in modern warfare, raising anew for us the question of life: how shall we live, how shall we exist?

War serves as a limit situation in another regard: it thrusts those who are involved in it into a confrontation with the possibility of their own deaths. War discloses mortality, and if – as Heidegger claims – awareness of one's own mortality is a defining characteristic of humanity, then war discloses our humanity. Most of the soldiers are aware of their mortality, their vulnerability and fragility, having been awakened to it through the imminent possibility of their deaths. They are aware that they do not occupy a privileged place in the cosmos or in nature. They struggle to understand their place in this order; they search for some sort of ground that secures their place and assuages their fear. Staros searches for a ground in God when he prays for the strength not to betray his men. For Bell this ground is his wife. The strength of his bond with her gives him a centre and a focus, and he does not feel alone because he is connected to her and she is there with him. Only when she writes that she wants to leave him does he seem lost.

For Heidegger, philosophy begins when Being and existence are thrown into question for us. This questioning leads to thought and introspection. Malick uses voice-overs to represent this inwardness in the film, and through the voice-overs we become privy to the characters' thoughts in a manner which augments the dialogue and gives us a deeper understanding of how their situation challenges them, the questions it raises for them and how they attempt to make sense of it. This inwardness is explored to greatest effect in the voice-overs associated with Witt and Welsh and their occasional exchanges in the film. Witt exemplifies how such an awareness can lead to the kind of questioning from which philosophy arises. He is contemplative and reflective, and perhaps more than any other character in the film, asks the question of Being in a decidedly philosophical manner. Witt seems to understand that life and death go hand

Can one man make a difference?: Sergeant Welsh embodies the psychological conflict of war

in hand, that this cycle is what connects us to nature, to other creatures, to one another and perhaps to Being. He wonders about the power, which may or may not be divine, which is the source of all beings, which is their ground. He wonders about our relation to this ground. He wonders about whether life and death are two faces of the same power or two different powers. Although at the beginning of the film, Witt says that he does not know of any immortality, he seems to think that nevertheless we should not be afraid of death because death connects us to life in a larger sense. Witt also wonders why there is hatred, why people – who are basically one family – have become divided against each other, why they search for salvation alone and not together. We gather that Witt would rather have no part in the war; he has gone AWOL several times and seems appreciative of what he perceives – although this perception is subsequently revised – to be the relative purity and innocence of the life of the islanders. But, having been returned to the army, Witt decides to try to make a difference in that context. He will stick by C-Company because they are his people. He says that he wants to be able to meet death calmly, and throughout the film he tries to allay the fear of death which his comrades experience.

Sergeant Welsh, at least on the surface, seems to disagree with Witt's reasoning. He tells Witt on several occasions that one man cannot make a difference, that in all of this madness, the only thing to do is to look out for oneself. Yet, despite this talk, Welsh clearly feels compassion for the suffering of the men and tries to make some difference – excusing a sick soldier from a mission which seems sheer suicide, and exposing himself to heavy enemy fire in order to help a dying soldier reach the morphine that will end his pain. Where Witt is able to see in war a play of life and death which is part of nature, Welsh sees only pointless suffering. Those whose interests the war serves try to justify it, but he rejects that it has any reason which might justify all this death.

Not only does the experience of war expose these men to their own mortality, it also shakes their forgetfulness of Being. When one's existence is called into question, one begins to ask what it means to exist; one asks why there is anything and not nothing; one asks what it all means. Such questions are concerned with Being, with the meaning of Being, and with the origin or ground of beings or entities. In short, we ask about the relation between Being and beings, and in doing so, we exist humanly.

Having chosen war as his subject, Malick specifically focuses on its potential to problematise human existence – not just in the trivial sense that those who go to war may die – but in the sense that our very humanity is challenged by modern warfare and by the loss of our sense of place in relation to all of nature and to Being which is evident in technological thinking. In *The Thin Red Line*, the characters all come to realise this in one way or another. But for the film to be poetry and for Malick to be a poet, the film must not merely represent this; it must present these questions and issues in such a manner that they become questions and issues for us. The film must poetically bring forth its subject, and since that subject is human existence or dwelling, the film must present this dwelling, and it must do so in a reflexive way that draws attention to this presenting.

The film's form and the cinematic techniques Malick employs are important in enabling *The Thin Red Line* to move beyond representation toward presentation. The images in the film draw the viewer into the questioning in which the film is engaged such that the viewer is not merely a spectator. Through the pacing of the film, the viewer experiences the tension of the situation and the soldiers' uncertainty during periods of quiet, which are then punctuated by brief explosions of fighting in which chaos and confusion reign. None of this is tied together by much of a narrative, and the viewer is thrown into the film as the soldier is thrown into battle. But we are not drawn into the film by the realism of its representation of the battle. The reality with which we are presented is a poetic creation: in many cases, the sounds of battle are muted so that we are required to focus on the image – on the faces wherein we see the truth that Malick wants us to see. Here Malick chooses not to allow the cinema's representational possibility to crowd out and prevent the realisation of other possibilities, specifically the possibility of presenting human existence. In this way, the film provokes in the viewer a questioning, and although we witness many different strategies or attitudes toward resolving these questions on the part of the various characters, the film does not clearly endorse any of them. The film, thus, does not answer for the viewer the question that it poses. The answer to the question of Being or ground around which the film swirls remains ambiguous, and this is necessary for the film to remind us of our humanity and of the question of Being. It also plays an important role in the film's presenting of its own presentational function.

Although Malick's film does not explicitly answer the questions it poses, it does point us in a direction. It encourages us to exist humanly, to dwell. To dwell on the earth – to exist – is to span the dimension between earth and sky through the preservation of the fourfold. In other words, we measure the space between earth and sky with an upward glance from the earth toward the sky above. We look up to the sky as the place where the gods are concealed; the distance between the earth where we dwell and the sky where the divine resides measures our distance from the divine and defines us as human (1971c: 220–2). In '... Poetically Man Dwells ...', Heidegger argues that poetry is a measuring in which our position with reference to the gods is assessed. In poetry, humanity takes measure of itself as human in relation to the divine, and to do so is to exist humanly. This suggests that we are only when we poetise (1971a: 138–9).

Malick conveys this sense of earthly dwelling in, for instance, having the camera effect the upward glance to the sky, to where the divine is intimated yet concealed. The underwater shots are all oriented skyward: we see sunlight diffusing through the sea and silhouetting swimming children. There are numerous shots of trees soaring to the heavens and of sunlight filtering through jungle canopy. In another shot, sparks from a roaring fire are sucked by the draft into the night sky. As the camera follows their ascent, the distance between earth and sky – the distance by which humanity is measured – is spanned.

In conveying the Heideggerian content of the film, Malick develops the possibility latent within the cinema to present and draw attention to its presenting and bringing forth, and in experimenting with this possibility of the cinema he can be seen to be extending into the language of the cinema the poetic and philosophical task which Heidegger described in relation to art and poetry. In reawakening a sense of our mortality and thus of ourselves as human through this poetic, filmic presentation, Malick assumes the role of the poet in destitute times and reveals the cinema's capacity to accomplish this poetic task.

Notes

1   This has generated a considerable amount of more or less serious speculation, as we have said, on the part of journalists and film critics, who have attempted to explain Malick's reticence, which has taken on legendary proportions, while characterising him as essentially reclusive and purposefully enigmatic. Examples include Bart (1998) and Handy (1997). Malick has commented publicly on his films on occasion. See, for example, the interview in *Sight and Sound* by Beverly Walker (1975).

2   Since *Sein* and *Seiendes* could both be translated as 'being' in English, it is customary to capitalise 'Being' when translating *Sein*, and to translate *Seiendes* as 'beings' or 'entities' to avoid confusion.

References

Bart, Peter (1998) 'The Silence of the Malick: What's His Line?', *Variety*, December, 21.

Cavell, Stanley (1979) *The World Viewed: Reflections on the Ontology of Film*, enlarged edition. Cambridge: Harvard University Press.

Handy, Bruce (1997) 'His own sweet time', *Time*, October 13.

Heidegger, Martin (1969) *The Essence of Reasons*, trans. Terrence Malick. Evanston, Il: Northwestern University Press.

_____ (1971a) 'What Are Poets For?', in *Poetry, Language, Thought*, trans. Albert Hofstadter. New York: Harper & Row, 90–142.

_____ (1971b) 'Building, Dwelling, Thinking', in *Poetry, Language, Thought*, trans. Albert Hofstadter. New York: Harper & Row, 143–161.

_____ (1971c) '... Poetically Man Dwells ...', *Poetry, Language, Thought*, trans. Albert Hofstadter. New York: Harper & Row, 211–229.

_____ (1977) 'The Question Concerning Technology', *The Question Concerning Technology and Other Essays*, trans. William Lovitt. New York: Harper & Row, 3–35.

Walker, Beverly (1975) 'Malick on *Badlands*', *Sight and Sound*, 44, 2, 82–3.

Whalen, Tom (1999) '"Maybe all men got one big soul": The Hoax Within the Metaphysics of Terrence Malick's *The Thin Red Line*', *Literature/Film Quarterly*, 27, 3, 162–6.

Zucker, Carole (2001) 'God don't even hear you', or Paradise Lost: Terrence Malick's *Days of Heaven*', *Literature/Film Quarterly*, 29, 1, 2–9.

CHAPTER FIFTEEN

Praising The New World

Mark Cousins

O tell us, poet, what do you do? – I praise…
How have you the right, in every disguise,
Beneath every mask, still to be true? – I praise.
How can the calm and the violent,
Star and storm, both know you?: – because I praise.
— Rainer Maria Rilke (1921)

We cannot separate our reading of a film, our sense of where it fits in culture and aesthetics, from the raw circumstances in which we saw it. I watched *The New World*, a film that flopped around the world despite headlining one of America's most famous movie stars, on a rainy Tuesday afternoon in the Vue cinema in Edinburgh. Usually a Colin Farrell movie would be booked into all the multiplexes simultaneously but this one was hard to find. It played in one suburb in Glasgow and on just a handful of other screens in Scotland, as if it had the plague and needed to be quarantined. For a prestige picture, it was booked with what seemed like reluctance, minimally, resentfully.

The film made me cry. I began to do so about thirty minutes after it started and continued, on and off, in waves, just like Yang Kuei-Mei sitting on the park bench in the last shot of Tsai Ming-liang's *Vive l'amour*. By the end of *The New World*, it seemed to me, I had experienced something like a Bach's Mass in B Minor or a poem by Percy Bysshe Shelley. It was about rapture and the end of rapture. It showed me seeing. It made me sensible. That week, I was to begin teaching at the Screen Academy in Edinburgh – Scotland's new film school. After seeing *The New World*, I realised that the best, most inspiring first class would be to watch it on the big screen. The Screen Academy negotiated a discount rate, and my students went.

None responded as I did. None cried, none thought that they'd seen a cinema masterclass, none seemed compelled to find words to describe how it went beyond cinema. Thus began *The New World*'s descent for me, its relegation, my growing suspicion that I went too far to meet it that rainy Tuesday morning, that I mingled too many of my ideas with its ideas, as if it was a lover for whom I had fallen, to whom I had not listened, in whom I had seen my own selfish sense of what lovers are.

The New World continued to become stale for me when I read the first edition of book you now have in your hands, whose subtitle is *Poetic Visions of America*. As I read Mottram's essay, then Patterson's, then Campbell's, McGettigan's, Orr's and McCann's, I realised that *The New World* was each of the things that the films they were writing about was. It is certainly Emersonian, as *Badlands* is, in that it is an essay about human subjectivity and its response to nature. It is also, surely, Heideggerian, predicated on the idea that deep down in the well of ourselves is Being, something rendered inaudible by the tinny sound of life modernising. It also uses commentary, as *Badlands*, *Days of Heaven* and *The Thin Red Line* do, to fetch water from that well and bring to the surface traces of deep thought and, as a result, render that surface numinous.

Like the other films discussed in this book, *The New World* is about having paradise and watching it slip away, the slippage caused by the very same stuff that allows us to feel the bliss of paradise in the first place. As in *Badlands*, *The New World* uses doorways and gateways to contend that the built world frames human beings in a different way to the bowers of the natural world, and causes us to re-see them because of this framing. Also, like some of the other movies conjured on these pages, *The New World* seems as if it could have been written by Herman Melville. Like Private Witt in *The Thin Red Line*, it asks the question 'This great evil, where does it come from? How did it steal into the world? What root did it grow from? Who's doin' this? What's killin' us, robbin us of life and light?' And, like the other films described here, its characters are often in a dream state, a condition that has 'gone upwards' to the movie itself, imparting to it their reverie.

This realisation that *The New World* is like the other films described deepened my deflation. That the fourth is like the other three is disappointing to me but then I am in and of a culture that values innovation and iconoclasm over continuity and confirmation. *The New World* does not value iconoclasm. It praises rather than destroys. Its glorious beauty is not fuelled by the desire to move forward into the future of ideas, but backward, as it were, or downwards into thoughts and wisdoms that are no longer apparent. This backwardness disappoints me. The film that made me cry began, on reading this book, to set off a train of thought that started with its over-familiarity, moved through its thematic and philosophical repetitions, on to question why another film had been made about Edenic America, and concluded with a bang, and some irritation, with another question: Why not produce a movie about something pressing on our modern age, like Iraq?

This point led to other thoughts: America has been irritating of late. Its centripetal self-regard has been showing too much and not been sufficiently outweighed by its openness, liberty of mind and optimism, so to see another film about its discovery by Europe, that politico-mythic next step that for so long was thought of (by Europeans) as a first step, seems like more navel-gazing. Who cares? Get over yourself. We've gotten over you. We no longer flock to see your horse operas, your primal law-makers, the stetsoned first-footers of what you consider to have been that splendid nineteenth-century party – America.

It is clear from its first scenes that *The New World* doesn't talk to America in this lippy, impatient, twenty-first century, teenage way. The film isn't 'over' the country. It elides the centuries since the 'founding' fathers as if they – the centuries – were a regrettable detour that, desirably, could be redressed. It is still calling those days 'new'. This last point, my attempt to be honest about the apparent conservatism of *The New World* conversely fails to be as depressing as it should be. The film shows that its director's worldview and philosophical assumptions haven't budged, but immobility can mean passionately, obsessively correct as well as blinkered. Once Gaugin found his style and situations, he strayed little because they took from the air around him, and made flesh, some of the discourses of his times. Maybe the writer-director of *The New World* has been doing the same thing all these years, precipitating timeless insights, just as Gore Vidal has been lobbing word bombs at his home country from the very same point since the 1950s.

With this thought – the longevity of the filmmaker's rightness – the deflation starts to reverse. The stature of *The New World* starts to grow again for me. It is time, today, also a Tuesday but sunny, to watch it once more.

The first shot, of the rippling surface of a pool, is scored to the ululation, twitter and squawk of a gigantic aviary. A Darwinian world, shoals of fish or eels, seem to slip and swim beneath the pool's surface, breaking and convulsing it. To stare at water in cinema is to expect a Spielbergian shark or contemplate a Tarkovskian void but here, in the first moments of this film, we are looking at a gene pool, the origins of life. A voice, that of Pocahontas, says 'Come spirit ... we rise out of the soul of you.' Then we are at her feet as she reaches to the heavens, hands apart, beckoning the spirit to descend. Then we are under the water, as if we have become the spirit she addresses, and are looking up at Algonquin Indians in Virginia in 1607, staring and pointing out to sea. They have spotted something. Deep down in the sound mix, softening and underscoring the aviary, are distant, gathering horns. Then violas join them in heralding what the Algonquins have seen, then violins rush to the scene, above the rest, and we cut to seventeenth-century boats drifting gracefully towards the land, the strain in their holds heard in the creak of massive beams and the click of rigging. Then we are in the black bowels of one of the boats, in whose gloom we see two white eyes of a dog, its wet hair hanging over its face as if it has been for a swim. Then we get closer and see that the dog is a movie star, Colin Farrell, who peers out into the light.

Then, six and a half minutes in to this gathering opera (the music is from Wagner's *Das Reingold*), we cut to a field of long grass which, given that it's this director, is photographed as if it is the sea. Wind rushes across it in waves, as it does in the trees at beginning of Tarkovsky's *Mirror* and the forest shots in David Lynch films. The field is alive, a corner of a slumbering planet. The Panavision lens makes the distant edge of the field, the horizon, curve as if it is a huge quadrant of the earth. Then Colin Farrell, playing John Smith, is walking through the field. The sun is behind him – this filmmaker usually shoots into the sun, giving his actors haloes, making their faces penumbral. Tribesmen arrive. With great gentleness, Smith reaches out his hand and they touch it and almost nibble it as if they are chickens eating corn or, as Smith says in close-miked voice-over, 'like a herd of curious deer'. When we hear his thoughts, they sound like he is praying to his European god. Interweave his prayers with Pocahontas's to her earth mother god and you get a theological duet, a song to two sirens.

At 12 minutes 40 seconds, in a sea-field, Smith sees Pocahontas. They look at each other. The light is to his right and behind him (of course), but his body is clocked at 45 degrees so the sun glances off his chest. We cut to her and, magically, impossibly, the light is to her right too. Sixteen minutes later she touches his lips. Smith says these people have 'no guile, no jealousy, no sense of possession', but how could he possibly tell? All he has is what he sees and feels in these moments, on that first day, a day that will change the world.

Two hours later, I am crying again, not as much as before because I am watching on DVD this time, on a screen too small to overwhelm. As I watch I get stuck at how beautiful Q'Orianka Kilcher, who plays Pocahontas, is, and Farrell too, and become suspicious of their casting because, in our time, the iniquities of the fashion and advertising industries have made us rightly uneasy about worlds where everyone is beautiful. I free myself to enjoy the film again by the thought that it, *The New World*, is explicitly asserting the beauty of this moment in Virginia in 1607, and that these beautiful actors are what John Orr calls 'the expressive externalisation of private emotions' – feelings of peace and harmony – that, themselves, are beautiful. Then I get stuck again, by Kilcher's age. She is fifteen. This filmmaker does fifteen well. Sissy Spacek was 24 when *Badlands* was released but seems fifteen in the film. The question in *The Thin Red Line*, 'Love, where does it come from, this flame in us?', is the question a 15-year-old would ask. This director keeps asking it, as if he himself is stuck at that age.

As I watch I think and scribble, mostly superlatives about people seeing and feeling and how the film depicts this and how it is mostly about seeing and feeling, their immediacy, their necessity and their limits. Again and again as I scribble, I write a name, David Hume. When I saw *The Thin Red Line* I also thought of the historian-philosopher Hume, who published *A Treatise on Human Nature* in 1740, *Enquiries Concerning Human Understanding* in 1748, *Enquiries Concerning the Principles of Morals* in 1751 and whose *Dialogues Concerning Natural Religion* was published posthumously, in 1779. The day after I saw *The Thin Red Line* I went to Hume's grave in Edinburgh, plucked a weed, taped it to a bit a paper and mailed it to the filmmaker's agent, with a note saying what it was and thanking him – the filmmaker – for what I considered to be a masterpiece.

A month later, as I left a theatre, I was met by my partner who said that I should hurry home because I would be getting a phone call at nine o'clock. I did so and, on the button of nine, the phone went and a high-pitched voice said 'Hi, it's Terry Malick here.' He asked if the weed was really from Hume's grave. He asked what the grave is like (a wide, squat Georgian tower). He thanked me again and again for the weed. He said he had read Hume as a student and admired him. I remember that in trying to explain why I sent the weed, I mentioned George Steiner's book *Real Presences*. We talked some more. Malick said he would call again, and hung up. He did call again. This time I asked if he'd agree to be interviewed for my television series *Scene by Scene*. He said that TV makes him nervous and that he is a bad speaker and, certainly, even in this least pressured of circumstances, a phone call with a cinephile, he was hesitant and diffident. I felt bad for asking, then, presumptuously, suggested a book-length interview, like the Truffaut-Hitchcock one or Faber & Faber's 'Filmmaker on Filmmaker' series. Again, he said that he wasn't sure, that he just liked talking about philosophy. Malick called a third time, then we said our goodbyes.

The connection, of course, made me alert to the Humeanism of Malick's work. Hume wrote that his mother was 'wake minded' and so is Malick and so are his films. Following in the footsteps of John Locke's Empiricism, Hume argued that passage beyond our sense perception is impossible. We have only these perceptions – he called them impressions – with which to construct our sense of the outside world. These impressions, argued Hume, imprint themselves on our mind and, when repeated, form ideas. An idea is an aggregate of confirmed impressions – that, for example, the sun in the morning will feel warm on my face. We do not build our understanding of the outside world logically (Hume criticised the concept of cause and effect), but by impressions accumulating into ideas. Each, said Hume, recalls the other. There is a flow between the two.

The lack of metaphysics in this empiricism, its non-essentialism sounds, at first, very un-Malick. That human beings are receivers of information, that there is nothing mysterious or soul-like inside the black box of themselves, seems to undermine the Heideggerean rapture that we see in Malick's films, their attempts to biopsy the human soul. But this is perhaps to misunderstand Hume and Malick. The mystery in Malick's work lies in his ability to use the medium of film to show that it is the process of receiving impressions of the world that is transcendent. He may in addition posit theories of self, but looking at Malick through the lens of Hume shows that the pre-cognitive experience of engaging sensually with the world is where at least some of the wonder lies.

So, in *The New World*, we see impressions turning into ideas. We see Smith feeling and hearing this new world, observing patterns of tenderness and openness in the Algonquins, patterns that, Hume would say, aggregate into ideas. They coalesce and take root. Through observing him, touching him and listening to him, Pocahontas's sense of what sort of man Smith is grows magically before us, as green shoots in the jungle do in time-lapse scenes in natural history programmes. And, over time, because Malick's films are cyclical and repetitive rather than forwardly directed, we see ideas becoming complex ideas – another Humean term. This tree is beautiful. The one I saw yesterday is beautiful. The one from the day before was too. We grow accustomed to this certainty, this beauty-hit, and come to expect it. It enters our nature, this assumption of constancy, of guaranteed rapture.

If Malick is in some sense stuck, and if in some sense I get stuck watching his films and reading about them, perhaps this is why. The constancy in his career, the ongoing

John Smith constructing a sense of this new world

praise he lavishes on the mid-moment in human experience when we are drinking in, with 'beaded bubbles winking at the brim, and purple-stained mouth', perhaps derives from that sense that because life has been beautiful so far, it should always be so. And in each of his films he gets knocked for six, bowled over by the un-expected, the post-Edenic, the scepticism at the very least, that is required in order to brace oneself for the tragedy of life.

In *The New World*, Malick gets knocked over yet again. Each time he goes away from our screens, he seems to unlearn what life has taught him and start again with new characters like Pocahontas who are too young to have learnt, or from a place that doesn't know or doesn't need to know. They are wide open, these characters, Humean sponges drinking in experience, glorying in the aviary that is life.

Whether we need more Malick films is an open question. I hate the thought that there might be no more but would, to be honest, love him to drop both Hume and Heidegger next time, and venture out into a new world. That's not to say that I don't adore the game of skittles he's played these last three decades, but isn't it time for another game? This one came courtesy of Time-Warner, just as the Vatican funded the paintings of Caravaggio in Santa Maria del Popolo.

CHAPTER SIXTEEN

Making Worlds, Making Pictures: Terrence Malick's *The New World*

James Morrison

The critical reaction to Terrence Malick's fourth film illustrates an entrenched critical habituation. According to most reviewers of *The New World* (2005), Malick – the cinematic 'nature' poet – is at it again in his rendering of the Pocahontas legend, compensating for narrative amorphousness with a lush array of pretty pictures. Whether in laudatory or censorious tones, critics treated the film as a 'transcendentalist visual symphony' (Jones 2006: 28) in which 'beauty transcends history' (Taubin 2006: 45), or as a 'heavily aestheticized' (Hoberman 2005) tone-poem that shows how 'to the innocent eye … every world is new' (Lane 2005: 151). If Malick were indeed rehearsing North America's myths of origin merely as occasions for neo-Romantic exercises in transcendentalism, or sporadic bouts of an accustomed lyricism, complete with Edenic pastorals and noble savages, the film would be worthy, on the grounds of terminal naivety, of the dismissals it earned from many quarters on the very different pretexts of its alleged tedium.

In fact, though, this appearance of naivety – poised between rapture and irony without subsuming either, on the order of the 'intelligent naivety' promoted by the Romantics themselves – sheathes a new kind of sophistication, nascent in *The Thin Red Line* (1998), that comes to fruition in *The New World*. In his consideration of the brutality and potential transcendence of 'world-making', in its relation to the chastened transcendence and extenuated brutality of 'world alienation' (in Hannah

Arendt's phrase), Malick risks the faults always potential in 'the cinema of exploration' (see Bazin 1967: 155) – exoticism, false romanticism, idealisation, a naïve faith in the transparency of mimesis or an exaggerated dependency on the ready-made picturesque – to mount an inquiry into the displacement of pre-Enlightenment myths of wholeness and cosmic integrity by a rising awareness, in the words of Michel de Montaigne, of 'the perpetual multiplicity and ever-changing vicissitudes of forms' (quoted in Ross & McLaughlin 1953: 158). Far from denying colonial violence in a welter of aestheticised myth-making, Malick explores the ways in which history, legend and ideology combine to produce possibilities for a pluralistic 'worldview' – and to subvert them. As history, the brutality of colonial conquest may appear to be slighted in the film, but as consciousness, it is everywhere, underlying the film's most radiant idylls and shadowing its gentlest and most volatile expressions of awe. In this meditation on the historical epoch of world-making, Malick shows how the inexpressibly violent becomes intertwined with the provisionally 'beautiful'.

Malick's films do indeed enquire into the dual character of 'nature' and 'beauty' in different historical, social and cultural contexts – consumerist mass culture in *Badlands* (1973), the rise of American industrialisation in *Days of Heaven* (1978), the onset of global warfare in *The Thin Red Line*. But these categories are hardly treated as an undifferentiated conceptual mass or a pair of constant quantities. If, for many viewers, 'nature' boils down in each case to the same aggregate of brush, sea and sky, Malick can hardly be expected to answer for a predisposition widespread since the seventeenth century – and indeed, this attitude ranks high among the provocations to his interest in modern diminutions of nature, a concern made evident in his alertness to how differently nature appears in each of the contexts he contemplates. In Malick's work, the theme of transcendence cannot be understood apart from that of alienation. Despite the film's overlay of rapture, this has never been the case more than in *The New World*, where the familiarity of the myth that furnishes the film's content enables an atomisation of narrative structure more extreme than in any of his previous films – more extreme, perhaps, than in any Hollywood movie ever made. Nature, once it takes its place in this radically sundered structure, can appear only as an image of failed transcendence, even if the film suggests the possibility of an authentic immanence with an ardency unmatched in this director's work.

In *The New World*, Malick portrays nature in much the terms in which so many have been inclined for so long to see it: as a preserve not of the specific but of the typical. Gone are the depictions in *Days of Heaven* of metamorphic natural processes or transformations of nature through human labour, with their attentions to growth and change, diurnal and seasonal cycles. Nowhere in evidence are the illustrations of natural multiformity of *Badlands* or *The Thin Red Line*, with their painstaking studies of dappled textures and variable surfaces or minute differences among leaves, trees, skyscapes, bodies of water. In *The New World*, the elements of nature remain the same – and an image of nature as an emblem of endurance remains constant across Malick's films – but they are portrayed as uniform and unchanging. Seasonal shifts occur not over time, but with startling abruptness, without transition, and if any processes are disclosed in the workings of nature, they are only those of repetition, as in one of the film's key images, recurrent shots of water flowing ceaselessly over rocks. In this film, nature endures by virtue of generating replications of the same types, and Malick makes this point most clearly by rhyming the various trees that Pocahontas communes with as, in effect, versions of the same tree, whether it grows in the wilderness of the New World or stands in a well-tended English garden.

This is not to suggest that Malick himself now portrays nature as a constant quantity, but that he imputes to it an aspect of inertness that renders newly pressing the question of how we are to look at it, or to be in relation to it. One possibility is to conquer it – to impress individual or collective will upon it in an imposition of intention or design, as the conditions of modernity so often incline us to act on what we define as inert. Another is to see it in its contingent qualities – its 'thing-ness' – as confronting us with an otherness against which we may define ourselves apart from the antagonisms of alien human will. The first of these alternatives entails a version of the colonial gaze, with its drive toward violent mastery. The second entails the gaze of a receptive consciousness attuned to nature's capacity, in time, to individuate and differentiate in its seeming reproductions of identity. These alternatives are, in large part, what the film is about: how worlds are 'made' as they are because of the ways that we look at them.[1] Depending on which option prevails, they might become home to a multifarious and flourishing humanity, or they might be destroyed.

These are the same alternatives that Martin Heidegger proposes as a response to crises of modernity in his philosophy, though his resolute pessimism makes clear that he does not believe the second could ever be realised. In *Being and Time*, Heidegger locates a decisive shift in human consciousness at the moment when the definition of 'truth' changed from a recognition of un-concealments in nature to a quest for absolute correspondence between the human mind and the things of the world. In the same moment, as a consequence, human beings became subjects, things became objects, and the differences produced in time fell to the subjective will to dominate the objective realm, in powerful assertions of identity between mind and thing – an identity which would have to be enforced if it could not be discovered. Thus, Heidegger located an impulse to 'imperialism' at the root of modern thought itself. What followed, in his view, was a history of violent solipsism, culminating in what Heidegger called 'the age of the world picture'.[2]

Historically coincident in Heidegger's account with ideas of 'new' worlds and the emergence of 'worldviews', the 'world picture' gives a 'structured image that is the creature of man's producing', reifying the 'conquest of the world' (1977: 134) toward which the drift of thought had led (particularly European thought, as Heidegger spoke contemptuously of the 'Europeanising' of the world). Heidegger does not mean here only the supersession of reality by representation; rather, he finds that the 'fundamental event of the modern age' is the construction of wide-ranging principles of measurement, axioms and decrees compelled to order 'everything that is' under the domineering subjects' assumed mastery of 'the whole' (1977: 133–4). To the extent that Heidegger offers a solution to this condition, it is that we give up the idea of wholes, make objects back into things – by coming to terms through reflection with their 'thing-ness' – and renounce the willfulness of subjectivity in an acceptance of our 'thrown-ness' (*Geworfenheit*), in an understanding of the conditions of being that enables discovery, in random encounters with natural contingency, of who, what or where we are.

In a sense, Malick's work has always been 'Heideggerean' in seeking means to depict natural beauty in 'the age of the world picture' and in its concern with the existential states of its protagonists.[3] These issues are linked by the films' convictions that nature is a site of alienation – that it is, perhaps above all, what people are alienated from in the schism of subject and object. In *Badlands*, *Days of Heaven* and *The Thin Red Line*, the 'beauty' of nature carries a penitential charge, as an aspect of the sense of irrecoverable loss these films convey. This penitential character persists in *The New World*, but it is synthesised with an unprecedented current of rapture, associated mainly with the figure of Pocahontas. In the previous films, nature stands as an image of what has been lost not because it is no longer available – the images derive much of their aesthetic force from their insistence that what they show is 'still there', at least as the raw material of the pictures – but precisely because it has become objectified. The pictures show this, too, in their very status as photographic images, 'composed' for aesthetic effect and reproduced for a human gaze.

In *The New World*, nature is integral to the film's structure in a new way. While in previous films Malick's nature imagery often appeared in dissociated interludes between narrative segments, here it is part of the narrative sequence, which is fractured not by their appearance, but from within. In *Days of Heaven* in particular, the nature interludes defer and confound the development of the story, by intruding as disruptive elements. They serve as transitions between narrative events that assert their own separateness from the narrative order. In *The New World*, with its emphatically paratactic structure, transition itself is abandoned, and the nature imagery falls back into the narrative, as an essential component of its progress. The effect is to raise the possibility, for the first time in Malick's work, that nature really could be somehow accessible to the people who inhabit it.

In *Badlands* and *Days of Heaven*, the inaccessibility of nature is demonstrated in narrative content as well as in form. The earlier film mocks the idea of a 'return' to nature as grotesque false consciousness, in the scene where the two young fugitives flee to the woods, while the later one portrays nature as the space of a profoundly disabled transcendence, alienated from the human action of the story. In both cases, the camera approaches nature warily, from an undefined, impersonal witness-point almost never connected to the points of view of the characters. Nature itself may be defined as dynamic, but there is something static in the manner of its representation, the camera remaining fixed before it, or scanning it from a sideways position, laterally tracking a coastal scene or a far horizon as if they were dioramas gliding slowly past – or as if the camera were engaged in an uncertain effort to find the vantage point on the landscape that will yield the most 'artistic' view. Indeed, the representation of nature is seldom free in any of Malick's films from the taint of the picturesque, but these assertions of technological or photographic mastery are often counterweighted by the tentativeness of their perspectives. In *The Thin Red Line*, nature is no longer a remote diorama but an encompassing surround, an environment in which the characters move, and the camera, its gaze less evocative of conventional depiction, penetrates it in smooth, forward-moving leaps that now suggest its innate capacity to create its own images, which need only be captured by the camera's gaze, not constructed for it. That the characters still cannot access it is shown not only by their tragic fates, but by the camera's tendency to exceed their physical motion. Shot after shot in the film is built around images of characters rushing into the frame – into the embrace of forest or field – until the camera following their path hurries beyond them, leaving them behind as it continues its survey of now-depopulated space, a technique that creates a pervasive and mournful sense of human oblivion. In its portrayal of nature as potentially 'present at hand' (in a Heideggerean phrase), *The New World* extends this technique in a precise reversal. Now it is the characters who exceed the roving gaze of the forward-tracking camera, entering the dynamic frame from behind the source of its vantage point, moving beyond it into nature's enfolding surround – whether for sanctuary or for conquest.

The potentiality thus expressed for nature's being 'present at hand' accounts for the film's streak of exuberance, while the terrible failure of this potentiality accounts for its overweening dejection. The bold synthesis of these conflicting tones is among the film's most extraordinary accomplishments, but they often diverge in formal terms. Many of the nature images again eliminate the human viewer, while Pocahontas is continually shown not just 'in' nature – as in one of the most beautiful shots, framing her against a sublime sky alight with bolts of lightning – but in a relation to it that the film contrasts with that of all others. That it is not the film's intent to portray Pocahontas as simply 'close' to nature is demonstrated by the contrast between the opening and the concluding sequences, scenes that answer one another directly. In both, she moves joyfully through natural landscapes, except that the first is 'unspoiled' wilderness, while the last is an English garden, severely groomed and filled with pruned trees, cropped hedges, topiary and sculpted simulations of natural rock. In a marked shift of tone, the film turns to an ironic mode as it cues us to see England as a site of grotesque de-naturalisation. At the same time, the film glorifies Pocahontas's sense of wonder in the garden, and it invests especially intense feeling in the moment when she places her hand at the base of the tree, so much like those she has loved in her home in the wilderness. The sequence is not just a celebration of nature's perseverance, though Pocahontas's joy suggests that the tree is to be seen not as a pitiful vestige but as a living presence. It confirms a palliative variety – the discovery in an appearance of sameness of a beloved difference, to be found in what is 'alien'. Viewed independently from assumed wholes, the objects of nature are harbingers of unclassed value, and what the film shows is Pocahontas's willingness to see them that way – neither making herself a masterly originator of meanings, nor becoming fixated before an absence that can be overcome only by being transcended. This, the film shows, is the 'sublime' process 'of being received into the steady bosom' (Ferguson 1992: 144) of the natural world.

Such reveries undoubtedly expose Malick to the accusation of naivety – a charge he courts openly in both *The Thin Red Line* and *The New World* – if only because of the displacement brought about in modernity of nature by culture. Yet it should be noted that the understanding of nature implied by *The New World* is anything but conventional. It is conceived not as that which places demands on people or preconditions human behavior to define and eliminate aberration, but as that which could, and should, be made to accommodate those who happen to live in it – an

Pocahontas is at one with nature in the 'unspoiled wilderness'

understanding that lies at the heart of the film's tender humaneness. Malick is so far from regretting the most obvious consequence of this displacement – the denaturalisation of universalism as ideology – that each of his films explores the destructive effect of imposing false generalities rationalised as nature.

Though *The New World* places great faith in the already known, it does so not to confirm prejudices but to explore the relation between myth and ideology. In the terms of the film, the myth of Pocahontas is situated squarely among the elements of the already known. In the demythologised context of modern history, this tale is best understood as an instance of false consciousness in which the conscription of a native girl as a hero of the colonial cause conceals her actual victimisation – the denial of her self-determination by means of her captivity and subsequent conversion to

Christianity, the stripping away of her native culture and her successive Anglicisation, her fate as a casualty of disease brought on by contact with the culture of the colonisers, whose own past circumstances living in urban settings protected them from pathogens capable of wiping out, as they did, millions of those whose very different history did not so immunise them, thereby easing the more deliberate strategies of elimination that were to follow.

Nothing in Malick's treatment of the story is at odds with – and much of it promotes – this understanding. But the film gives popular conception a slight turn to render the myth as a story about the possible reconciliation of diverse 'worlds' as they confront each other at a time when received paradigms about the make-up of the world of this encounter – and about the destruction of this meagre hope of reconciliation. The direst accounts of the myth celebrate Pocahontas's assimilation as a victory for the colony and a valorisation of the business of empire to shore up Christianity; Malick understands both the colonisers and the natives as people with a culture and a history, differentiated mainly by the extent of their technologies and the provenance of their exploits. In this light, the tale is about the prospect of cultural exchange, through mutual education and sympathetic consort – and about how this prospect falls under the dominion of an ascendant will to power.

The film begins with the 'dream' of a human collective life in an early voice-over of John Smith, as he looks upon the New World, a monologue that recalls the reveries of Montaigne or Shakespeare's *The Tempest*:[4]

> Here the blessings of the earth are bestowed upon all. None need grow poor. Here there is good ground for all, and no cause but one's labour in the true commonwealth – hard work and self-reliance and virtue ... We shall have no landlords to extort the fruit of our labour, or wrack us with their high rents. Men shall not make each other their spoil.

Thereafter, Smith's growing affection for Pocahontas is portrayed as an avenue toward the realisation of this dream. Scene after scene, lovingly rendered, shows the two of them engaged in repeated intimate concourse – walking hand in hand, or embracing while looking into each other's eyes – wordless and chaste but sensual and charged with erotic possibility. In the course of these interludes another voice-over reveals Smith's inner reflection: 'Real – what I thought was a dream.' Later, after Smith returns to the colonial settlement following a long period with the Powhatan, he considers the change in circumstance that is registered in the film's increasing emphasis on grueling work in the expansion of the colony: 'It was a dream; now I am awake.' At the end of the film, in a final colloquy with Pocahontas when she has been brought from England to receive honours from the king, Smith tells her, 'What I thought was a dream – it's the only truth.'

Creating the most consistent thematic arc in the film, this nexus of words represents in a more general way how the characters talk: plainly yet obliquely, with hints of cliché and tinctures of a superannuated artlessness amid the philosophical reverie.[5] That these words are not presented overtly as examples of 'naïve' speech cannot prevent their being heard that way any more than it necessarily implies an ultimate intention one way or another. The naivety of speakers in voice-over, however, has always been a key issue in the interpretation of Malick's work. In his first two films, according to critical consensus, this naivety is unquestionable. In *Badlands*, the voice-over narrator's flighty clichés are belied by the action in a direct ironic contrast. In *Days of Heaven*, the voice-over narrator's account may illustrate a guileless candour instead of a chilling false consciousness, but the narration remains defined by its obvious failure to grasp the meanings of the story being told, which we can comprehend only by looking beyond the frame we have been given. These explorations in limited perspective give way, in *The Thin Red Line*, to a very different method, with multiple voices juxtaposed, each prone to passing meditations and freed of narrative obligations or the pressures of counteraction. In the evolution of Malick's work, this decisive turn is felt as a withdrawal of irony, a mounting refusal to assert a superior sophistication as a corrective to wrong thinking. It is supported by a change in the content of the speech, which devotes itself to interior speculation instead of to the rationalisation of action or event.

The New World follows the model of *The Thin Red Line*, and irony remains so much in abeyance, for the most part, that if we hear the speakers' words as naïve all the same, we re-enter the sphere of dialectic – with its rhythm of competitive statement and counterstatement and its movement toward closure – that the film seems at such pains to suspend. Of course, there is good reason to suspect the vision Malick gives to Smith of a harmonious community in the New World, because we know that the society that developed there in fact was founded on the blood of those with whom Smith conceives the creation of a civil unity based on their own model.[6] Yet the history of North America might have been very different if the indigenous populations had been equal to the savagery of their conquerors, or if the hope of a humane collective existence, of which this history and this myth give us a glimpse, had been in any way sustainable. In *The New World*, Malick asks us to remain mindful of the fact that things might have gone differently even as the film recounts how and why this fleeting hope evaporated.

Smith's role as something of an unwitting agent of empire underscores the film's meditation on the emergence of a kind of 'world alienation' that a long tradition of thinking has located precisely at this point of history. This idea is perhaps most notably outlined in Hannah Arendt's *The Human Condition*, a book that shows the pervasive influence of Heidegger, where Arendt traces the development of this concept alongside the evolution of Renaissance humanism and colonial world-making. Aligning the birth of the modern age with 'the discovery of America and the ensuing exploration of the whole earth' (1958: 248), Arendt argues that these explorations joined with advances in European science to undermine a formerly held reliability of humanity's collective capacity to apprehend the universe. One response to this condition was the violent world-making of empire, a reaction-formation that aspired, in part, to negate cultural relativity and recover cosmic integrity by enlarging the power of allegedly unified nations across diverse territories, and eliminating or appropriating whatever was viewed as extraneous to the imposed world order. Yet the fact that it had to be imposed, instead of being found as an 'authentic order' (1958: 287) given in nature, served to confirm doubt and produce counter-conceptions of a secular world system, unguided by a divine plan, operating according to a hidden logic of its own. Thus deprived of a clear goal, this system turned circular, repetitive and arbitrary instead of progressing dependably toward a known apotheosis. As a result, according to Arendt, self-discovery took on a new priority – albeit on a colonial model, since it was identified with a capacity to transcend local perspective – while the 'expropriations' of colonial expansion 'did not simply result in new property or lead to a new redistribution of wealth, but were fed back into the process to generate further expropriations, greater productivity, and more appropriation' (1958: 255). Thus, the notion of individual agency took shape at just the time when it could only be abrogated by the intricate violence and impersonal force of the world system. For this reason, for Arendt, 'world alienation, and not self-alienation, as Marx thought, has been the hallmark of the modern age' (1958: 254).

As *The New World* portrays him, Smith is one type of the world-alienated modern subject, an individual agent acting as an envoy for a large system of power with objectives that do not coincide entirely with his own desires. He begins as a rebel against the system, soon establishes an ideational autonomy roughly compatible with it (in his fantasy of utopia and his consort with the natives), and ends by being reabsorbed into it (when he returns to the fort and later resumes colonial expeditions). Throughout, his mercurial introspection, as heard in voice-over, arises from a perplexed effort to come to terms with a reality seen as divested of material substance, caught between appearance and illusion, decidable only through a subjective leap. Smith's constant arbitration between dream and reality recalls explicitly the legacy of Cartesian doubt – especially in its origins in Descartes' own well-known dreams – a heritage which Arendt cites as a primary symptom of world alienation in its effort to relocate within consciousness an Archimedean point of view capable of mediating between local perspective and 'universal' truth (1958: 273–80). Smith appears in the film as an example of this standpoint, illustrating something of its positive value in his inclination to find commonality between the settlers and the natives. Yet it is also the source of both his complicity in structural violence and his own restlessness or rootlessness, as he repeatedly contemplates a land without end, beyond the immediate scope of his own vision – even as he gazes on the ubiquitous natural beauty of the New World.

Smith thus exemplifies world alienation as an impetus to mastery, a loss of present-ness calling for the restitution of an artificial wholeness. Confronted with the splendid landscapes before his eyes, he can only imagine the still more glorious ones that lay beyond them. Every 'here', in this worldview, is only the intimation of a superior elsewhere – and because the human mind is now supposed to be equal to both, the obvious end of conceiving them must surely be conquest. As Arendt suggests – in a phrase that recalls Heidegger's 'thrown-ness' – world alienation 'throws back' (1958: 254) people upon the self, but it is a self constrained by a newfound sense of its own limits, brought about, paradoxically, by novel proclamations of its power. From this perspective, empire is the aspiration to remake worlds in the image of the minds that contrive, according to this model, to arrogate the most power to themselves. When Smith returns to the settlers' fort after his time among the Powhatan, his bitterness is manifest in a direct expression of world alienation: 'That fort is not the world', he says. Thereafter, the coerced labour of the colonists is carried on under threats of withheld sustenance, as ceaseless, mundane activity pursued with no concern or enjoyment of the world, no intrinsic pleasure in cultivating land, but enforced only through a concerted exploitation of worry about the fate of the self.

Pocahontas exemplifies another kind of world alienation. In her literal displacement, she is an object of its drive to mastery yet, like Smith, she too is 'thrown back' upon the self. When her father warns her against aiding the settlers – 'Promise me you will put your people before all else' – she answers in a peculiar *non sequitur*: 'I know myself.' She is portrayed as the most reflective character in the film not only to belie the colonists' claims to enlightened superiority, but to suggest an ambivalence in the exercise of colonial power in its encounter with native subjects who both fulfil and undermine the desire of the coloniser.[7] In the myth and the film, Pocahontas 'loves' Smith and, eventually, Rolfe, who are both 'kind' pilgrims. 'Are you kind?' she asks Rolfe on their first meeting, and as the film depicts him, he is – to a fault. In one sense, this depiction further illustrates the compromise of individual agency, since Smith and Rolfe, 'kind' as they may seem, mainly represent the limits of a familiar kind of pseudo-benevolent humanism. They remain emissaries of her displacement as surely as her acts of intermarriage and exogamous childbearing remain predicated on her own oppression – a point made clear in the portrayal of her acculturation into colonial society, loving yet enforced, as a process of learning compliance and shame.

Perhaps for these reasons, she too experiences subjectivity as a schismatic crisis, a withdrawal of spirit from nature – 'You took the god in me', she intones in one voice-over – that compels her to find the grounds for action in consciousness, in thoughts that recall Cartesian principles of being as directly as some of Smith's ruminations: 'I will be given to you. True. Two. No more. One. One. I am. I am.' Throughout, our access to her thought disposes us to see the denials of her subjectivity that attend even the 'kindest' gestures toward her on the part of Smith or Rolfe. When her future husband presumes to teach her, for instance, she asks a question – 'What is a day, an hour…?' – that we know to be a philosophical inquiry, prompted by her great sadness, into the nature of time, but that he is capable of hearing only as sweetly naïve, an expression of primitive curiosity. Like Smith's, her introspection is largely given over to pensive and alienated reflections on the possibility of a recovered unity, and by the end it is clear she thinks she has found it. Her last words are a benedictory invocation answering an earlier expression of doubt: 'Mother, now I know where you live.' Despite the film's discrediting of the search for wholeness as a from of ideology, her final epiphany is powerfully credited – but what is it she thinks she has learned, and can we take it as anything more than a reflection of the naivety that Malick himself appears to foster so avidly?

In the last sequence, Pocahontas is transported to an England out of Stanley Kubrick's *Barry Lyndon* (1975), in all its sterile pomp and processional circumstance. As the geographical origin of the colonial gaze, this England harbours throngs of seemingly undifferentiated masses, a proto-Malthusian density homogenised by conditions of misery or strictures of class. Kubrick's film is an apt point of comparison not just for its direct correspondences of imagery but because, like Malick's, it is an anatomy of preconditions for modernity by a director otherwise concerned with existential crises arising after modernity's onset. For Kubrick, in film after film, that outcome is a rampant dehumanisation, in which virtually nothing of the meaningfully human

Pocahontas in an England of 'sterile pomp and processional circumstance'

remains, and *Barry Lyndon* – the director's only film with even a hint of lyricism, in its inconsolable dissection of a pivotal moment in human typology – means to reveal how this came about, systematically illustrating an all-encompassing change from a state of Rousseau-like 'naturalness' to one of Benthamite instrumentation; from a human selfhood characterised by empathy, humility, resourcefulness, disinterested curiosity and reason, to a dire subjectivity defined by deception, cunning, estrangement, self-interest, self-assertion and rationalisation.

Alienation remains Malick's primary subject, but his work – by stark contrast with Kubrick's – is about possibilities for human endurance under conditions of modern oppression. Like Kubrick, Malick in the final sequence of *The New World* archly satirises the habits, customs and traditions of England as a nucleus of colonial enterprise. This appearance of satire is surprising in a film that otherwise seems so resolute in its exclusion of irony, but the real question is how this tone can register at all against what proves to be the dominant affect of the sequence: a strange exhilaration that coincides with a fervently mounting grief. Until then, Pocahontas has been borne along into the supposed progress of civilisation – and the film makes clear, in the end, that there is no going back, no question of any 'return to nature'. Its hope is a different one, located in Pocahontas's recognition of difference amid the identity and sameness that the imperial mind imposes. In an invigorating 'reworlding'[8] that is what she finds – in her charged encounter with an African man on the street of a slum, in the looks of sympathetic curiosity she constantly exchanges with individuals among the seemingly faceless mobs, in her frolics in the garden in the final shots. She looks on this urban environment not with the horror at its denatured uniformity that we are signaled to observe, but with a sense of wonder at its manifest multiplicity, which we too may perceive, through the medium of her gaze. If Smith sees every 'here' as an elsewhere, she sees every elsewhere as a 'here', and the intense love the film expresses for the figure of Pocahontas derives from her role as a reminder of what might have happened – a peaceful coexistence – and did not.

But she is also a reminder of what did happen, not just a celebrant but a principle of difference and a casualty of empire. The film's sense of exhilaration is made possible by the conceit that the worst horrors of empire, in the present of the narrative, have not yet arrived, and its gravity is incited by the counter-knowledge that from any other standpoint, they have long since been accomplished. The film's ardent fragmentation reaches an apogee in the final sequence when, in a Yeatsian moment of intense individual feeling thrust suddenly under the aspect of eternity, at the height of Pocahontas's joy, we learn of her death: without submitting either to the indignity of an expedient dualism, this commemoration of a lost potentiality is brought simultaneously into focus with an unswerving awareness of oppression, suffering and mortality. A question the film raises is whether, from this standpoint, we must regard any dreams of a humane collective life as nothing but sentimental fantasy. If there is any answer in *The New World*, it can only be found where it cannot communicate: in the inspiriting fusion the film achieves of ecstasy and sorrow.

Notes

1   This point recalls Nelson Goodman's *Ways of Worldmaking*, in which Goodman domesticates the concept for modern philosophy by viewing it as an everyday activity of human understanding to be glorified in order to bring about a pragmatic acceptance of 'the multiplicity of worlds' (1978: 1) and to promote an authentic pluralism. Though Goodman says nothing about the colonial history of world-making, it haunts his discourse – as in his discussion of Vachel Lindsay's poem 'The Congo' (1978: 18). Malick retains some of Goodman's sense of the word but untames it by returning it to its historical contexts.

2   When Heidegger wrote 'The Age of the World Picture' in 1938, he was an apologist for Nazism. It is one of the great failings of modern philosophy that the author of these arguments, and their subsequent developments in the 'Parmenides' lectures (1942/43) did not see how the genocidal solipsism of the Nazis realised them. The blindness of Heidegger's own political life is irreconcilable with his critique of imperialist thought and the modern will to domination.

3   Malick translated Heidegger's *The Essence of Reason* from German into English in 1969. For a discussion of the Heideggerean influence on Malick's work, see Morrison & Schur 2003: 97–101.

4   Shakespeare's colonial fantasy notoriously paraphrases the virulently anti-colonialist writing of Montaigne, who is also a key source for *The New World*. John Smith's reveries on the natives directly cite Montaigne's essay 'Of the Cannibals' (see Montaigne 1991: 233).

5   On the roles of dialogue and cliché in Malick's films, see Morrison & Schur 2003: 73–5.

6   Even so, there is evidence in the historical record of Smith's initial wish to form

just such a community. In his first account of the establishment of Jamestown, published in 1608, he speaks repeatedly of his desire to enhance the 'publike good' (I: 43) – in which he includes both settlers and natives. By the time of his final account, published in 1624, he assumes the conquest of the natives as a foregone conclusion: 'It might well be thought, a Countrie so faire (as Virginia is) and a people so tractable, would long ere this have been quietly possessed' (II: 136).

7   For discussion of this point in a more general context, see Bhabha 1994: 72.

8   The idea of 'reworlding' is a post-colonial concept derived from the notion of word-making, and advised as a means of resistance to the legacies of empire. See especially Gillman *et al*. 2004: 262 and Muthyala 2006: 29–66.

References

Arendt, Hannah (1958) *The Human Condition*. Chicago: University of Chicago Press.

Bazin, Andre (1967) 'Cinema and Exploration', *What is Cinema?*, vol. I. trans. Hugh Gray. Berkeley: University of California Press, 154–63.

Bhabha, Homi (1994) *The Location of Culture*. New York: Routledge.

Ferguson, Frances (1992) *Solitude and the Sublime: Romanticism and the Aesthetics of Individuation*. New York: Routledge.

Gillman, Susan, Kirsten Silva Greusz and Ron Wilson (2004) 'Worlding American Studies', *Comparative American Studies*, 2, 3, 259–70.

Goodman, Nelson (1978) *Ways of Worldmaking*. Indianapolis: Hackett.

Heidegger, Martin (1977) 'The Age of the World Picture', in *The Question Concerning Technology and Other Essays*, trans. William Lovitt. New York: Harper and Row, 115–54.

Hoberman, Jim (2005) 'Mr. And Mrs. Smith', *Village Voice*. Available at http://www.villagevoice.com/film/0551,hoberman,71140,20.html [accessed 13 January 2007].

Jones, Kent (2006) 'Acts of God', *Film Comment*, March/April, 24–8.

Lane, Anthony (2005) 'The Other', *The New Yorker*, 23 December, 149–51.

Montaigne, Michel de (1991) *The Essays of Michel de Montaigne*, trans. M. A. Screech. London: Penguin.

Morrison, James & Thomas Schur (2003) *The Films of Terrence Malick*. Westport, CT: Praeger.

Muthyala, John (2006) *Reworlding America: Myth, History and Narrative*. Athens, OH: Ohio University Press

Ross, James & Mary McLaughlin (eds) (1953) *The Renaissance Reader*. New York: Penguin.

Smith, John (1986) *The Complete Works of Captain John Smith, vols I–III*, ed. Philip L. Barbour. Chapel Hill, NC: University of North Carolina Press.

Taubin, Amy (2006) 'Birth of a Nation', *Sight and Sound*, 2, 44–6.

CHAPTER FOURTEEN

Approaching The New World

Adrian Martin

Two immediately striking details about Terrence Malick's *The New World* (2005): firstly, the character played by Q'Orianka Kilcher is named Pocahontas, for the first and only time, in the final credits. Before that, 79 minutes in, there is an explicit barring of the utterance of this indigenous name, when Mary (Janine Duvitski), who is about to speak the name ('My name's Mary, and yours, I believe, is…'), is interrupted: 'She says it's not her name anymore. She hasn't got a name' – to which the kindly woman replies: 'How unfortunate. Well, we shall have to give you one!' What defines this central female character across the film, then, is not the essence of a single, original, 'true' name, but a succession of names. So, from start to end, Malick structures the film around a displacement of – and investigation into – personal identity, and the typical cinematic means of signalling and characterising that identity.

An even subtler example of this process occurs in relation to John Smith (Colin Farrell). For the first twenty minutes of the shortest (and still most generally available) version of the film,[1] Smith does not 'come together' as an ordinary filmic subject – as, quite simply, an individual who can be unambiguously identified via the act of opening his mouth and speaking lines of dialogue. Over and over, when addressed, he merely grunts, or laughs. The first few times that we hear his 'inner voice' on the soundtrack, we are thus unable to compare it, or ground it, in relation to any instance of this character talking aloud. And the editing and sound mixing – which form a truly complex weave of elements through the entire film – constantly create detours, enigmas and misdirections that derail the standard attributions or reinforcements of identity within scenes: other characters call his name, address him or talk about him, look or point in his direction, but there are no reverse-shots to clearly, cleanly close off the articulation. And the same goes for the character's potential point-of-view shots which – in a manner we know well from Malick's previous films – tend to wander off from a purely individual function in order to embrace a more external, even cosmic, vantage point.

One of the worst habits of film commentary amounts to an ultra-conventional congealing of all the different levels that create a cinematic character into a single, coherent, univocal, common-sense 'personhood' – with every imaginable metamorphosis of that character, every structuring contribution made by the multi-levels of cinematic artifice, and every 'spacing' or complication in relation made possible by the actor's performance, thinned out into a banal, psychologistic humanism (see Bersani & Dutoit 2004). Such an approach brutally short-changes the work of Malick – although some of his actors offer a better sense of how to approach this dimension of his *œuvre*, as when Sam Shepard (in the documentary *Rosy-Fingered Dawn*) describes his role as the Farmer in *Days of Heaven* (1978) as one of playing a ghost, someone immaterial. But what is the problem with assuming Malick's characters to be more-or-less conventional screen characters, with experiences and thoughts and drives and agendas – as we rightly assume of around 90 per cent of the films we see from week to week? What we miss, through the imposition of such a grid, is everything that is ambiguous, halting and above all constantly changing in Malick's constitution of his characters.

These characters are (far) less 'three-dimensional people' than they are cinematic figures – perpetually drawn, withdrawn and redrawn, created and devoured, in the play of contour and shadow, light and colour, rhythm and montage, image and sound. And this is not merely a formal demonstration of a general cinematic principle; it goes directly to the heart of Malick's most profound philosophical propositions. Instead of grasping this flux, we project retrospectively the coherence that has accumulated (in case of *The New World*, precariously and fitfully) by the end of the film back into its first, most tentative and mysterious steps (Kilcher is Pocahontas); and/or we come in with too much pre-knowledge fed by trailers and press kits, spots on *E! Entertainment* and items in *Premiere*, already filling in, from the world go, the plot's moves and the character's identities (Farrell is Smith).

I have argued elsewhere (Martin 2007) that what makes Malick's characters so ghostly is the sense that they scarcely seem to belong inside the stories that carry them along, past such momentous events of murder, migration, invasion, industry. Figures of history, or myth, or both (as is the case with Pocahontas), they never assume the grandeur that their names and identities have been granted by the passage of time and mass communication. Malick shows them in the uncertain, twilight, becoming state before such a congealing of identity. This congealing is a historic development which, frequently, they do not live long enough to see – since, from Starkweather/Kit in *Badlands* (1973) to Pocahontas, via the soldiers at Guadalcanal, Malick is clearly drawn to the tragic-romantic aura of heroes and heroines who die young. But one of the elements that marks *The New World* as a distinctive departure in his career is that, for the first time, it is a woman who takes this charged, quasi-sacrificial role – and who therefore becomes the cosmic centre of the film.

Studies of a director's career often impose a tidy evolutionary trajectory upon precarious production opportunities that are, in reality, far more chaotic and contingent, at the mercy of the industry's sense of 'timing'. As is the case with many filmmakers, Malick's filmography – the four feature works he has so far managed to realise – is informed by many projects that he has imagined, scripted, worked up to various levels, and still could conceivably make if given the chance (for, as with Stanley Kubrick, one senses that, for Malick, no project is ever altogether dead – *The New World* itself is a script dating back a quarter-century). Looked at this way, the decision to address the story of Pocahontas is not such a departure for Malick as it might seem. In particular, *The New World* bears the traces of his project for a German-language film about psychoanalysis, 'The English-Speaker', for which he auditioned actors in Austria in the mid-1990s. Although it is perilous to extrapolate too much from accounts of Malick's script drafts – which tend to be mere springboards for the films that are actually, finally made at the end of a long and elaborate creative process – it is nonetheless clear that *The New World* is, at some level, a displacement or transformation of many core elements in 'The English-Speaker'.

Like the so-called 'Anna O.' – the fictively renamed subject of a famous therapeutic case discussed by Freud and led by his colleague, Josef Breuer – Pocahontas comes to us as a figure of popular myth (that mythic quality signalled, in the first instance, by the telegrammatic brevity of their names). Relatively little is actually known about either woman; what we have, largely, are the extrapolations and projections woven upon their shadowy outlines by successive waves of storytellers, whether psychoanalysts, historians, novelists, poets or filmmakers – most of them male. (In Anna's case, Malick does have at his disposal the myth's epilogue or sequel: the re-creation of this figure as the real Bertha Pappenheim who, as Jacques Lacan reminds us, 'is one of the great names in the world of social welfare in Germany' (1979: 157).) Malick's approach to the 'legends' of these women is to take them on, precisely, as legends, not at all to demystify them as Robert Altman did in *Buffalo Bill and the Indians, or Sitting Bull's History Lesson* (1976) – in fact, he imaginatively expands the fictional share that has attached itself to these characters, picturing the dreams that Anna relates to Breuer, and luxuriating in the possibility of a romance between Pocahontas and Smith to a degree that would make even the Disney Corporation blush. Both characters undergo massive, dramatic changes in their identity – and both, strikingly, become 'English-speakers' in a disconcertingly strange and sudden fashion. (Pochontas's rapid assimilation of the English language is a deliberate unreality which many initial viewers and reviewers of the film found it hard to get past.) And both characters, ultimately, allow Malick a way to enter into and interrogate the highly charged, mythic-spiritual figure of the 'Earth Mother', cosmic carer and nurturer (Pocahontas as dying mother, Anna's final metamorphosis into a Mother Teresa-style worker for the sick and the poor) – just as his male characters allow a channelling and renegotiation of the crucified Christ figure.

Any diligent researcher into Malick's creative process quickly realises that any text or document, fictional or non-fictional, that can be consulted – on Fugate and Starkweather, Guadalcanal, Anna O., etc – has not only been previously well-read and digested by Malick, but also (and this is the creative part) somehow absorbed, incorporated, woven into the surface texture or deep structure of his film on that subject. This gives his work a palpable depth or volume that is rare in world cinema – comparable only to Kubrick, Carl Theodor Dreyer, Víctor Erice and a very few other filmmakers (perhaps what unites this 'family' are the amounts of time these directors usually had to wait before realising, in their lifetimes, a relatively small number of major projects). In Malick's case, even if his approach to the material adopts an overall line, orientation or agenda, the wealth of research creates subterranean echoes of other, neighbouring interpretations of the subject at hand. In *Badlands*, for instance, what normally forms the centre of every telling of the Starkweather-Fugate case (as in the tele-movie *Murder in the Heartland* (1993)) – the mystery of how complicit Fugate was or was not in the 'murderous spree' – is utterly displaced, even (many viewers might conclude) entirely disregarded; yet, the more one looks at the film, the more one sees and hears odd images, gestures, pauses and silences that hint at what Brian Henderson once tantalisingly described as a 'larger pattern of evasions, suppressions and silences' (1983: 49).

The New World exhibits a similar comprehensive weave of studied references – and the same pay-off of subterranean richness. Only two examples of this vast process must here suffice. The first relates to Malick's use of artistic sources – pre-existing versions of the Pocahontas legend, some grandiloquently ambitious in their intent. As if in response to those who (not always kindly) compare Malick's aesthetic to that of silent cinema, *The New World* kicks off with a fleeting citation-rewriting (his freedom with source material rivals, in a different register, that of Jean-Luc Godard – but aren't both of them collage artists in a peculiarly modern vein?) of a poem by that great on-the-spot theorist of silent film, Vachel Lindsay (1917). Where Pocahontas, over the opening pre-credit images, intones, 'You are our mother/We, your field of corn/We rise – from out of the soul of you', Lindsay's 'Our Mother Pocahontas' – which itself begins from the citation of a meditative passage by Carl Sandburg on 'Pocahontas's body' in its English tomb – contains the line, 'We rise from out of the soul of her'; there is a great deal of imagery from the rest of the poem ('Held in native wonderland/While the sun's rays kissed her hand') which seems to find its correspondence in Malick's film. In a more general way, the passion and anger animating Vachel's projection onto Pocahontas – he successively 'renounces' his white American civilisation's 'Saxon blood', 'Teuton pride', 'Norse and Slavic boasts', 'Italian dreams' and 'Celtic feuds' in order to be reborn as her descendant – resonate throughout *The New World*. Yet let us not elide the small but significant difference entailed in this particular citation-rewriting, which is important as the fact that the many questions uttered throughout *The Thin Red Line* (1998), taken as thundering pronouncements by antipathetic commentators, remain just that, 'unanswered questions' (as in the Charles Ives musical piece, 'The Unanswered Question', sampled during the film). To Lindsay, Pocahontas is the holy Mother figure; but to Pocahontas herself, in Malick's re-vision, this Mother is something or someone else – the 'spirit' whom she invokes in order to 'sing the story of our land' – precisely not her; she is not the mythic centre of the cosmos, more like its ephemeral vessel.

Another sort of example involves the use of historical documents. In an erudite discussion of the film, Pierre-Yves Pétillon (2006), a French specialist in American culture, describes his sense that Malick simultaneously dramatises quite different interpretations of the scant, elliptical historical traces of Pocahontas's life. For example, was Smith really rescued from certain, imminent death by the impetuous intervention of Pocahontas? It is easy to read Malick's version of the event in this way – but perhaps this is a too-easy capitulation to myth, and more precisely to a myth as told and viewed through white, Western eyes. Pétillon raises the cross-cultural debate among historians – a debate we must assume Malick knows well – that what happened to Smith (even if he did not understand it properly himself) was the performance of a 'pretend' execution, a kind of 'rebirth' ritual signalling the adoption of an outsider or foreigner into the tribe; in this scenario, the girl's actions would have been a premeditated part of the spectacle. And there is much to Malick's highly theatrical *mise-en-scène* in this sequence that supports this contrary reading: the elaborate construction of the dwelling that allows such dramatic lighting (it is one of the few emotionally warm interiors in any Malick film), the choreography of the bodies, the ambiguous facial reactions and gestures of the chief of the tribe...

More generally, Pétillon poses a range of interpretations of the subsequent relationship between Smith and Pocahontas that tallies well with Malick's increasingly radical mode of storytelling, fraught with mystery and suggestiveness: either nothing (or nothing much) happened, and Smith fantasised it as an immortal story to be forever told; or something (perhaps many things) happened, but Smith discreetly withheld an account of the whole truth from his various memoirs. The fantasy that accompanies (and often precedes) a relationship, and the secrecy that follows it, posthumously: this is a familiar dialectic in Malick's cinema, where the basic facts of any event – whether an intimate relationship, an act of killing, a military manoeuvre or a collective historical incident – are frequently, deliberately obscured.

Yet it is the complex nature of a special event – the event of falling in love – which is at the heart of *The New World*. Intimate relationships between men and women figure in all of the films he has directed to date (far less so in those he has co-produced in recent years, such as *Endurance* (1999) and *Undertow* (2004)) – but, as a love story, this is his least inhibited, his most rapturous (although any explicit depiction of sexual relations is, as usual for this rather tactful director, omitted). This constitutes something strikingly new in his work: beyond the largely alienated or 'affectless' union of Kit and Holly in *Badlands*, the periods of lyrical rapture allowed his characters are either furtive (*Days of Heaven*) or brutally ephemeral (the flashbacks in *The Thin Red Line*); either way, a harsh reality-principle imposes itself as the victor in the game of passing time.

It is an intriguing and instructive exercise to draw out the panorama of depictions of love in Malick's films. *Badlands* is entirely anti-romantic from the outset: the love that Kit and Holly have for each other is purely a matter of alienated fantasy-projection – mutually felt (which is why it can minimally function as romantic love, as coupledom), but quick to disintegrate. In *The Thin Red Line* and *Days of Heaven*, love is like quicksilver: it moves through people, and then moves on. Love's attraction suddenly shifts, leaving the abandoned party devastated. The films present this shift in

John Smith and Pocahontas: an emblem of the reconciliation of vastly different cultures

amorous attachment as simply another hard fact of the cosmos, like death or the passing seasons: 'She loved the farmer' is all that can be concluded, with naïve yet infinite wisdom, by the child-onlooker-narrator in *Days of Heaven*; while the dumped soldier in *The Thin Red Line* staggers, the whole natural and human world moving around him, as he reads the kiss-off note from his ex-lover far away.

The New World widens the picture on Malick's perception of love. Love is more than a mutual intoxication; it is (to use the terms of philosopher Alain Badiou (2006)) a full-blown event to which its participants must strive to be faithful. This is not fidelity of a moral, religious or social order; rather it is a testament to the transformative, even utopian power of this emotional entanglement. In *The New World*, the love of Pocahontas and John Smith is, of course, an emblem of the reconciliation of vastly different cultures, indigenous and settler – something that the film shows without ever explicitly spelling it out. It would have been easy to overload and overdetermine this aspect of the film – the utopian dream of racial union crushed by social pressures – but Malick avoids it by demanding (as Pocohontas herself demands) that the intimate participants be faithful to the event of love. Smith is here, once again, brother to Breuer in 'The English-Speaker': in that story (which hinges on the ambiguity of psychoanalytic transference as a basis for – even a definition of – love, a relation that Hitchcock frequently dramatised in both explicit and displaced terms), it is the man who 'fails the event' of love (through fear, obligation, compromise…), reneges on its contract, and turns away from its utopian, world-changing potentiality. Malick's work is in fact haunted by characters who 'bail' on love – Miranda Otto in *The Thin Red Line* (the closest to *The New World* in this regard, since we are shown the montage of rapturous union between the lovers), even (to take a perverse logic internal to the film) Holly in *Badlands*. But when it is a man who fails love – men enmeshed with the progress of history or civilisation, like Breuer and Smith – there is a significance that strikes at the core of a Western 'symbolic order', with its codes of rationality, discernment and stable identity.

Being faithful to the event of love implies taking a huge gamble – trusting that the mutual fantasy-projection element inherent in this relationship (the Other as the sole possible saviour, as the figure of the New World in all its exotic delight of difference) can survive across into time and reality, inventing in its wake an appropriately transformed social arrangement. *The New World* is constructed on a constant, painful seesaw between these stark options of reality and dream – where it is asserted, variously, that the dream can replace reality, or overcome it, or change it ('Real – what I thought a dream') – which is, in another register of twentieth-century lyricism, the great Surrealist creed of the 'marvellous', of permanent revolution; or, by contrast, that the dream is ephemeral, illusory, that it falls away and reality rushes in once more ('It was a dream – now I am awake'). It all leads to the great, immensely sad dialogue couplet (part of a *mise-en-scène* and shot *découpage* that rigorously insists on the 'separate worlds' now inhabited by the characters) in which Smith's passion for exploration, for opening new vistas on the maps of his culture, becomes – in its very failure – a metaphor for his failure to remain strong and faithful to the love-event: Pocahontas asks, 'Did you find your Indies, John? You shall', and Smith replies, 'I may have sailed past them.'

As I write, *The New World* still feels like a new film, a young film – and this piece takes the form of notes, of approaches, because the rush to judgement so typical of contemporary film criticism (more than ever, in the Internet age) seems particularly ill-equipped to take the measure of Malick's achievement here. We do well to remember that no Malick film was received unanimously well at the moment of its initial release. Key critics and major publications have always had massive reservations on first seeing Malick's work: re-read *Jump Cut* on *Badlands*, *Sight and Sound* on *The Thin Red Line* – and, now, *Cahiers du cinéma* on *The New World*. In fact, some of the same critiques have circulated, almost verbatim, since 1973: Malick cannot tell a story coherently; you cannot care about the characters; his films are too pretty and too vague; they express a phony, nostalgic innocence for a simpler time; they are ideologically naïve, even reactionary; they are formless and meandering in their structures – both undercooked (in the scripting) and overcooked (in post-production). Pauline Kael said of *Days of Heaven*: 'The film is an empty Christmas tree: you can hang all your dumb metaphors on it' (1982: 137), and her acolytes have been happy to recycle the terms of that abuse of Malick's work beyond her death. But even some of the world's finest and most progressive critics safeguard their sceptical reservations, as when Jonathan Rosenbaum muses: 'When he resorts to some of the exquisite visual syntax of F. W. Murnau's silent cinema, as he did in *Days of Heaven* and *The Thin Red Line*, does that mean he also wants us to revert to a 1920s understanding of what these films are about? And if not, how, exactly, does his understanding go beyond the 1920s?' (2005).

Where *The Thin Red Line* accumulated its cult reputation quite rapidly (it is the most written-about Malick film), and was widely considered a masterpiece within two or three years (judging by the many 'canon' polls on the Internet), *The New World* has experienced a boringly inevitable backlash. The twenty-year wait for the former massaged widespread excitement and goodwill, but the (only!) seven-year interval before the latter has invited, bizarrely enough, a jaundiced, seen-it-all-before disenchantment, as if Malick 'filmed too soon'. As well, a curious note of technological savvy had entered, in the interim, the consciousness of many critics: *The New World* was taken by some (including such normally astute commentators as Dave Kehr (2006) and Thierry Jousse (2006)) as the worst embodiment of that modern phenomenon known as the 'AVID film' – edited (and perpetually re-edited) on digital computers, which (according to these commentators) encourages maximum freeform sloppiness in the filming, and results in the lack of a strong, overall rhythm or structure in the global montage. Of course, the film also attracted immediate champions (including critic Matt Zoller Seitz (2006) and filmmaker Wim Wenders (see Chaw 2006)), but their assertions of love were polemically fuelled – and perhaps skewed – by the general indifference that they heroically hurled themselves against. Within the first year of its after-life, however, sensitive revaluations of *The New World* began to appear – including two, rigorously argued, in *Cahiers* itself by two critics relatively new to the magazine, Stéphane Delorme (2007) and Cyril Béghin (2007), both influenced by the school of 'figural analysis' that emerged in France during the 1990s. They articulate the central aspect upon which subject and form are married in the film: the kind of ceaseless montage described at the beginning of this chapter, a swirl of fragments that create a lyric swirl of perpetually metamorphosing identities – on the condition that the process of metamorphosis can either fulfil itself or become tragically stalled, on the basis of whether the individual 'subject' stays true to the love-event that is taking him or her apart.

Of course, there are risks, as well as rewards, in the aesthetic path that Malick appears – especially in light of *The Thin Red Line* and *The New World* – to now be on. Placing so much store on a certain kind of on-location improvisation – less of storyline or dialogue than of gesture, of expressive action – and leaving the filming wide open in its options with a view to exploiting all-over discontinuity in post-production, creates rich possibilities for a radical, decentred montage structure, but also places unfamiliar and heavy demands on his actors, and on his own 'impulsive inspiration' at the moment of filming the gesture of an actor's body in natural space. Like many viewers, my feeling on first viewing the film was that the choreographic work with Kilcher, and the gestures of love between her and Farrell, was far more inspired than the sometimes schematic presentation of the British colonisers in their foaming, decrepit anger (although this makes logical, systematic sense: the colonisers are 'too much themselves', too static, too fixed in their social roles). Yet I firmly believe – and time has proven this true of Malick's three previous films – that one needs to suspend, at this point, conventional 'normative' judgements of what works and what does not in *The New World*. For what is truly experimental in it – its polyphonic weave of image and sound, its exploration of a philosophy of love, its subtle evocation of the weave of and breakdown between cultures – is far more difficult to grasp, and far more open to cinema's future, than what seems (perhaps deceptively) familiar.

Writing ten years after the appearance of *Badlands*, Brian Henderson began his discussion of the film by attempting to bracket off all those distortions introduced by what he termed 'polemical dispute': defensiveness, anger, dismissal, over-invest-ment. The appearance of subsequent Malick films, according to Henderson, merely 'further complicated' the emotional murk on this battlefield. 'This is not a favourable background for the serious criticism of any work,' concluded Henderson, 'still less for that open-ended exploration which a new and unstudied work invites' (1983: 38). Actually, pondering Henderson's sage advice, it strikes me that love of a Malick film is rather like love *in* a Malick film – especially *The New World*. The element of fantasy-investment – the haste to enshrine the film, secure it a place within a precariously shifting cultural history – is an unavoidable drama, hard to separate one's 'better self' from. This drama leads, inevitably, to both an 'inner experience' of intense euphoria and a kind of aphasia that can only speak its name in the ineffable language of love – a sort of lyric dance around what is 'unspeakable' in the work, beyond words, beyond rationalisation, a pure potential or possibility which registers as a kind of utopia.

At the same, staying faithful to the profound event of each Malick film (like each Dreyer or Erice film) imposes on the lover the obligation to say more, to speak clearly, to move from assertion to analysis and thus somehow ground in reality the verifiable 'concrete materiality' of the work – without snuffing out the feeling that it prompted within oneself in the first place. Malick's films take time, in every sense: they carve out a sense of time beyond everyday reality as well as everyday cinema, and they require a long, slow intimacy, successive periods of appreciation, description, critique and revaluation. Every Malick film still beckons, to those of us who love them, as some-thing 'new and unstudied', an experience demanding its witnesses and its testament.

Note

1   There are three versions of *The New World*: the general international release version of 135 minutes; a 150-minute version briefly circulated at the start of its public life (at the 2006 Berlinale and as a 'screener' to achieve eligibility for Academy Award nomination) and then withdrawn; and a definitive three-hour 'director's cut' (although all three were cut by the director!) that has (according to authoritative reports) been prepared for future DVD release. The first, 'intermediate' cut, which bears some fascinating differences to the second version, is available as a bonus on the Italian DVD release of the film.

References

Badiou, Alain (2006) *Being and Event*. London: Continuum.
Béghin, Cyril (2006) 'Princesse montage', *Cahiers du cinéma*, 617, 95–6.
Bersani, Leo & Ulysse Dutoit (2004) *Forms of Being: Cinema, Aesthetics, Subjectivity*. London: British Film Institute.
Chaw, Walter (2006) 'Wim, with Vigour', *Film Freak Central*. Available at http://www.film freakcentral.net/notes/wwendersinterview.htm [Accessed: 23 September 2006]
Delorme, Stéphane (2007) 'Un lyrisme élégiaque', *Cahiers du cinéma*, 619, 86–8.
Henderson, Brian (1983) 'Exploring Badlands', *Wide Angle*, 5, 4, 38–51.

Jousse, Thierry (2006) 'Munich, Malick et la politique des auteurs', *Panic*, 3, 25–7.

Kael, Pauline (1982) *5001 Nights at the Movies*. London: Zenith.

Kehr, Dave (2006) 'Malick as Messiah'. Available at http://davekehr.com. [Accessed: 21 December 2006]

Lacan, Jacques (1979) *The Four Fundamental Concepts of Psycho-Analysis*. London: Penguin.

Lindsay, Vachel (1917) *The Chinese Nightingale, and Other Poems*. New York: Macmillan.

Martin, Adrian (2007) 'Things to Look Into: The Cinema of Terrence Malick', in *Rouge*, 10. Available at http://www.rouge.com.au/10/malick.html [Accessed: 8 May 2007]

Pétillon, Pierre-Yves (2006) 'Trajectoires à propos du Nouveau Monde de Terrence Malick', *Panic*, 3, 88–101.

Rosenbaum, Jonathan (2005) 'The Movie Club 2005', *Slate*, 28 December. Available at http://www.slate.com/id/2132498/entry/2133364/ [Accessed: 14 September 2006]

Seitz, Matt Zoller (2006) 'One "World"'. Available at http://mattzollerseitz.blogspot.com/2006/01/one-world.html [Accessed 19 February 2007]

FILMOGRAPHY

Terrence Malick has been involved in filmmaking as a writer and producer, sometimes uncredited. Below are details of the four features he has both written and directed.

Badlands (1973, USA)

Director: Terrence Malick
Screenplay: Terrence Malick
Production Company: Pressman-Williams Enterprises
Executive Producer: Edward Pressman
Producer: Terrence Malick
Director of Photography: Brian Probyn, Tak Fujimoto, Stevan Larner
Editor: Robert Estrin
Associate Editor: William Weber
Art Director: Jack Fisk, Ed Richardson
Music composer: George Tipton
Sound Editor: James Nelson
Length: 95 minutes
Lead Cast: Martin Sheen (Kit Carruthers), Sissy Spacek (Holly), Warren Oates
   (Father), Ramon Bieri (Cato)

Days of Heaven (1978, USA)

Director: Terrence Malick
Screenplay: Terrence Malick
Production Company: O.P. Productions, Paramount Pictures Corporation
Executive Producer: Jacob Brackman
Producer: Bert Schneider, Harold Schneider
Director of Photography: Nestor Alemendros
Additional photography: Haskell Wexler
Editor: Billy Weber

Art Director: Jack Fisk
Music Composer: Ennio Morricone
Length: 95 minutes
Lead cast: Richard Gere (Bill), Brooke Adams (Abby), Sam Shepard (The Farmer),
    Linda Manz (Linda), Robert Wilke (Farm Foreman)

The Thin Red Line (1998, Canada/USA)

Director: Terrence Malick
Screenplay: Terrence Malick
Production Company: Twentieth Century Fox, Fox 2000 Pictures, Phoenix Pictures
Executive Producer: George Stevens Jr.
Producer: Robert Michael Geisler, John Roberdeau, Grant Hill
Based on novel by: James Jones
Director of Photography: John Toll
Editor: Billy Weber, Leslie Jones, Saar Klein
Production Designer: Jack Fisk
Art Director: Ian Gracie
Music: Hans Zimmer
Length: 170 minutes
Lead Cast: Sean Penn (First Sergeant Edward Welsh), Adrien Brody (Corporal Fife),
    James Caviezel (Private Witt), Ben Chaplin (Private Bell), George Clooney (Cap-
    tain Charles Bosche), John Cusack (Captain John Gaff), Woody Harrelson (Ser-
    geant Keck), Elias Koteas (Captain Charles 'Bugger' Staros), Nick Nolte (Lieuten-
    ant Colonel Gordon Tall), John C. Reilly (Sergeant Storm), John Savage (Sergeant
    McCron), Paul Gleeson (First Lieutenant Band), Arie Verveen (Private Dale),
    Dash Mihok (Private Doll), John Travolta (Brigadier General Quintard), Jared
    Leto (Second Lieutenant Whyte)

The New World (2005, USA)

Director: Terrence Malick
Screenplay: Terrence Malick
Production Company: New Line Cinema, Sunflower Productions LLC, Sarah Green
    Film Corp, First Foot Films, The Virginia Company LLC
Executive Producer: Toby Emmerich, Trish Hofmann, Bill Mechanic, Rolf Mittweg,
    Mark Ordesky
Producer: Sarah Green
Director of Photography: Emmanuel Lubezki
Editor: Richard Chew, Hank Corwin, Saar Klein, Mark Yoshikawa
Production Designer:
Art Director: David Crank
Music: James Horner
Length: 135 minutes
Lead Cast: Colin Farrell (Captain John Smith), Q'Orianka Kilcher (Pocahontas),
    Christopher Plummer (Captain Christopher Newport), Christian Bale (John
    Rolfe), August Schellenberg (Powhatan), Wes Studi (Opechancanough), David
    Thewlis (Wingfield), Yorick van Wageningen (Captain Argall)

BIBLIOGRAPHY

Books
Chion, Michael (2004) *The Thin Red Line*. London: British Film Institute.
Martin, Adrian (forthcoming) Terrence Malick. London: British Film Institute.
Morrison, James & Thomas Schur (2003) *The Films of Terrence Malick*. Westport, CT: Praeger.

Articles & reviews
Abramowitz, Rachel (1998) 'War Story', *Premiere* (USA), 11, 9, May, 62–3.
_____ (1999) 'Présence de Malick…', *Premiere* (FR), 264, March, 77–80.
Adair, Gibert (1999) '*The Thin Red Line*', *Independent on Sunday*, 28 February, 5.
Almendros, Nestor (1979) 'Photographing *Days of Heaven*', *American Cinematographer*, 60, 6, June, 562–5, 592–4, 626–32.
Amiel, Vincent (1999) '*Badlands*: La fuite et le cliché', *Positif*, 466, December, 97–8.
Andrews, Nigel (1974) '*Badlands*', *Financial Times*, 1 January.
Anon. (1973) '*Badlands*', *Variety*, 10 October, 12.
_____ (1978) 'A preview of *Days of Heaven*', *Films and Filming*, 25, 3, December, 26–9.
_____ (1998) '*The Thin Red Line*: Movie Info' [Internet]. Available at: http://www.foxmovies.com/ thinredline/htmls/movie_info.html
_____ (1999) 'Alive and Kicking', *Sight and Sound*, 9, 12, 3.
Atkinson, Michael (1999) '*Days of Heaven*', *Village Voice*, 30 March, 126.
_____ (2006) '*The Thin Red Line*' [Internet] *Village Voice*. Available at: http://www.villagevoice.com/film/ 0604,atkinson,71907,20.html
Bart, Peter (1998) 'The Silence of the Malick: What's His Line?' *Variety*, December, 21.
Béghin, Cyril (2006) 'Princesse montage', *Cahiers du cinéma*, 617, 95–6.
Benjamin, B. (2006) 'Uncharted Emotions', *American Cinematographer*, 87, 1, January, 48–52, 56–57.
Bilbow, Marjorie (1979) '*Days of Heaven*', *Screen International*, 193, 9 June, 23.
Biskind, Peter (1998) 'The Runaway Genius', *Vanity Fair*, December, 460, 116–25.
Bourget, Jean-Loup (1979) 'American Gothic: *Days of Heaven*', *Positif*, 218, May, 65–7.
Bradshaw, Peter (2006) '*The New World*' [Internet]. *Guardian*. Available at: http://film.guardian.co.uk/ News_Story/Critic_Review/Guardian_review/0,,1695483,00.html
Bristol, Mark (1997) 'And you are?', *Premiere* (USA), 11, 3, November, 4–2.
Brown, Colin (1997) 'Executive Suite: An interview with Robert Michael Geisler and John Roberdeau',

Screen International, 1127, 26 September, 52.

Buckley, Michael (1974), '*Badlands*', *Sight and Sound*, 25, 4, 245.

Buscombe, Edward (1979) 'Breaking out of "story"', *Tribune*, 15 June.

Cain, Jimmie E. Jr (2000) '"Writing in His Musical Key": Terrence Malick's Vision of *The Thin Red Line*', *Film Criticism*, 25, 1, 2–24.

Canby, Vincent (1973) 'The movie that made the festival memorable', *New York Times*, 21 October.

Christopher, James (2006) '*The New World*', The Times, Times 2, 26 January, 16.

Ciment, Michel (1975) 'Entretien avec Terrence Malick', *Positif*, 170, June, 30–4.

_____ (1979) '*Days of Heaven*: le jardin de Terrence Malick', *Positif*, 225, December, 18–24.

_____ (1975) 'Entretien avec Terrence Malick', *Positif*, 170, June, 30–4.

_____ (1998) 'Entretien: Robert Michael Geisner et John Roberdeau', *Positif*, 446, April, 54–8.

_____ (1998) 'L'absence de Malick', *Positif*, 446, April, 52–4.

Ciment, Michel & Hubert Niogret (2000) 'Entretien Mike Medavoy: De Woody à Terry', *Positif*, 457, March, 14–16.

Clarke, Roger (1999) 'The return of the maverick', *Independent*, 20 February, 5.

Coleman, John (1974) 'All Goes to Show: *Badlands*', New Statesman, 21 December.

Combs, Richard (1974/5) '*Badlands*', *Sight and Sound*, 44, 1, 53–4.

_____ (1978) 'In the Picture: *Days of Heaven*', *Sight and Sound*, 47, 2, 84.

_____ (1979) 'The Eyes of Texas', *Sight and Sound*, 48, 2, 110–11.

Cook, G. Richarson (1974) 'The Filming of *Badlands*: An Interview With Terry Malick', *Filmmakers Newsletter*, 7, 8, 30–2.

Corliss, Richard (1978) 'Every Picture Tells a Story', *New York Times*, 2 October, 68–70.

Critchley, Simon (2002) 'Calm: On Terrence Malick's *The Thin Red Line*', Film-Philosophy, 6, 48. Available at: http//www.film-philosohy.com/vol6-2002/n48critchley

Cumbow, Robert C. (1979) '*Days of Heaven*', *Movietone News*, 155, 41–3, 60–1.

Curtis, Quentin (1999) 'Shy auteur comes out shooting', *Daily Telegraph*, 22 January, 25.

Danks, Adrian (2000) 'Death Comes as an End: Temporality, Domesticity and Photography in Terrence Malick's *Badlands*', *Senses of Cinema*, July–August, 8. Available at: http://sensesofcinema.com/contents/00/8/thinredline.html

Dean, Joan (1999) '*The Thin Red Line*', *Film West*, 35, February, 18–19.

Delorme, Stéphane (2007) 'Un lyrisme élégiaque', *Cahiers du cinéma*, 619, 86–8.

Docherty, Cameron (1998) 'Maverick Back From the *Badlands*', *Sunday Times*, 7 July, 4–5.

Doherty, Thomas (1999) '*The Thin Red Line*', *Cineaste*, 24, 2–3, 83–4.

Donougho, Martin (1985) 'West of Eden: Terrence Malick's *Days of Heaven*', *Postscript*, 5, 1, 17–30.

Ebert, Roger (1999) '*The Thin Red Line*' [Internet]. Chicago Sun Times. Available at: http://www.suntimes.com/ebert/ebert_reviews/1999/01/010802.html

_____ (2001) '*Days of Heaven*' [Internet]. Chicago Sun Times. Available at: http://www.suntimes.com/ebert/greatmovies/heaven.html

_____ (2006) '*The New World*' [Internet]. Chicago Sun Times. Available at: http://rogerebert.suntimes.com/apps/pbcs.dll/article?AID=/20060119/REVIEWS/51220006/1023

Fillipidis, Michael (2000) 'On Malick's Subjects' [Internet]. *Senses of Cinema*. Available at: http://www.sensesofcinema.com/contents/00/8/malick.html

Fox, Terry Curtis (1978) 'The Last Ray of Light: *Days of Heaven*', *Film Comment*, 14, 5, Sept–Oct, 27–8.

Freer, Ian (1999) 'Soundtrack review: *The Thin Red Line*', *Empire*, 118, April, 124.

_____ (2006) '*The New World*', *Empire*, 201, March, 42.

Fuller, Graham (1998) 'Exile on Main Street', *Observer Review*, 13 December, 5.

Gargett, Adrian (2002) 'Is this darkness in you too?' [Internet]. *Talking Pictures*. Available at: http://www.talkingpix.co.uk/Article_Thin%20Red%20Line.html

George, Sandy (1997) '*The Thin Red Line* draws cash into Australia', *Screen International*, 1099, 14 March, 8.

Gillis, Joe (1995) 'Waiting for Godot' [Internet]. Available at: http://www.eskimo.com/~toates/malick/art5.html

Gleiberman, Owen (1999) 'Soldiers' Story', *Entertainment Weekly*, 466, 8 January, 44–5.

Gow, Gordon (1974) '*Badlands*', *Films and Filming*, 21, 3, December, 35–6.

_____ (1979) '*Days of Heaven*', *Films and Filming*, 25, 9, June, 28–9.

Graham, Johnny (1977) '*Badlands*', *Moving Target*, 1, June, 10–12.

Handy, Bruce (1997) 'His own sweet time', *Time*, October 13, 150, 15, 92–9.

____ (1998) 'Back from the *Badlands*', *Daily Telegraph Weekend Magazine*, 15 August, 20, 22, 24.

Henderson, Brian (1983) 'Exploring *Badlands*', *Wide Angle*, 5, 4, 38–51.

Henry, Michael (2000) '*The Thin Red Line*: reverie d'un cineaste solitaire', *Positif*, 457, March, 6–10.

Hoberman, J. (1998): 'The Wars Within', *Village Voice*, December 23–29.

____ (2005) 'Mr. And Mrs. Smith' [Internet]. *Village Voice*. Available at: <http://www.villagevoice.com/film/0551,hoberman,71140,20.html

Hodenfeld, Chris (1978) 'Terrence Malick: *Days of Heaven*'s image maker', *Rolling Stone*, 16 November.

Hodgkins, John (2002) 'In the Wake of Desert Storm: A Consideration of Modern World War II Films', *Journal of Popular Film and Television*, 30, 2, Summer, 74–84.

Hodsdon, Barrett (1999) 'Where Does War Come From? Reprising the Combat Film: *Saving Private Ryan* and *The Thin Red Line*', *Metro*, 119, 40–9.

Hunter, Stephen (1999) 'The thin long movie' [Internet]. *Washington Post*, 8 January 1999. Available at: <http://www.washingtonpost.com/wpsrv/style/movies/reviews/thinredlinehunter.htm>

Hutchinson, Tom (1974) '*Badlands*', *Sunday Telegraph*, 22 December.

Insdorf, Annette (1978) '*Days of Heaven*', *Take One*, 6, 12, 8–9.

Irwin, Lew (ed.) (1999) 'Studio Briefing: Despite Oscar nods, *Thin*'s biz thins out' [Internet]. Available at: http://www.imdb.com/SB?19990224#4

Johnson, William (1974) '*Badlands*', *Film Quarterly*, 27, 3, 43–6.

Jones, Kent (2006) 'Acts of God: Naturally Wondering About Terrence Malick and his new Transcendentalist Epic', *Film Comment*, 42, 2, March–April, 24–26, 28.

Kael, Pauline (1977) 'Sugarland and Badland', in *Reeling*. London: Marion Boyars, 300–6.

Katelan, Jean-Yves (1999) 'La Ligne Rouge', *Premiere* (FR), 264, March, 37.

Kauffmann, Stanley (1978) 'Harder Times', *The New Republic*, 16 September, 16–18.

____ (1999) 'On Films After Twenty Years', *The New Republic*, 25 January, 24.

Kehr, Dave (2006) 'Malick as Messiah' [Internet]. Available at: http://davekehr.com.

Kendall, Lukas (1999) '*The Thin Red Line*', *Film Score Monthly*, 4, 2, February, 39.

Khoury, George (1998) 'Script Comments: *The Thin Red Line*', *Creative Screenwriting*, 5, 6, November–December, 14.

Kinder, Marsha (1974) 'The Return of the Outlaw', *Film Quarterly*, 27, 4, 2–10.

King, Michael (1974) '*Badlands*', *Jump Cut*, 1, May–June, 5–6.

Klawans, Stuart (1999) 'The Thin Red Line', *The Nation*, 268, 1, 4 January.

Landau, Jon (1974) 'I Fought the Law and the Law Won', *Rolling Stone*, 9 May.

Landrot, Marine (1999) '*Badlands*', *Télérama*, 2581, 30 June, 25.

Lane, Anthony (2005) 'The Other', *The New Yorker*, 23 December, 149–151.

Lee, Hwanhee (2002) 'Terrence Malick' [Internet]. Available at: http://www.sensesofcinema.com/contents/directors/02/malick.html

MacCabe, Colin (1999) 'Bayonets in Paradise', *Sight and Sound*, 9, 2, 10–14.

Macnab, Geoffrey (1999a) 'Soldier Stories', *Sight and Sound*, 9, 2, 14.

____ (1999b) '*The Thin Red Line*', *Sight and Sound*, 9, 2, 53–4.

____ (2000) 'The 100 days' war: an interview with John Toll', *Sight and Sound*, 10, 2, 9.

Maher, Kevin (2006) 'You paleface; me male fantasy', *The Times*, *The Knowledge*, 28 January, 9,11.

Malcolm, Derek (2006) '*The New World*', *Evening Standard*, 26 January, 34.

Martin, Adrian (2006) 'Things to Look Into: The Cinema of Terrence Malick' [Internet]. *Rouge*. Available at: http://www.rouge.com.au/10/malick.html

Maslin, Janet (1998) 'Beauty and Destruction in Pacific Battle', *The New York Times*, 23 January, E1.

McCarthy, Todd (1998) '*The Thin Red Line*', *Variety*, 21 December, 73, 80.

____ (2005) '*The New World*' [Internet]. *Variety*. Available at: http://www.variety.com/award central_review/VE1117929092.htmlnav=reviews07&categoryid=1986&cs=1&p=0

McGettigan, Joan (2001) 'Interpreting a Man's World: Female Voices in *Badlands* and *Days of Heaven*', *Journal of Film and Video*, 52, 4, 33–43.

Milne, Tom (1974) 'From *Badlands* to Bond', *The Observer*, 22 December.

____ (1979) '*Days of Heaven*', *Monthly Film Bulletin*, 46 (544), May, 93–94.

Morrison, James (1999) '*The Thin Red Line*', *Film Quarterly*, 53, 1, Autumn, 35–38.

Mottram, James (2006), '*The Thin Red Line*', *Film Review*, 667, March, 93.

Nathan, Ian (1999) 'Review: *The Thin Red Line*', *Empire*, 117, March, 16.

Newman, Kim (1994) 'Whatever Happened to Whatisname?', *Empire*, 56, February, 88–9.

____ (1999) '*The Thin Red Line*', *Empire*, 123, September, 127.

Norman, Barry (1991) '*Badlands*', *Radio Times*, 269, 3523, 29 June, 26.

Orr, John (1999) 'Poetic Enigma: The Films of Terrence Malick', *Film West*, 37, 24–6.

O'Toole, Lesley (1999) 'You can look but you can't touch', *The Times*, 25 February, 39.

Patterson, Hannah (2003a) '*Days of Heaven*', *Kamera*, 1, 17–18.

____ (2003b) '*Badlands*', *Kamera*, 1, 78–9.

Patterson, John (2005) '*The New World*', *Guardian Film and Music*, 13 December, 2.

Pétillon, Pierre-Yves (2006) 'Trajectoires à propos du Nouveau Monde de Terrence Malick', *Panic*, 3, 88–101.

Petric, Vlada (1978) '*Days of Heaven*', *Film Quarterly*, 32, 37–45.

Pizzello, Stephen (1999a) 'The War Within', *American Cinematographer*, 80, 2, February, 42–8, 50, 52, 54–60, 62.

____ (1999b) 'A cinematic honour roll: *Days of Heaven*', *American Cinematographer*, 80, 3, March, 134.

Polan, Dana (1999) 'Auteurism and War-teurism: Terrence Malick's War Movie', *Metro*, 119, 58–62.

Powell, Dilys (1974) '*Badlands*', *Sunday Times*, 22 December.

Probst, Christopher (1999) 'Award-worthy Images', *American Cinematographer*, 80, 6, June, 70–88.

Pulver, Andrew (1999) 'The Resurrection Man', *Guardian*, Section 2, 10 December, 5.

Rich, Frank (1978) 'Night of the Locust', *Time*, 12 September.

Riley, Brooks (1978) 'The Last Ray of Light: Interview with Nestor Almendros', *Film Comment*, 14, 5, September–October, 28–31.

Robey, Tim (2006) '*The New World*', *Daily Telegraph*, 27 January, 29.

Robinson, David (1974) '*Badlands*', *The Times*, 20 December.

Romney, Jonthan (1999) 'Treading the Line' [Internet]. Available at: http://www.guardian/co/uk/Archive/Article/0,4273,3834076,00.html

Rosenbaum, Jonathan (1974) '*Badlands*', *Monthly Film Bulletin*, 41, 490, November, 245–6.

____ (1999) 'Malick's Progress' [Internet]. *Chicago Reader*, 1 January. Available at: http://www.chireader.com/movies/archives/1999/0199/01159.html

Roud, Richard (1973) '*Badlands*', *Guardian*, 27 November.

Schaffer, Bill (2000) 'The Shape of Fear: Thoughts after *The Thin Red Line*' [Internet]. Available at: http://sensesofcinema.com/contents/00/8/thinredline.html

Schilling, Mark (1999) 'Uphill struggle in Japan', *Screen International*, 1207, 7 May, 18.

Schreger, Charles (1985) 'Altman, Dolby, and the Second Sound Revolution', in Elisabeth Weis & John Belton (eds) *Film Sound: Theory and Practice*. New York: Columbia University Press, 348–55.

Shepherd, Jim (2003) '*Badlands* and the "Innocence" of American Innocence', *The Believer*, 1, 1, March, 39–47.

Shtier, Rachel (1994) 'The Elusive Playwright', *Village Voice*, 11 January, 84, 86.

Sibley, Adrian (1996) 'Director's cut – and run', *Observer*, 9 June, 11.

Sigal, Clancy (1984) '*Badlands*', *The Listener*, 111 (2858), 17 May, 35.

Simon, John (1974) '*Badlands*', *Esquire*, June.

Sineux, Michel (1975) 'Un cauchemar de douceur', *Positif*, 170, June, 26–9.

Smith, Gavin (1999) 'Let There Be Light: *The Thin Red Line*', *Film Comment*, 35, 1, January–February, 8–11.

Spelling, Ian (1999) 'Red Peril', *Film Review*, April, 58–61.

Stark, Susan (1999) '*The Thin Red Line* takes war to a stirring level' [Internet]. *Detroit News*, 15 January. Available at: http://detnews.com/1999/entertainment/0115/redline/redline.html

Stein, Michael Eric (1995) 'The New Violence or Twenty Years of Violence in Films: An Appreciation', *Films in Review*, January-February, XLVI, 1–2, 1, 40–8.

Taubin, Amy (1993) '*Days of Heaven*', *Village Voice*, 8 June, 63.

____ (2006) 'Birth of a Nation', *Sight & Sound*, 16, 2, February, 44–45, 72.

Taylor, Charles (1999) 'The Big Dead One' [Internet]. Available at: http://www.salon.com/ent/movies/reviews/1999/01/cov.08reviewa.html

Thomson, David (1999) 'Malick: the prodigal returns', *Independent on Sunday*, 24 January, 1–2.

Turan, Kenneth (1998) '*Red Line*: A Distant Epic' [Internet]. *Los Angeles Times*, 23 December. Available at: www.calendarlive.com/top/1,1419,L-LATimes-Movies-X!ArticleDetail-5039,00.html

Uffelen, René (1999) '*Badlands* en *Days of Heaven*', *Skrien*, 231, March, 13–15.

Van de Graaf, Paul (1999) 'The Thin Red Line', Skrien, 231, March, 13–15.
Viviani, Christian (2000) 'Terrence Malick, l'harmonie de la disharmonie', Positif, 457, March, 11–13.
Walker, Beverly (1975) 'Malick on Badlands', Sight and Sound, 44, 2, 82–3.
Wells, Jeffrey (1991) 'I may be some time…', Empire, 26, August, 42–3.
Whalen, Tom (1999) '"Maybe all men got one big soul": The Hoax Within the Metaphysics of Terrence Malick's The Thin Red Line', Literature Film Quarterly, 27, 3, 162–6.
Wistanley, Cam (1999) 'War is Hell. Discuss…', Total Film, 27, April, 64–71.
_____ (1999) 'The Thin Red Line', Total Film, 27, April, 84–5.
Wolcott, James (1998) 'Tanks for the Memories', Vanity Fair, 456, August, 38–44.
Wondra, Janet (1994) 'A Gaze Unbecoming: Schooling the Child For Femininity in Days of Heaven', Wide Angle, 16, 4, 4–23.
Wood, Gaby (1998) 'Out of Sight', Guardian, 29 May, 2–3.
Yellen, Linda (1973) 'Badlands', The Hollywood Reporter, 228, 31, 24 October, 16.
Young, Josh (1998) 'Hollywood's Prodigal Son', Sunday Telegraph Review, 5 July, 7.
_____ (1999) 'Days of Hell', Entertainment Weekly, 467, 15 January, 28–35.
Zaller, Robert (1999) 'Raising the Seventies: The Early Films of Terrence Malick', Boulevard, 15, 1–2, 141–55.
Zucker, Carole (2000) '"God Don't Even Hear You", or Paradise Lost: Terrence Malick's Days of Heaven', Literature/Film Quarterly, 29, 1, 1–9.

Chapters and segments in books

Almendros, Nestor (1984) 'Days of Heaven', in A Man with a Camera. New York: Farrar, Straus and Giroux, 167–86.
Andrew, Geoff (1999) Directors A–Z: A Concise Guide to the Art of 250 Great Filmmakers. London: Prion Books, 140–1.
Bersani, Leo & Ulysse Dutoit (2004) Forms of Being: Cinema, Aesthetics, Subjectivity. London: British Film Institute, 124–178.
Biskind, Peter (1998) Easy Riders, Raging Bulls. London: Bloomsbury.
Cavell, Stanley (1979) The World Viewed: Reflections on the Ontology of Film, enlarged edition. Cambridge: Harvard University Press, xiv–xv, 11, 245–6.
_____ (1981) Senses of Walden. Chicago: University of Chicago Press, 156.
Clarke, James (2006) 'The Thin Red Line', in War Films. London: Virgin Books, 128–137.
Cohan, Steve & Ina Rae Hark (1997) The Road Movie Book. London: Routledge, 90–109.
Cohen, Hubert (2003) 'The Genesis of Days of Heaven', Cinema Journal, 42. 4, Summer, 46–62.
Corrigan, Timothy (1991) 'Genre, Gender and Hysteria: The Road Movie in Outer Space', in A Cinema Without Walls: Movies and Culture After Vietnam. London: Routledge, 137–60.
Critchley, Simon (2005) 'Calm: On Terrence Malick's The Thin Red Line', in Rupert Read & Jenny Goodenough (eds) Film as Philosophy: Essays on Cinema After Wittgenstein and Cavell. Basingstoke: Palgrave Macmillan, 133–148.
Doherty, Thomas (1999) 'Taps at the Millenium: Saving Private Ryan and The Thin Red Line', in Projections of War: Hollywood, American Culture and World War II, revised edition. New York: Columbia University Press, 300–15.
Emerson, Mark & Eugene E. Pfaff, Jr (1998) 'Changes', in Country Girl: The Life of Sissy Spacek. New York: St Martin's Press, 31–46.
Foreman, Alex & R. Barton Palmer (2000) 'Terrence Malick', in Tom Prendergast & Sara Prendergast (eds) International Dictionary of Films and Filmmakers Vol. 2 – Filmmakers, fourth edition. Michigan: St. James Press, 643–4.
Gilbey, Ryan (2003) 'Terrence Malick', in It Don't Worry Me: Nashville, Jaws, Star Wars and Beyond. London: Faber & Faber, 75–87.
Homden, Peter (2002) 'Terrence Malick', in Yoram Allon, Del Cullen & Hannah Patterson (eds) Contemporary North American Film Directors: A Wallflower Critical Guide, second edition. London: Wallflower Press.
Katz, Ephraim (1998) 'Terrence Malick', in The Macmillan International Film Encyclopedia. Revised by Fred Klein & Ronald Dean Nolen. London: Macmillan, 890.
Laderman, David (2002) 'Gothic Irony and the Outlaw Couple: Badlands', in Driving Visions: Exploring the Road Movie. Texas: University of Texas Press, 117–27.

McCrisken, Trevor & Andrew Pepper (2005) 'Saving the Good War: Hollywood and World War II in the post-Cold War world', in *American History and Contemporary Hollywood Film*. Edinburgh: Edinburgh University Press, 89–130.

Orr, John (1998) 'American Reveries', in *Contemporary Cinema*. Edinburgh: Edinburgh University Press, 162–87.

Pfeil, John (2004) 'Terrence Malick's war film sutra: meditating on *The Thin Red Line*', in Steven Schneider (ed.) *New Hollywood Violence*. Manchester: Manchester University Press, 165–182.

Pilowsky, Marian (2000) '*Badlands*', in Tom Prendergast & Sara Prendergast (eds) *International Dictionary of Films and Filmmakers Vol. 1 – Films*, fourth edition. Michigan: St. James Press, 96–7.

Polan, Dana (2005) 'Auteurism and War-teurism: Terrence Malick's War Movie', in Robert Eberwein (ed.) *The War Film*. New Brunswick: Rutgers University Press, 53–61.

Reeves, Tony (ed.) (2001) *The Worldwide Guide to Movie Locations*. London: Titan Books, 48, 104–5, 354.

Riley, Lee & David Shumacher (1989) '*Badlands*, Good Times', in *The Sheens: Martin, Charlie and Emilio Estevez*. New York: St Martin's Press, 17–22.

Sargeant, Jack (1999) 'Killer Couples: from Nebraska to Route 666', in Jack Sargeant & Stephanie Watson (eds) *Lost Highways: An Illustrated History of Road Movies*. London: Creation Books, 148–68.

Thomson, David (2002) 'Terrence Malick', in *The New Biographical Dictionary of Film*. London: Little Brown, 552–3.

Williams, Mark (1982) '*Badlands*', in *Road Movies – The Complete Guide to Cinema on Wheels*. New York: Proteus, 26–8.

Wood, Robin (2000) '*Days of Heaven*', in Tom Prendergast & Sara Prendergast (eds) *International Dictionary of Films and Filmmakers Vol. 1 – Films*, fourth edition. Michigan: St. James Press, 292–4.

Visual sources

Absence of Malick (2003), featured on *Badlands* (1973). Directed by Terrence Malick. Los Angeles, Warner Bros [Film, DVD].

Rosy-Fingered Dawn: A Film on Terrence Malick (2002). Directed by Luciano Barcaroli, Carlo Hinterman, Gerardo Panichi & Daniele Villa. Italy, Citrullo International.

Visions of Light: The Art of Cinematography (1992). Directed by Todd McCarthy. Los Angeles, The American Film Institute [Film, DVD].

INDEX